The Life and Times
of

God's Friendly Servant

Biography

of

Canon Alleyne George Bradshaw

Malcolm H. Bradshaw

and

Shirley I. Bradshaw

PREFACE

There are not many people over eighty years of age who have such recall of their earlier years as Alleyne George Bradshaw did. The family feels very fortunate that so many events and happenings were recorded on a small tape recorder while "Braddy" was able to do so. Throughout the book he shall be known as Braddy as that is what is wife and friends always called him. To his family he was Dad.

This book is the print out of those recordings and many other interviews and recordings done by others in later years.

A special thanks to family and friends who have assisted in any way to make this as complete as possible.

It was a pleasure to share the various segments of the book as they were prepared for printing with the late Right Reverend George Arnold. He was quite prepared to write the forward for the book but that was not to be as he died before the manuscript was ready. His replies and apparent enjoyment from reading the excerpts gave us joy too.

Many more people have stories to add to these as Braddy affected so very many lives but we have tried to include a part of each era of Braddy's life and times. We hope we have succeeded in sharing some happy and yet often trying times with an audience who treasures the past and knows that the present is better because of people like Braddy.

The Life and Times of God's Friendly Servant
Copyright © 2003 Malcolm H. Bradshaw and Shirley I. Bradshaw

Published by The Big B Publishing Company, 2003
17 Porter Street
Yarmouth, Nova Scotia
Canada, B5A 2Y7
Printed in Canada by Sentinel Printing Ltd.,
Yarmouth, N.S.

Bradshaw, Malcolm Henry, 1931 -
Bradshaw, Shirley Isabel, 1934 -

The Life and Times of God's Friendly Servant
ISBN ISBN 0-9699622-3-1

1. Biography - Adult literature. 2. Anglican Church. 3. Church
Communities. 4. England 5. Barbados 6. Alberta. 7. Nova Scotia 8.
Church History
I. Bradshaw M.H., II Bradshaw S.I. III Title

Contents

FAMILY BACKGROUND

1

An English Background

Alleyne George Bradshaw (Braddy) was born in Tunbridge Wells, England, February 3rd, 1891 (d. Sept. 21, 1978), the sixth child of Henry Lee Bradshaw and Katherine Alice Dawson Bradshaw.

In April 1877, Henry had inherited quite a substantial farm in Wakerley, in the county of Northampton. However, in September, 1890 Henry and family were living at Liphap Farm, Tunbridge Wells.

Braddy's mother died two years after Braddy was born - less than three months after his sister, Mary, was born. She had a bad case of measles at the time of the birth,

Katherine and Henry

and in those days measles, especially with an adult, was quite a serious disease. Following his mother's death the family moved back to Lincolnshire, his parent's original home. Lincolnshire was an agricultural county and both of his parents had come from farmers' families. His father died when Braddy was six. He had been thrown from his horse while hunting and died from injuries he received.

Braddy remembered the old farmhouse in Lincolnshire - a low-lying, very pleasant house - with a lawn in front and a hedge at the bottom of the lawn. Beyond the hedge was a duck pond. When the ducks were on the duck pond at dusk, and wouldn't come in, Braddy's brothers would take a piece of bread tied to a long string and throw it in. The ducks would gobble it up and then they could pull them to shore by the string. They would pull gently and the bread would not come out of the ducks' mouths. If they left them on the water at night, they would gradually come to shore and roost there and would be easy victims for foxes.

Braddy was told another story about the duck pond by his brother. They had a cousin who was ordained and was curate in one of the London churches. He used to come and visit them and was very proud of his athletic abilities. Braddy's brothers once kidded him that he could not jump over the hedge at the bottom of the lawn. He said he could. They didn't tell him anything about the pond on the other side of the hedge. It must have been on one of his first visits to the place before he had looked around properly. He tried it and did jump the hedge and landed into the pond. Afterwards he probably learned the truth of the saying, "Look before you leap."

Braddy did not know if his brothers carried on the farm after his father's death, but Mary, the new baby, and Braddy were taken to live with Aunt Sarah, the next oldest sister of his mother. His mother had four brothers and one sister. Aunt Sarah then lived in a small village called Castle Bytham. Braddy remembered the days there quite well.

His Aunt Sarah had a very pleasant, fairly good-sized thatched cottage which stood on a hillside by the side of the road that went down into the main part of the village. The wall of the cottage came right down to the edge of the road. On the other side there was quite a large and pleasant garden with plenty of trees, vegetables, and fruit trees. In the house there were three upstairs bedrooms. Down stairs there were two sitting rooms, a dining room, kitchen and scullery. Off the kitchen the scullery had a huge cement cup-shaped thing which was used for washing. There was a little fireplace under it to heat the water in it. In the kitchen was an old fireplace with a rod across and hooks hanging down to hold the pots. At the side was what was called a Dutch oven, built into the side of the fireplace. In later years there had been a grate put into the bottom and it was there that his aunt cooked their meals. All the bottom floor of the house had stone flag floors. Upstairs the floors were wooden.

In the center of the village was the usual general store that was always found in old English villages. Also there was a baker's shop and the post office. The bakery was quite interesting, not only because they turned out wonderful crusty loaves of bread, about twice the size of the present day loaves; and he thought they cost about six cents each (two pence), but also on Sunday, when the majority of people went to church, they used to leave their Sunday dinner at the bakery to be cooked and ready for them to put on the table when they came out of church. Braddy always remembered his aunt's delicious dinner of roast beef and Yorkshire pudding. The beef was cooked on top of the pudding. There were also roasted potatoes around the beef. They called at the bakery after church and the baker handed them out the large container with the whole "works" in it. They took it home and would sit right down to their meal.

There was no plumbing in the cottage. They relied on water from a well not very far from the door into the garden. The well did not have a pump but had over it a winch system to draw up the water. The bucket was on a chain and the water was drawn up by first lowering the bucket, then winding it up with a crank handle. That was their only water supply.

8

At the bottom of the garden path was the usual old outhouse. Braddy remembered that his cousin, Parson William, was visiting once and nearly burnt the outhouse down. It seemed that it was the habit to take the London paper there, sit comfortably, and smoke cigarettes and read. Also the newspaper served as the toilet tissue of the day. There were two toilet seats - one small one for children and a larger one for adults. William threw a cigarette butt down the small hole without troubling to put it out. Next thing he knew he had set fire to the paper down below. He came out rather hurriedly. Braddy and Mary had just come home from somewhere and saw the smoke coming out of the outhouse and saw William hurriedly trying to adjust his pants. They went to the well and fortunately there was a bucket down in it so they hurried and wound it up and the two of them staggered along down the garden path with the bucket of water. There was sufficient water to put out the conflagration before it consumed the whole building.

Two other events, Braddy recalled - neither of which were much to his credit, he admitted. There was a small boy friend who had something which Braddy envied very much. He had two small partially fledged, baby birds - thrushes - he thought. They had fallen out of a nest and he was taking care of them and trying to raise them by feeding them with an eyedropper. They fascinated Braddy and he wanted baby birds to look after too. The only thing he could think of was that not far under the eves of his bedroom upstairs, there was a nest of swallows. He knew that there were two or three in it as he could see them stick their heads out the hole when the parents fed them. So Braddy decided on a terrible thing and admitted that he was conscience-stricken afterwards. It was the kind of thing a child would do without thinking of the consequences. He got a long pole, leaned out the window and poked the nest down. It fell into the road and the small birds fluttered out of it. Braddy ran down stairs for all he was worth, around the side of the cottage and out into the road. When he arrived, there was a cat going off with one of the birds and he could not find either of the other two. It was a long, long time that he sorrowed over his act of destroying those three little birds.

The other thing happened, not very long before they left Castle Bytham. By that time, Mary had gone to live with Aunt Susan in Peterborough. Queen Victoria died in 1901 in the Isle of Wright and she was buried at Balmoral in Scotland. The train came up bearing her body on its way to her last resting place in Scotland. The school children were taken out onto a big bridge that went over the railway, so that they would be able to see the train go by. The bridge had stone parapets and they were warned not to get up on them. When the train came along they would be able to see it as the parapets were not very high and, as well, had holes in them so that they could see through. Braddy insisted on going against authority and so he climbed up onto the wall. He remembered the teacher so well. She took him down, placed him in the middle of the roadway so that he couldn't see the train go by except to see it coming in the distance and disappearing in the distance. That was a heartbreaking experience, but was one that he felt he thoroughly deserved.

Another thing that he remembered about Castle Bytham was the parson, Myerhouse, at the village church. He was one of the last of the old hunting parsons, and was quite well known for his eccentricities. He used to wear a surplice, when taking the services, and was probably one of the first in the country villages to do so, especially in the pulpit. Most of them wore a black gown only. This surplice was something that was considered to be very high church. Braddy could recall his appearance vividly. He used to dress in a black coat, knee breeches, and high boots as if he were riding on the hunting field, which he did a good deal of the time. He had two white bands around his neck, not the clerical collar of the present day. Braddy remembered that he had continual warfare with the Salvation Army, and to his disgust, they generally came and played their band and sang the loudest hymns during the sermon in the church. The sermon in those days lasted the best part of an hour. One Sunday he got extremely annoyed, took off his surplice, and flung it over the pulpit wall; went outside and grabbed the Salvation Army captain and threw him into the center of the big drum. The band didn't play outside of the church after that. Soon after that there was a law passed that no Salvation Army band should play within a certain distance of a church building where a service was being held.

A number of years after this when Braddy lived in London, they read of the death of Parson Myrehouse and they recorded some of his many eccentric doings. He was a great friend of Sir William Harcourt, the then Home Secretary and he used to go shooting with him. There came the time when he found that there was no more room for graves in the village churchyard, so he applied to the Home Secretary to supply another place for burials. Like most government offices they were a bit slow in doing this. Finally, there was a baby, stillborn, and the parson had no where to bury the body. So what he did was pack it in a game hamper and sent it to the Home Secretary, Sir William Harcourt. He had been in the habit of sending him presents of game-pheasants, hares, partridges and things. The story went that the Home Secretary's butler received the parcel

- a little hamper of what he thought was game, and he told Sir William that Parson Myrehouse had sent him a present of game. The butler was told to hang it up in the game room where they hung meat, until it was "high" enough, as they called it, to eat. He came back very distressed after he had opened the hamper and he told Sir William that there was a baby's body in it. The Home Secretary said, "Good God! What is that man going to do next?" Then he remembered the request for the extra land for the churchyard and he said that he had better look after that at once before "he gets showering more corpses on me."

During Braddy's days at Castle Bytham, he remembered that he only had one particular friend, a boy about his own age, Guy Armstrong. He was the son of a very prosperous farmer. He had one brother, Horace, younger than himself and a sister, Gussie, younger; and there were twins about two or three years old. They had a beautiful home, an old farmhouse that was right under the hill on which the ruins of the old castle were. There was just an old foundation and a bit of old walls and that's what gave the village its name-Castle Bytham. The house was quite large - library, sitting room, nursery school (They had a Governess.) and like the cottage where Braddy lived, it had flagstone floors on the ground floor. They had a very large kitchen with a large table at which they had most of their meals. Over the table, in the beams of the roof, there were hanging quite a number of cured hams. Also on the ground floor was the game room in which pheasants, hares, rabbits and the like were kept. This was a cool room and game could be kept there for quite sometime. There was also a dairy room in which there were huge pannikins of milk. Braddy remembered them as a very delightful family but he could not remember what any of them looked like except the father. He was a tall spare-built man and appeared very austere and frightening to Braddy. He generally wore a Norfolk jacket and knee breeches and leggings and he always had with him a quirt which he used when he was riding his horse. He did a lot of riding around the farm. He didn't mind using the quirt on any of the children who were at all delinquent. Braddy used to eye him with a good deal of suspicion when he saw him walking through the household still slapping his leg very frequently with the quirt.

In later years after moving to London, Braddy spent some summer holidays with the Armstrongs, sometimes all the school holiday time - generally the month of August. They used to have a great time playing around the farmyard which was filled with big stacks of hay and they had great fun playing hide and seek and sliding down the haystacks. There was one inhabitant of the barnyard that was allowed to run freely and he

11

was the children's constant enemy. Braddy remembered one day when they were playing hide and seek and Braddy was hiding behind a bush, trying to see where the others were and trying to get "home" before they saw him. He forgot about the billy goat. Behind him was a bank edging a creek which ran through the end of the farmyard. He was stooping down waiting to make a break for "home" when he got a tremendous shove in the rear end and went over the bank into the creek. Mr. Billy Goat had seen his opportunity and had taken Braddy in the rear.

Towards the end of August or the beginning of September, the large fields of wheat, oats and barley would be reaped. There were horse-drawn reapers that would drive round and round the square sides of the fields gradually drawing towards the center. There were generally four men with guns, one at each corner of the fields, because there were a lot of rabbits and hares in the grain and as the square got smaller these animals would begin to run out and then the men would shoot them. After one morning shoot they had about 187 rabbits and about 45 hares. These were sent to the nearest town, which was Stamford, to the market and received a very quick sale. They got about six pence or a shilling for a rabbit and probably half a crown for a hare.

It was an interesting fact, that practically wherever Braddy had been - in England, Barbados and Canada - he always had intimately known an Armstrong. Beginning with Guy as his special friend in Castle Bytham and then when they went to Barbados, both Braddy and his wife, Maggie, were intimate with a family of Armstrongs. Charles Armstrong was Maggie's father's executor in Barbados. In Alberta, Braddy's first church warden at Nanton was George Armstrong. The Bradshaws and Armstrongs were very friendly there. When Braddy was first appointed there the Armstrong's had one small son, who was also called George, but everyone called him Gay. Braddy often tended him while Mrs. Armstrong was busy getting dinner or supper or whatever it was. Years later, after the Bradshaws came to Yarmouth, Gay became a member of the army camp here preparing to go overseas. Strangely enough, the times Braddy and Maggie spent with their daughter, Dorothy, and her husband, Earl Patte, in Scarborough, the almost next door neighbours were Clarence Armstrongs. The name Armstrong had played a pretty important part in Braddy's life and all of them were very fine memorable friends.

Many years later he was to recall Castle Bytham. There were a number of English brides of Canadian soldiers who used to come to Canada. The clergy were notified of their arrival and were asked to get in touch with them and make them feel as at home as possible, in what was to them a

12

strange country. One girl came to Arcadia, Yarmouth County, and as Braddy had received notice of her coming, he went out to see her. They began talking and when he asked her what part of England she came from she told him a little place that he would not know anything about, and probably had never heard the name of - a little place in Lincoln, called Castle Bytham. That was a strange coincidence that she should come from the village which Braddy remembered clearly during his early life.

Braddy's siblings were George (b. 13.10.1877, d.?), James (b.25.5.1879, d. 1.4.1939), John (Jack) (b. 23.8.1881,d.25.3.1885), Charles (b. 7.4.1883,d. 13.4.1917), Frank (b. 10.10.1885,d.?), and finally after Braddy, a girl Katherine Mary (b. 29.9.1893, d. 3.9. 1937)

Braddy's Father's Family

Braddy's father, Henry Lee (d. 1897) son of James Bradshaw, married Katherine Alice Dawson (d. 26.12. 1893), daughter of John Dawson, July 19, 1876 in the parish church at Castle Bytham. Henry Lee was known as a "Gentleman Farmer".

Henry had one brother, John Thomas, whom Braddy recalled had a farm and lived in a small village called Tinwell, not very far from Stamford. Henry had five sisters, Elizabeth (never married and died in Stamford on 1.4.1879), Ann, Mary, Jane and Susannah (Susan). When Elizabeth died, she too left a fairly substantial sum that was equally shared between her brothers and four sisters. Aunt Susan, Braddy remembered, was quite well off and had a nice home in Peterborough. He could not recall the other sisters at all.

Braddy's Mother's Family and More Childhood

Braddy knew more of his mother's family. Beside three aunts, Aunt Polly (Mary), Aunt Sarah and Aunt Annie, there was another aunt, Aunt Fanny, who had a boarding house in Hastings on the South Coast. Of the boys, Uncle John was the oldest of the family and he emigrated to Collingwood, Ontario, a number of years before Braddy was born. He had quite a large family. He visited England once with several of his children. When Maggie and Braddy were visiting their daughter, Dorothy, in Ontario, they came in touch with the last of his children living then, Cousin Julia. She was a retired nurse and was living in a residence for retired nurses in Toronto. They visited her often and she would visit them at Dot and Earl's home. When Maggie and Braddy were not there Dot still kept in touch and finally when she died, Dot attended her funeral in Collingwood where she was buried. Braddy and Maggie did visit nearby Collingwood and attended the church where his uncle had attended and they saw the family burial plot in the cemetery. They met several people who had known members of the family. Cousin George, another of John's sons, was in Alberta and Braddy met him at one time in Okotoks when he was going out on his bicycle on one of his parochial visits in the morning. On the bridge over the river going out of town, Braddy met a Canadian car from Ontario and he stopped and asked Braddy, who was wearing his clerical collar, where he would find the parson in the town. He said his name was Bradshaw. Braddy told him that he was the parson of the Church of England. (It was not yet called the Anglican Church of Canada.). The person in the car said, "I am your cousin, George". A number of years after that while the Bradshaws were at St. Clements, in Barbados, Braddy received a telephone call one day from the manager of the Bank of Commerce who told him that his Cousin George was passing through on a tourist cruise ship and would like to see him. They didn't have time to go to St. Clements as they weren't staying long enough, so wondered if Braddy could get to town. So Braddy went to town. The bank manager took them around St. John's parish a bit and they had lunch together. He remembered that Cousin George gave him a pound to treat his children. He couldn't recall whether he had spent it on his children or spent it on something else and wished the children good luck. Afterwards when Bishop Kingston came to Nova Scotia, he told him that one of his great layman, one of his greatest helps in Algoma, Ontario, Canada was Percy Dawson. He was another of Uncle John's sons.

There were two other brothers of Braddy's mother that died before he was born. One was George who was a captain of a sailing schooner that used to go between England and Barbados. On one of the trips home, in rough seas, he was washed overboard and never heard of again. That was the first time Braddy had heard of Barbados, when he was told the story of where Uncle George was coming from, when he was lost at sea. Uncle Charles was killed in one of the skirmishes with native tribes in North Africa. The Prince Imperial of France, the only son of the Empress Eugenie, was at that time with the British army and wanted to go out for a little hunting in the district and there was a guard of men sent with him. Among them was Uncle Charlie. They were ambushed and the Prince Imperial and Uncle Charlie were both killed.

The fourth brother was Dick. He was sort of a commercial traveler but didn't worry about doing much of anything. Braddy thought he was

14

rather addicted to the bottle. He was a very jolly specimen but Braddy did not know when and how he died.

Braddy did have a good deal to do with Aunt Fanny Simpson down in Hastings. She had a boarding place there for summer visitors. When Braddy met Mrs. Colburn at Journey's End in Queensland, Nova Scotia, he thought she reminded him very much of Aunt Fanny, a Polly Anna type, although he thought probably Aunt Fanny had a much better business head than Mrs. Colburn had. She ran the house very well and did quite a good job of her boarding house. She was always cheerful and happy, no matter what happened to her. Braddy could not remember her husband but said he was a rather ineffectual specimen, a little man, and Braddy did not know his work and could not recall his name. When Braddy knew him his chief business seemed to be traveling around the house with a hammer and tacks and he tacked down bits of carpet that were sticking up afraid that people would trip over them. Aunt Fanny treated him almost like one of the children. She did get cross with him once when she found that he had nailed down the scatter rugs in the drawing room. Braddy

Braddy's Family
Left to right, standing: Annie (wife of James), brother James, sister Mary (age 10),
brother Charles. Left to right, sitting: Aunt Annie, Aunt Sarah, Aunt Mary "Polly",
Ada (wife of George) with daughter Katherine on her lap, brother George.
Child standing at right with watering can is Fred (Ada and George's son).
Braddy (age 12) is sitting on ground in front.

remembered it as a beautiful drawing room with a beautiful floor and he decided that the rugs weren't safe so he tacked them all down. Aunt Fanny was very annoyed and she chased him with his hammer and tacks to some other part of the house, where he couldn't do much damage.

Aunt Fanny had a large family too. Winnie was the oldest and a school teacher. Braddy could recall her as being very much a school teacher and could remember her face clearly. She was always very correctly dressed. Her chief object in life seemed to be to see that Braddy's hands were always clean when he went to the table. He also saw her peering behind his ears to see that he had washed behind his ears and did not have a high-water mark on his neck.

The next child was Ted, who was Braddy's idol. He was at that time a Sergeant in the Household Cavalry, the Lifeguards. Braddy used to have a picture of him showing him and a fellow Sergeant riding right behind the Royal carriage at the coronation of King George V.

Next son was Noel, who was in the Coldstream Guards, but he left them and became a comedian on the Music Hall stage. He made quite a name for himself but later got into a dissolute way of life. He drifted away and Braddy never heard anything about him until while in Alberta Braddy met someone who came across him as a hired hand at one of the western ranches. The people were very kind to him and took him in. He was "pretty down on his uppers" and Braddy understood that he died there (either in Manitoba or Saskatchewan) and was buried there.

After Noel, there was Kathleen, who was working in one of the stores in Hastings when Braddy knew her. There was a boy, George, and another daughter, Ruby, who was about Braddy's age so they used to travel around together a great deal. Braddy would often spend his whole school holiday of August down at Aunt Fanny's house in Hastings. Ruby and Braddy used to spend a lot of time on the beach shrimping and doing other things together. They were always warned to be back in time for lunch and sometimes they were rather late and would try to crawl in without washing and would try to steal their place to the table. All the summer visitors and tourists - could be a couple dozen - had their meals together with the family in the big dining room. They never got past Winnie who chased them off to put shoes and stockings on and also wash hands, behind ears and so on.

Braddy had many happy memories of Hastings. It was a beautiful old town. It was really a twin town; there was St. Leonards, right next to it; the two piers of Hastings and St. Leonards were only about a quarter of a mile apart. They used to enjoy concerts held on the piers every afternoon and evening. In the mornings there were often, what was called then "black minstrels", that performed down on the beach.

Braddy remembered one amusing incident that happened while he was down there. The manager of the Hastings Pier was leaving so they had a big going-away party - a sort of testimonial to him - and were giving him presents. The town gave him a present and visitors gave him presents. All had quite a good time; but the town council of Hastings were very annoyed the next day when they found out he had taken up the management of the St. Leonards' Pier right next door. There was a tremendous amount of rivalry between the two twin towns, so the town council was not at all pleased that they had given him such a tremendous send-off and he had kept "under his hat" that he was only going to St. Leonards' Pier right on their doorstep.

Braddy remembered visiting the little village of Battle, not very far from Hastings. That was the site of the Battle of Hastings when Harold was unfortunate enough to catch a Norman arrow in his eye. That was the time when William of Normandy became King of England in place of Harold.

One of the most exciting incidents in Braddy's life was Ted's wedding. As Braddy said earlier, Ted was in the Lifeguards, and he couldn't get enough leave to go down to Hastings to get married so it was arranged that he should be married from Aunt Polly's house, in the parish church there - St. Andrew's. He arrived with six fellow Sergeants from the Household Cavalry, all from the Lifeguards, Ted's own regiment. Braddy was about twelve or thirteen at the time and he was quite impressed by these big men. They weren't allowed to wear their ceremonial dress that they used for parades and royal occasions but they were in their chief best uniforms and they were a very striking lot of men. They had tight white doeskin breeches, big hip boots, but they did not have big helmets and elaborate tunics. Braddy remembered the service at the church and Ted had such difficulty kneeling down because his breeches were so tight. He did manage to get down but used his hands on the top chancel steps to prevent falling forward. Afterwards, Braddy was very impressed with the six escorts outside with their arch of swords under which Ted and his bride passed. Braddy could not recall how many were at the wedding - but probably about twenty; he recalls that their small house was absolutely packed in every corner. They all had a gay old time. Ted and his bride lived somewhere across the other side of London. Whitehall was the

Headquarters of the regiment where Ted was. Braddy did remember that Ted's wife was a model and was one of the most beautiful women he had ever seen. Her chief work in modelling had been as the Blessed Virgin Mary in stained glass windows. There were a number of windows in various London churches in which she had figured as the Blessed Mother. Some of these would have been destroyed during the war.

Braddy could not recall ever seeing them again but he was quite sure that Ted, at least, had visited them when he and Maggie had been in England on their honeymoon in 1919.

Once a month at the church, they had what was called a "Penny Reading". You only paid a penny admittance at the parish hall and there was a lecture, recitations, and other things. On one occasion when Cousin Noel was appearing at the local Music Hall, the Lewisham Hippodrome, Father Rice went to Braddy and asked him if he could get his cousin to come up and give them a couple of songs at the next Penny Reading. Braddy's aunt was not particularly anxious about it as she didn't approve of Noel very much. She was a little too straight-laced for some of his jokes and she was a bit afraid of what he might do at the church concert. Anyway, she didn't like to say no so they asked him and he said that he would. Braddy said he "brought the house down" and it was so very different from anything they had ever had. One of the songs he insisted on singing, which was one of the songs of the time, was called "Seaweed". Braddy remembered some of the song when he was 84 years old. The idea of the song was that if you had a piece of seaweed and felt it, you could tell by its feeling whether it was wet or dry, or soft or hard, what kind the weather was going to be. It was supposed to be sort of a Nature's barometer. One verse was this and was the type of the kind of song it was. It seems there was a fire in this man's house or hotel where he was staying; and:

...
I quickly tumbled out of bed, though I could hardly stand
My seaweed hung upon the wall I grabbed it in my hand.

Chorus:

And rushed upon the roof - forgot to take my clothes;
The fireman down below was squirting with his hose,
He hit me where I stood - right on the parapet,
And as soon as I touched my seaweed
I knew it was going to be wet.

That brought the house down and Braddy recalled the look on Father Rice's face. He didn't know whether he was supposed to laugh or show disapproval but he carried through very well. The vicar, Father Philpotts, was not present on that occasion or they thought they might have heard something about the type of song that Noel had sung.

The local music hall, the Lewisham Hippodrome, was not very far from Braddy's home, and the family used to go there quite often - probably once a month. The highest fee was one and sixpence. In those days one could get a reserved seat in the first gallery or in the orchestra stalls for a shilling. The best time of the English Music Hall was probably those days. There were comedians and others, like Dan Leno, Harry Randall and it was the beginning of Charlie Chaplain's prominence. Braddy remembered seeing Sir Henry Irving who was a great actor. They did have some very good shows. There were also local cinemas with movies. Braddy recalled seeing the first feature picture they had, called "Lines of White on a Sullen Sea". It was a story of the sea and Braddy and the others thought that was a great thing. There were other sorts of entertainment too but they could not afford to do too much.

Braddy's pocket money, out of his five shillings he earned a week, when he began to work, was only sixpence a week. Aunt Polly used to keep the rest of it for household expenses, which were probably considerable. At this time there were Charlie, Braddy and the three aunts living together.

George's oldest boy was Fred and the eldest girl, Katherine, (called Sissy) had been named after Braddy's mother. There was also a sister, Elsie, with whom Katherine lived later in life.

Jim had two children, Harold and Winnie. Harold was living at the time of Braddy's death and, in fact, in 1986 when Braddy's youngest son, Malcolm and his wife, Shirley, visited England, they had a most pleasant dinner at the Hotel Kenilworth with Harold and his lovely wife, Mary, who were living in Surrey, just outside London. Braddy saw Harold when he was in England during his

From right Harold, his wife Mary, and Malcolm

19

daughter's (Joan) illness in the fifties. They kept in touch at Christmas time and Braddy corresponded with his two daughters, Ann and Ruth. Braddy always sent them a little present each Christmas. Braddy had lost touch with other family members and did not know if any other were still living. Thought that perhaps Ruby and Ted would still be alive (when he taped much of this information in 1974).

Sometime during the late 1890's, around the turn of the century, Aunt Sarah and Braddy left Castle Bytham and went to live with Aunt Mary, or as they called her, "Aunt Polly". Charlie also lived with Aunt Polly. He and Braddy had always been very close as they were kept together in Catford after their parents' deaths and Braddy's short stay at Aunt Sarah's. Another unmarried brother, Frank, next in age to Braddy, was living with Aunt Susan, in Peterborough. Charlie and Braddy shared a bedroom for those years around 1900 to 1913 at Aunt Polly's.

Aunt Polly had recently moved up to the district of Hithergreen, a new development and a subdivision of the borough of Lewisham called Catford, in South East London. There was a small river or stream that ran through the district, the Ravensbourne. Catford got its name from the name Cattleford because it was here that the farmer's cattle in the district crossed the stream. The word eventually got shortened to Catford.

Aunt Polly had been housekeeper for a number of years to an ecclesiastical lawyer, Mr. Law. In those days the church and state were closely connected and still today the Church of England is still the State Church. There were certain lawyers that had to look after the peculiar laws of the church. Mr. Law died and that decided Aunt Polly to take this house in Catford on Arngask Road and look after her sister, Katherine's (Braddy's mother) brood of children, as much as she could. Aunt Polly's household was made up of Aunt Polly, Aunt Sarah, Aunt Annie, Charlie and Braddy. This house was not very far from the open fields where London extended very rapidly. When Braddy and Maggie went to England on their honeymoon in 1919, there must have been forty or fifty thousand new houses between them and what had once been the open fields. Hithergreen was a new development.

Frank was in a Naval Cadet School, somewhere in the Midlands probably near Peterborough. Mary was to go to live with Aunt Susan, her father's sister, who lived in Peterborough.

George and Jim had a good carpentry business. Jim was a very good cabinet maker. Their workshop, as well as both their homes, were near Aunt Polly's.

When the folks moved in to Aunt Polly's there was the beginning of a parish and there was only a parish hall that had been built so services were held there. The priest in charge was Rev. Ernest Cantelo Burt Philpott. He took a great deal of interest in Braddy. During the thirteen or more years that Braddy lived there the family was all very closely connected to the church. A beautiful church, St. Andrew's, was built around 1904 and Braddy went back and saw it when he was there in 1919. In the Lady Chapel there he found very much of his brother Jim's work. He thought the altar and a lot of the furnishings of the chapel were done by Jim.

Aunt Polly was a very keen church woman and she saw that they all went regularly to church and Sunday School. They often went to the eight o'clock service, then Braddy went to Sunday School at ten, and then they went to the eleven o'clock service. There was Sunday School again in the afternoon at three and then they always attended the evening service. Aunt Annie was fairly long in age then and she did not go out to the evening services but occasionally went to the others.

Braddy could not remember a time when his mind was not set on getting into the ministry. For many years there didn't seem to be much chance of it, but when one is determined on anything, ways and means are found. At the age of fifteen, Braddy was asked to become Superintendent of the morning Sunday School. That was really the beginning of his sincere church work. He went to a local school until the age of fifteen and by then he had passed through all the Standards, and his aunt then had to look around and get work for him. Her income was very small, a small annuity from Mr. Law, and they relied on what Charlie brought in. Braddy never saw it but Charlie worked in a store; had to go to work by tram; and went somewhere near the actual city of London.

Braddy's First Job - at Cheesmans

Aunt Polly would search through the daily newspapers and see what jobs were being offered for boys. She thought she might be able to get Braddy a job in some office, maybe even in London. Two or three times they took a trip up to London to go and see possible employers but none of the jobs seemed to be what Aunt Polly thought would be good for him.

Finally he got a job in a local department store, Messrs. Cheesman Brothers, and it was rather an interesting job. Cheesman's was the biggest department store in Lewisham. They had quite a number of departments - dry goods, hardware and the like. The Art Department was in a house by itself on a side street behind the store. In those days all the price tags and announcements of prices and suchlike were printed by hand and in this house, with a staff of about four, they made the price tickets for all the different departments. It was quite a job. A couple of the older men did art posters advertising some special items. These were very decorative and very pretty to be put in the window. Braddy's job, when he started, was to fill in the spaces on the price tags, and it was very easy to run over the edges. The boss told Braddy he didn't want his numbers turned into bloody fretwork. The pay was rather startling - five shillings a week, or a dollar twenty, Canadian. His hours were from eight o'clock in the morning until eight o'clock at night. He had Thursday afternoons off.

He had a mile and a half to two miles to walk to work every morning and come back at night. He enjoyed it and found it quite interesting work.

Besides doing the tickets and show cards for the windows, they also looked after the decorating department and they - two or three at a time - would go out to dances or other social events and would decorate the halls for the occasion, with flags, muslins and other things. If the event were a church bazaar, they would put up all the stalls and decorate them. They charged so much for the whole job. One job Braddy was involved in was at the time of George V's coronation. The whole of the city of London and all the boroughs were decorated for the occasion. Braddy had to go around to all of the various pubs that were owned by one brewery over quite a portion of South East London and put up a Union Jack at each place. It took about three days as they travelled by a horse and van.

There were many interesting things at work. There were two bosses, Harry and Frank. Harry was older than Frank. Frank was the busy man and Harry amused himself by going around to see that everyone was doing his job. They were both very kind and Braddy enjoyed his time with them. There were three water colours, that David (Braddy's son) has now, which were painted by Fred Wicks for Braddy and given to him and Maggie at the time of their wedding, January 18, 1919. Fred was one of the senior men in the department. They were a happy company. There were several other apprentices other that Braddy. They would take their lunch and eat in at noon and then would get their main meal around five o'clock in the evening in the big dining room attached to the store. During sale time, especially the big White Sale, they would be asked to go into different departments of the store and help out with the sale's work. There was one thing that Braddy hated and that was wrapping parcels as he could never make a neat parcel. They did make a little extra cash as they had to add their initials or signature to every sales slip, and after the sale was over they would each get a bonus according to the amount of the sales they had made.

One part of the work, in connection with Cheesman's that Braddy always remembered was that every Christmas, beginning about six weeks before Christmas, they had a special toy department and the art department built what they called a cave. It was taken down in sections and was rebuild the next year by putting the sections back together. This cave was running through several of the basements under the store and you wandered through this cave. Each year there was a special subject that the cave was about. One year Braddy recalled it was Alice in Wonderland and various nursery stories were depicted by scenes through the cave. The cave was made of canvas, painted in different colours to look like rocks and at the beginning of it a cashier sat in a cashier's cage. The charge to go through it was sixpence. Before you got very far into the cave there was Santa Claus and for several years Braddy had the job of Santa Claus for six weeks. At the end of the cave was a bazaar of Christmas gifts. There were a couple of counters on each side with fairies behind them and they gave each person when they went out a present which was well worth the six pence you paid on going into the cave. The idea of the whole business was to take the people into the bazaar where they would buy more expensive presents and gifts. Every Saturday, the cave opened at eleven o'clock and closed about nine o'clock and there were six to seven thousand people who went through. It would be packed for most of the day. Braddy calculated that during the six weeks each year he shook hands as Father Christmas with about fifty thousand or more people. Mr. Harry Cheesman loved the cave and used to wander through continually and would stand and listen to what Braddy said to the people. If he thought Braddy had done well, at the end of the week, there would be an extra ten shillings in his pay envelope. He had received a raise by now, anyway, and was now getting about ten shillings a week instead of the five he received when he started.

Braddy felt there were many important visitors that went through the cave each year. One day Braddy heard a male voice ask the cashier, "Is this St. Matthew or is this Lady Matthew at the seat of Customs?"

Name ALLEYNE BRADSHAW

School PLASSEY ROAD Dept. ART.

Age 12 YEARS - 1903~

We hereby certify that this _____ is absolutely and entirely the work of the scholar whose name it bears.

_____
Head Teacher.

_____
Teacher of subject.

Example of Braddy's art at age 12.

When he got to Braddy, he saw that he was a bishop and he had two little girls with him. It was the Right Rev. Winnington Ingraham, who was then Bishop of London. When he saw Braddy, he said, "I think this must be Father Christmas or should we say, Good King Wenceslas, who looked out on the feast of Stephen." Then he went off with the little girls. He was a bachelor and Braddy found out afterwards the little girls were children of his brother who was a rancher in Alberta, Canada.

Braddy's keen sense of humour lasted throughout his whole life. Frank and Ruth Stockwell tell us that whenever her father, Harold Bradshaw, spoke of his Uncle Alleyne, he did so with a smile. They were left with the impression that Braddy had been well known for his lively, not to say mischievous, sense of fun. Harold recalled a story Braddy told him about Cheesmans. While he was working there he came around a corner one day to be confronted by the rear end of a figure bending over a counter. He had been unable to resist the temptation so he nudged the figure forward with his boot. Then - as the victim let out a yell - he took to his heels because from the voice it dawned on him that he'd picked on one of his proprietors - one of the Cheeseman brothers! Apparently after that, Braddy lived in fear for several days of being found out and losing his job.

Braddy's three oldest brothers:
left to right, George, James, Jack.

Beginning His Chosen Profession- Holy Orders

Braddy continually hoped that somehow to could get into college so he could study for Holy Orders. About that time there was a new curate who came to help at the church. There were two or three assistant priests as there was a large congregation. The new curate, Father Rice, took a great deal of interest in Braddy and after he finished work at night, for two or three nights a week, he would go to Father Rice to be coached in Latin. Braddy had learned a little Latin in school but not much. On one other night a week Braddy went to night school and took mathematics that he was weak in, as well as one or two other subjects. Leaving home around half past seven in the morning and working until eight at night, except on Thursday, Braddy did not have much time to mope about anything. He was generally ready for bed at half past ten or eleven.

A New Beginning - Study Abroad

A scholarship had been received from the Society for the Propagation of the Gospel (S.P.G.), for Chad's Hall, Durham University. Codrington College, Barbados, was associated with Durham University and it was from Durham University that Braddy would receive his degree. Dr. Anstey, principal of Codrington at this time, was in England asking for students for Codrington, and a number of applicants for the ministry were contacted and asked if they would go. Among them were Alleyne Bradshaw (Braddy), Cashmore and Hodgekins. They were the first group to go and they left England early in January, 1913 by the Royal Mail Steam Packet (R.M.S.P.) Magdalena from Southhampton.

The three of them went down from London by train. With them was Braddy's brother, Charlie, and a young deacon, the Rev. Sebastian Hall-Patch, who was to complete his training at Codrington. Charles and Braddy had been very close ever since their Aunt Polly had made a home for them and their sister, Mary, in Catford, following the deaths of their parents.

The ship had two classes. They travelled second class, which was quite comfortable. The food aboard ship was good. Their cabins had four berths. Hodgekins and Braddy shared one with two others. Cashmore and Hall-Patch were in another cabin. All got settled. Braddy had a cabin trunk, which was made of cane and fibre so it was quite light and was made to fit under the bottom bunk in a ship's cabin. He also had a wooden box which his brother, Jim, had made for him to carry his books. When the ship left the dock it was smooth going but during dinner the ship began to heave and toss as they got out of the channel. Braddy was not prepared for the rough seas and soon had to leave the saloon and make a dash for his cabin.

On the stairs going down he met a steward coming up who took one glance at him and said "Sir! You can't be sick here".

Braddy said, "Can't I"? and promptly was. He did not leave his cabin for the next three days as matters got worse as they sailed through the Bay of Biscay.

Hodge was a good sailor as he had been in the army and had had to rough it. He took good care of Braddy and even spent sixpence on a small bottle of champagne, which he had been told was good for seasickness. Braddy drank it and promptly threw it up. This rather peeved Hodge as he had wasted his hard come-by sixpence. However, Braddy soon recovered and enjoyed the rest of the voyage.

When they arrived in Barbados, Dean Berkeley, afterwards Bishop, met them and hustled them through Customs and Immigration, then took them to the deanery where they had a meal.

One thing Braddy especially remembered of that evening was while waiting for the meal they sat out on the lawn and heard, for the first time, the frog chorus. They thought it was mosquitoes making all that racket and were rather appalled to think what size they must be!

They finally reached Codrington about nine o'clock in the evening - not a particularly pleasant hour to enter into a new life. They were met by the senior student, Jimmy Gittens, who did his best to make them welcome. Braddy had been allotted a room known as "four square". It was one of four small rooms over the belfry - the space between the dining hall and the chapel. Braddy's room looked up the gap with a view of Society Chapel on the hill. Being on the leeward away from the breeze, it was quite warm; but, he was fortunate

Braddy in his room at Codrington

in the fact that at the end of the term a student on the other side looking out over the Atlantic moved and without asking any questions he moved into this vacated room and kept that room until he left college in 1917. These rooms were about 10 feet by 10 feet and furnished in bare simplicity - a bed, a table, a chest of drawers over which there was a mirror, a wash stand with basin and jug, also a jerry and slop pail, a small book shelf and one kitchen chair. The bed was covered with a thin mattress over wooden slats - no spring. Among the furnishings of the room was a kerosene lamp. One of Braddy's first purchases was a better reading lamp.

For about one week Braddy was desperately homesick, but like the seasickness, he got over it and settled into a new and very different life.

Codrington College, Barbados

Codrington College

The average number of students at Codrington during Braddy's time there was 35, about half of which were divinity students. The staff consisted of the principal, Dr. A.H. Anstey, who also lectured in various subjects; Professor Wippell took divinity. The tutor was Rev. E. Lee who fitted in where he was wanted. Honour students, that is those who were taking honours, were looked after by the classic master of Lodge School, Mr. Dunlop. A vicar of a neighbouring church went in once a week and lectured in mathematics. The parochial medical officer, Dr. Briggs Clark, went in weekly to give them a smattering of medical knowledge. Although they were a small student body, with a small staff, each student did get a lot of individual attention which was lacking at large universities. He arrived at Codrington knowing a smattering of Latin, no knowledge of Greek, and weak in mathematics. The first thing he had to do was take entrance exams. He passed these in three months and received his B.A. degree in four years.

There were three terms per year at Codrington as there were at Durham University. Each one was ten weeks, the first before Christmas, the second from January to Easter, and the third from Easter until May or June depending on the date of Easter.

The day at college was a full one. The rising bell went at six o'clock

Society Chapel

in the morning, when everyone went to the large bath - what would now be called a swimming pool. There was only one shower in the college - in the principal's lodge. After the "bath" there was a daily Holy Communion in the chapel at 6:30, followed by tea and hard biscuits at 7:00. Matins were held at 7:30 and breakfast at 8:00. Lectures were from 9:00 to noon when they had noonday prayers in the chapel followed by lunch. At three o'clock the students worked on the grounds, tennis court, ball fields or worked in the printing shop on the quarterly magazine. At five there was Evensong at Society Chapel on the hill.

Dinner was at 6:00 followed by a free period until 8:00 when there was a lecture or private study until Compline at 9:00. After that the students had chats in various rooms before bed which was generally at 10:00 or a little after. Braddy always was ready for bed and the hardness of the bed did not keep him awake.

The theological students kept an abbreviated version of the old seven daily hours of the monasteries. The ones at Codrington were Holy Communion, Mattins, Sext, Evensong and Compline. Although attendance at the daily service was required from the divinity students, many of the others used to attend also.

On Friday afternoons, theological students were required to do visiting in the tenantries around the college, on the two sugar plantations that belonged to the college - Society and College. Braddy had the tenantry between the college and Consetts Bay.

A Special Remembrance of a Tenantry

Once when on these weekly visits, a peculiar thing happened. Braddy was visiting a very old woman, whose husband had been dead over fifty years. She was cared for by a granddaughter in a very small house with the usual two small rooms. The small living room had the usual clutter of various pieces of china and the gatherings of many years. In looking through things, Braddy came across a mug with H.M.S. Victory on it. He asked the old lady where it had come from and she told him that when some of the British fleet were anchored off Bridgetown in Carlyle Bay, the officers would come ashore and sometimes bring mugs with them to get a drink of liquor from the mill boiling-house nearby. Of course, that had happened before her time but her husband told her that this happened before the battle of Trafalgar. Nelson and his fleet arrived in Barbados in 1805 and he was killed later that year at the battle of Trafalgar. Years later in 1925, when Braddy went to St. Mark's he tried to find the small house again, but was not successful. No one seemed to know what had become of it or its inhabitants of his college days. He often thought what he had missed in failing to obtain a wonderful relic of the Nelson Days. He always wondered what became of it.

College Life Continues

At the end of the first term there was a short break from Friday evening until Tuesday. It was the custom of the principal (the "old man"), to treat any who remained in college to a lunch at the Beach Mount Hotel at Bathsheba. Braddy was in college for several such half terms and thus took advantage of this enjoyable trip. To get this treat it meant that they had to walk to and from the hotel. They generally went through St. Joseph's and then walked home by the train line and then walked up from Bath Station. These were quite enjoyable because it was really the only times the students had a chance to talk to the "old man" about various things. He was a different person when he seemed to get away for a time from the college itself. There were usually eight or nine who went on these lunch trips. Professor Whippell was often with them too if not engaged otherwise.

The Staff of Codrington

Reverend Dr. Anstey

Braddy felt that the staff at Codrington had done so much to set him on the right path for his ministry. The principal, the Rev. Dr. A. H. Anstey was a bachelor, about forty-two and, in some respects, a complicated individual, but at the same time, a very dedicated one. He generally knew what he wanted and usually got it. Some called him in this respect a Jesuit. He had not much use for women. He really had only one aim in life, at least while Braddy knew him, and while principal of Codrington, and that was to do all that he could to extend the usefulness of Codrington and the education of all the people of the island, in general. He was concerned with education at all levels - a first for the island of Barbados. To this end, he had built the teacher's training school for both men and women. Because he was disgusted with the poor local elementary school on Society Hill, he had built a stone commodious building and finally the beautiful Girl's Grammar School (Codrington High School) on the brow of the hill next to what was then Society Chapel, (The society was the S.P.G.) All of this was accomplished, in most part, from his own large private income; but, he also managed to snaffle some funds from private givers. He was a great disciplinarian and ruled in college with a firm hand. Study and work were the order of the day. No one could leave the college during term without permission. Occasionally, they did sneak out when they thought they could get away with it. He was also good in sports, especially football, which was his favourite. He pulled many games against Lodge School from defeat by his own efforts.

Braddy remembered the total disregard as to what he did with his teeth - his dentures, that is. No! He did not bite opposing players. One day before going into a game, Braddy saw him drop them into the lap of the daughter of the Headmaster of Lodge School. Braddy said he had never seen a more disgusted look on the face of any young lady. Another time when no accommodating lap was available, he put them down in the grass at the edge of a field and then when he heard the bell of Society

Chapel ringing for Evensong, he picked them up and put them in his mouth and as quickly took them out as they were filled with ants. Visitors, being shown around his Lodge, especially noting his many pieces of beautiful furniture in the drawing room, would be surprised to see his teeth nestling in some fragile cup.

Like many a scholar, he was always losing his glasses. Generally he had them attached with a piece of red tape and when not in use, he pushed them up on top of his head. Braddy remembered seeing him with as many as three pairs on top of his head at the same time. Professor Wippell called them his periscope. When he ran short of glasses he would begin the search for them on his head.

Although a young man in his forties, Braddy always thought he looked all of sixty, especially without his teeth.

The students once played a trick on him and got away with it. He used to go in the swimming pool about six in the morning. Hodge, Cashmore and Braddy went very early to the bath too and it got so they would race to see who could get there first. Harvey Read, during vacations, used to go to St. Philip, Georgetown, British Guiana (now called Guyana), and once brought back to Barbados for Braddy a small stuffed alligator. The three "tricksters" decided to get to the bath before the principal and put Mr. Alligator in the water just under the springboard. Braddy attached a small weight to its tail so that it would float with its head high in the water. He got it in just before the principal arrived and he greeted the three of them with a smile and some unnecessary comment on it being a fine day. Then he stripped off his pyjamas and dived in. Evidently he saw the alligator as he was diving but could not stop the dive. While he was under water, Braddy got in and hurriedly seized the little beast and hid it under his pyjamas. The "old man" came out sputtering and said, "Bradshaw, did you see a little beast in the water?" Of course, Braddy - all innocence - denied it. He looked puzzled but did not say anything more but later in the day he had the bath emptied.

Another interesting story involved the principal. Although he had a very comfortable lodge, during term time he occupied an attic room in the college building with the rather false impression that, because of his presence, the after-hours "ragging" might be reduced. Then at the end of the term before vacations started he would move back to the lodge. One morning, at the end of term, Braddy was waiting for the buggy to arrive to take him to the rectory. The principal was busily moving and asked Braddy to help. It was not a long job and they had reached the last few items. Braddy had an armful of books and the "old man" had his lamp in his right hand and his jerry in the left. When they came around to the front of the lodge, they discovered that Governor Leslie Probyn and Lady Probyn were making an unexpected morning call. The "old man", entirely unmindful of what he was holding in his left hand, had put down the lamp on a nearby stone post and still waving the jerry proceeded, with a beam on his face, to shake hands with Lady Probyn and say how glad he was to see them. Over his shoulder, Braddy caught her ladyship's eye, and then, to make matters worse, Sir Leslie winked at him. Braddy nearly exploded with laughter. Afterwards the principal said,

"Why, Bradshaw, didn't you do something?"

Soon after Braddy left college, Dr. Anstey was elected Bishop of Trinidad and served there for several years. On his retirement he went back to England. He died, probably before he was seventy; Braddy said, "Probably worn out".

Professor Wippell was a nephew of the great clerical furnishing firm in Exeter, England. For years after, Braddy got their catalogue. In his words, "I don't think that I've met a more lovable person that John Cecil Wippell, a great scholar, innocent and simple in his living, full of fun and always a friend in need." He became principal of Codrington after Anstey's departure for Trinidad and eventually went to Jamaica where he lived doing church work and lecturing in the college. He lived to be over ninety. If Braddy and Maggie's second child would have been a boy they would have named him John Cecil, but as they were blessed with a daughter instead, they named her Joan Cecilia. Joan was baptized in Society Chapel by Canon Clark-Hunt and Wippell was her Godfather.

The third member of the resident staff was Father Lee. Braddy did not see so much of him. He was a friendly soul but rather delicate. He married the younger daughter of the vicar of St. Mark's, Jessica Barnet. He returned to England shortly after Braddy left college and died there not many years after.

Of the visiting staff, Professor Dunlop used to go down from Lodge School to take honours in classics. Braddy did not see much of him. While Braddy was in Canada he drowned at Cattlewash trying vainly to save another swimmer who had gotten into difficulties with the undertow. Wippell married his widow.

Father Briggs, vicar of St. Margaret's, used to teach mathematics. Braddy thought of him as a peculiar soul. When he went to Barbados, he did not expect to live long as one lung was gone and the other one damaged. The doctors had told him that his only hope was to be in a mild tropical climate and suggested Barbados. There for a number of years he lived a very controlled life with rigid ideas with regard to diet. One idea was that fresh bread was harmful and he never ate any that was not at least four days old.

When he went to college he always carried his own bread in a paper bag and placed it on one of the serving tables in the dining hall until lunch time. Stanley Reece, a prankster, once got some bread and kept it until it was very dry and mouldy and substituted it for that of Father Briggs.

Braddy said he never forgot the look on the principal's face when Mr. Brigg's produced the substituted bread. The principal said, "Surely you're not going to eat that."

Briggs looked at it a little puzzled and said, "It does look a little old but it should be good," and he proceeded to chew it. He was the only person Braddy ever saw who would put an egg, shell and all, in his mouth and crunch it up. He claimed that hens had to have grit to help the digestive organs and so their shell was good for our similar organs.

Last, but not least, of Braddy's professors was Maggie's Uncle, Briggs Clark. He was always cheerful and full of fun, but sometimes he was absent-minded and unpredictable. To his disgust, the principal sometimes attended his lectures so he thought he would try and discourage him. One occasion when he was lecturing on tooth extraction, he seized the principal by the neck to illustrate how to extract teeth, but it did fall a little flat when he discovered that the principal had dentures. On another occasion, when the principal insisted on the elementary female teachers attending the lectures, the doctor lectured on the reproductive organs of both sexes, a subject in those days rather taboo. The principal and the women hurriedly withdrew. Braddy wondered if the "old man" was afraid that the doctor might once again use him to illustrate. The women never attended another of Dr. Briggs Clark's lectures.

While at college Braddy had one encounter with the doctor that "scared the daylights" out of him. It was during one of the vacations, and Aggie Greenhage, the rector's youngest daughter, married to Nat Greenhouse, the Assistant Inspector of Schools, was pregnant. She and her husband were living in town and she had been under the care of a town doctor. While visiting at the rectory she began labour and Braddy was dispatched hurriedly, in the middle of the night, to get Dr. Briggs from Villa Nova. He went on his bicycle and when he got there, by ringing the bell and shouting, he aroused the doctor who came to the window and let fly with the most appalling language. Mrs. Briggs appeared behind him and tried to calm him down. Braddy said, "Briggs, it's Braddy, You are wanted at the rectory". He let go another blast and said he did not care who "— — — —" stars it was and then yelled for his man to get the car ready. When he came downstairs fully dressed, with his little bag, he cheerfully grinned at Braddy. By this time, Braddy was at least expecting a physical assault. Mrs. Briggs told Braddy afterward that he always blasted those who came to call him in the night but he always went.

Braddy remembered another incident that occurred while he was at Codrington College. There was near the beach, south of the rectory, the other side of Sandy Lane, a little cottage called Rhodes Villa. Later on the Sydney Nurse's occupied it for some years while he was district magistrate. At the time Braddy was telling about it, it was what was known as a Bay House. Tim Tarilton and his wife and sisters-in-law, Daisy and Dolly, were there for a short holiday and invited Braddy for a few days of Christmas vacation. He arrived there the same day as they did. That evening when the lamps were lighted, the centipedes began to come out of the walls and they arrived in scores. They were busy for over an hour killing them or chasing them away. That night Braddy bunked down on a small cot in the living room and towards daylight he felt something wet and rough on his cheek. He said, "I woke up standing!", he nearly fell over a calf that had wondered in through the open door. He was relieved to find out the harmless cause of his waking; he'd had fears of some giant centipede.

The College Media

The college had two magazines - one printed in the printing shop for distribution among old Codringtonians and the other for college perusal only. This latter, called *DeBus*, was produced each term and only had one copy which was kept in the Common Room. It had all kinds of personal jibes and comments and was illustrated. When it became known that Braddy could draw, he became the editor of illustrations. One of his hardest chores was, not the cartoon, but the cover which had to be a work of art more or less. He wondered if any of the *DeBus* existed to the present time but he felt that many of them would have been lost in the college fire of 1926. (Mac and Shirley Bradshaw looked extensively for a copy of this while doing research in Barbados in the 1990's, but could find none.)

In "College News", the Codrington magazine, Braddy was first listed in residence during the Lent Term which began on January 24, 1913. "It read 'The New Year has brought over with it several new faces from the Mother Country to our dear

Domus (Latin for dormitory). We welcome to our midst Messrs. Hall-Patch, Cashmore, Bradshaw, Hodkins'.

In the same magazine dated April 24, 1913 was "the Royal Visit of H.R.H. Princess Marie Louise of Schleswig-Holstein".

Michaelmas Term of 1913 reported that "its college contemporary *"DeBus"* was under the able editorship of the Rev. J.S. Hall-Patch with Messrs. Narracott and Bradshaw as art editors" and that "it had gained a higher pitch of excellence than we think it has ever gained before". Later in the Trinity Term 1914 the following was reported:

The latest copy of "DeBus" has won the highest praise from all that have seen it. The editors last term were Messrs. A. Bradshaw, M. Peritt and H.J. Hutchinson.

During the Michaelmas Term, 1915, the Codrington College magazine reported that Braddy has successfully passed his first year Arts Course.

Some interesting notes during 1917 appeared in the college notes:

Mr. Bradshaw was a very capable representative last year".

Braddy and Classmates at Codrington.
Back row, left to right Price, Rev. Sebastian Hall-Patch
Front Row, left to right Hodge, Townsend, Braddy

We heartily congratulate the following on their success in their examinations - Theological Special - A. Bradshaw and T. Cashmore.

Then from the Debating Society:

On February 23rd Mr. Cashmore used his influence to convince the House that "Clergy should not marry". Mr. Bradshaw led the opposition, which eventually secured all the votes. Two other resolutions for debate at the time were "Cremation is desirable" and "The allies were justified in refusing Germany's proposal for peace.

The New Rifle Range

About mid February, soon after their arrival at college, an interesting event took place. The principal gave a cocktail party to welcome to the island, Princess Marie Louise of Schleswig, Holstein. She was to open the new rifle range which was situated on the college grounds opposite the football field.

This event had a personal interest to Braddy as at the event he got drunk or nearly so, for the first time in his life.

In the presence of many of the important people in the island, including the governor, Sir Leslie Probyn and his wife, Lady Probyn, her Highness fired the first shot and to everyone's surprise, it was on the edge of the bullseye. Afterwards Braddy asked Cuthbert Peterkin about this, as he had his doubts about her Highness' marksmanship. Peterkin told him that he had fixed a target before hand and changed it for the one she fired at. Her shot missed entirely and went into the woods behind. The Princess was delighted when Peterkin handed her the target and said, "Wait until I show my husband this!" Peterkin got her to sign another target for the college which may still be in existence.

Braddy's Fall - From Grace

Now to clarify Braddy's fall from grace. As usual at such social affairs, there is a bountiful supply of rum punch. It was the first time either Hodge or Braddy had been confronted with its deceptive powers. They enjoyed their first taste from the usual cocktail glasses and went back for more and then some more. Braddy had never imbibed anything stronger than port wine or weak whiskey and suddenly the punch "punched" him. Hodge seemed to be in better shape than Braddy, and together they went to sit on some benches in the belfry. As Braddy was wondering where all the wind had come from to make all the palm trees shake and dance around, Professor Wippell, brought up Cecilia Gardener, the younger daughter of the rector of St. Phillip to introduce her to them. Braddy did not dare to try to stand and vaguely saw three hands being extended in greeting. After considering the matter Braddy shook the middle one. Some time after this, when Braddy again met Cecelia, she remarked that she was surprised that he did not stand to be introduced. He told her that perhaps she would have been more surprised if he had done so and fallen flat on his face. After that experience, it was a long time before he summoned up enough courage to tackle another Bajan rum punch.

3   FIRST CHURCH EXPERIENCE

Matriculation and Church Work

Soon after this Hodge, Cashmore and Braddy passed their matriculations and the principal told them he wanted them to go as lay readers to St. John's, St. Joseph's and St. Mark's. Cashmore went to St. Joseph's, Hodge to St. Mark's and Braddy to St. John's. The principal thought that now they had enough experience to be able to do some practical work in the services of the church.

The arrangement was that Hodge and Braddy were to change after six months. However, as it turned out both Canon Clark-Hunt at St. John's and Father Barnett at St. Mark's were satisfied and they remained on at each church. They would go there each Saturday afternoon and return to the college on Monday morning. Braddy felt he was very lucky to come under the direction of such an outstanding priest as Canon Clark-Hunt. He saw that during vacation time when Braddy stayed at the rectory, that he spent the mornings in the study.

In Braddy's words, "I believe that I got more out of the time spent there than I did from college in term times". The canon was an outstanding scholar and would always help Braddy over difficult times. Mrs. Clark-Hunt was "a dear lady" and contributed to Braddy's happy days at the rectory.

Braddy's first year at Codrington went without incident. He gradually integrated into a very different way of life and enjoyed the regular daily routine during the week and spending every weekend at St. John's. There he preached every Sunday, alternating mornings and evenings with the rector. Twice a month at the nine o'clock morning service, he went to St. Gabriel, a small church on the hill overlooking St. Philip's parish. A Miss Tarilton drove him in the rectory buggy and she also played a little organ in the church for the hymns. She lived with her father in a little house across from the rectory glebe. Her father was poorlaw inspector for the parish. She had a good voice and sang in the choir at St. John's.

Braddy recalls one such memorable Sunday when Miss Tarilton sang out a very peculiar rendering of a verse in the psalms. Her seat was next to his stall, so he got the full force of it. The words should have been "the polished corners of the temple" but she changed them to" the colished porners of the temple". After that occasion he never read that particular psalm without thinking of her. Braddy wondered in later years what had happened to her. He knew that she had gone to the United States but then lost track of her.

Braddy had concerns about sermons. All the divinity students had to preach a sermon once a term before the principal, for his comments. It was just the two of them. The principal and the student went up to Society Chapel one afternoon during the week for this trial run. On one occasion Braddy had forgotten that it was his turn until the day before. He hurriedly boned up on one of the sermons of Dr. Winnington Ingraham, Bishop of London, one of the great preachers of his time. He delivered it with vim and vigour and got quite a shock when the old man said that he had never heard such rot; the theme was bad, the conclusions worse and the delivery putrid. Braddy suspected that he knew the sermon and its author. Braddy admitted that throughout his whole ministry, preaching was one of the things he liked least.

First Earning's "In The Ministry"

Braddy spent the vacations that year - the first year - at the rectory, studying and helping as Lay Reader in the work of the parish. The rector paid him $10.00 per month which was practically his only income while at college. He got an occasional gift from the parish at home in Catford, but his expenses were few so he actually was able to save some money.

The Clinic at Codrington

During the first year Hodge and Braddy, under the guidance of Dr. Briggs Clark, later to be his uncle-in-law, started a small clinic at the college to help people, especially children. In those days when shoes or any kind of footwear were mostly unknown for the children, many of them suffered from bad ulcers on their feet and legs. The doctor told Braddy and Hodge that they could be treated easily and he gave them some corrosive tablets which were very strong and had to be diluted - one tablet to a quart of water. They used a ground floor room opposite the kitchen and there, directly after lunch each afternoon, they would treat a number of children and sometimes adults. All they had to do was wash out the ulcer with the solution and bandage it. Some ulcers, especially in the older people, would be quite large. It was surprising how after a few weeks of this simple treatment the ulcers would heal. Sometimes they also attended to cuts and other such ailments. Braddy remembered one small girl who had fallen out of a cherry tree onto a sharp stake and had a nasty hole in her upper thigh. They treated her with a diluted tincture of iodine and it healed; but because of its position the bandaging was the worst part.

The principal was very pleased with their work; and of all things, he took them a set of dentist's forceps to try their hands at tooth extraction. Braddy let Hodgekins tackle this and he did so with glee. Of course, they had no anaesthetic and the "victim" had to bear it. The patients were nearly all older people and their yells, he felt sure, could be heard for miles, although, in most cases, the teeth were loose anyway.

Another thing the doctor showed them how to do was rather peculiar. In those days many of the children had six fingers on one hand, sometimes on both. The sixth was a little boneless one that jutted out from the real little finger. All they had to do was tie a little dental floss around it and pull and it would drop off without bloodshed.

"Ragging" at Codrington

One common "rag" that Braddy recalled was to toss sleepers out of bed in the middle of the night and decamp before the sufferer could retaliate. As previously mentioned, the beds were just a thin mattress on thin slats and the "ragger" would crawl under the bed and jump up; the unfortunate one on the bed would be deposited on the floor with the mattress.

It was at this time that the Briggs Clarks of Villa Nova, gave Braddy a little black and tan terrier. It was a tiny thing, named Nicky. He got permission from the principal to keep him in college as long as he kept him under control. The dog always slept under Braddy's bed.

One night "Boots", as Peterkin was called (His brother, Percy, was called "Shoes", and his youngest brother, "Dirt", because he was always under foot.) came along and backed under Braddy's bed, so that he could escape more easily after he tossed Braddy out. Nicky, when confronted with "Boots'" rear end, did not like it so he bit it. Braddy was awakened by the ensuing racket, with "Boots" trying to see how much he had lost of his seat. "Boots" finally left muttering about fair play in keeping man-eating dogs under the bed.

Legends of Codrington

There were some legends that were rife at Codrington when Braddy graced it with his presence. One had its source in tragedy. It was stated that about one hundred years before, there was a student named Chisolm, whose practice it was to go down to the bath each morning before daybreak. Some of the "young idiots" in the college thought that it would be a great

40

joke to let the water out of the bath one night and when Chisolm dived in he would get an unpleasant shock. He did and broke his neck. Ever since then any untoward happening at college had been laid to the charge of the ghost of Chisolm. An example was the "quaking" - the name given to the tossing of unsuspecting Freshmen out of their beds in the dead of night.

Another legend was that the founder of the college, Sir Christopher Codrington, had occupied a room in the Principal's Lodge and that in it was still a bed in which he had slept. The truth of this was always open to doubt because it was stated that the lodge was burned down in one of the college fires and had been rebuilt; in the new building the Founder's Room was replaced as nearly as possible to the original. During Braddy's first year of college, because of overcrowding in the college proper, owing to an influx of English students, several senior students were given rooms in the Principal's Lodge. One of the students was Stanley Reece, who occupied the Founder's Room. It was Reece's custom after working on the grounds and probably playing tennis or football, to go to his room, strip off his clothes and hop across the hallway to the shower bath. One afternoon while doing this, the principal took into the lodge some American visitors and was showing them the Founder's Room and spinning the old yarn about it, when stark naked into the group, jumped Reece. In relating the incident, Reece told that he found himself within inches of a pretty girl; and he jumped out of the room as quickly as he had entered but he heard the girl ask, "Was that the Founder?"

Chapel Altar

Christmas and "Love at First Sight"

Examinations for the B.A. degree were divided into two parts - the preliminary and the finals. The preliminary was sat before the first Christmas there and Braddy passed. Examinations were sent to Durham for correction. After the exams, the term closed a few days before Christmas and he went to the rectory for the vacation which lasted a little over a month. Before the Festival of Christmas, there was the usual Christmas at the alms-house where there were about eighty old people and a number of orphan children. The rector, Mrs. Clark Hunt, and Braddy went to the party. There were also present some of the planters and their

Maggie, Braddy - 1916

families. It was at this gathering that Braddy first saw his future wife, Margaret (Maggie) Greenidge, who was there with her mother, not long back from the United States. He wondered in later years, "Was it love at first sight? Probably!" In later years he looked back to that meeting and the succeeding years as, in his words, "a meeting pregnant with results". Mrs. Clark Hunt introduced them and "that was it". A few days after Christmas Braddy received a note from Haynes Hill (the home of the Greenidges) from Maggie saying that that afternoon she was going to tennis at Villa Nova and would be glad to take him if he would like to go. Indeed he did! She called for him and he went to "that beautiful home" for the first time.

Many of the family, in later years, including Braddy, visited Villa Nova and as Braddy noticed, the house had not changed much over the years but the grounds did. There was a very good tennis lawn behind and to the right of the house which had a wall on two sides and a high wire fence on the third and fourth. It was a single court and kept in excellent

Villa Nova

order. The club met there twice a week - on Tuesdays and Saturdays. It was at Villa Nova that Braddy met, for the first time, many whom he was to know for years - the Armstrong girls from Cliff; the Peterkins from Kendai; (Their brother, Cuthburt was at college with Braddy.); the Johnsons, nieces of Mrs. Briggs Clark; Emsie - afterward married Jack Simpson; Nora - now living in Trinidad married to Worley Bradshaw; Maggie - married to Dudley Clark; the eldest girl Dorothy was not there. Strangely enough, Braddy met this Dorothy for the first time in Yarmouth, Nova Scotia, when she was a Mrs. Clark. They became very good friends.

When Braddy went to Codrington, he had never touched a tennis racquet, but during the years, by playing nearly every day, he became a fair player. In fact, during his last term, Hodge and he met in the finals for the college championships but Hodge won. Dr. Briggs Clark was a fine player and generally he, with three other men, played together as they were far above Braddy's class of player.

After the first tennis "date", whenever Braddy went to the rectory for weekends, Maggie called for him on Saturday afternoons for tennis at Villa Nova. Sometimes there would also be games at the rectory court.

During term if Braddy knew that "the old man" (meaning the principal of Codrington) was out of the way he would sneak up to Haynes Hill, for tea. Anyway, he and Maggie met very often both in term time and more frequently during vacations.

Braddy recalled that it was probably during the Whitson half term that year, that a picnic was organized at Long Bay Castle. Braddy remembered that the building was very much the same in later years but back then there were no grounds, just pasture lands around the castle. Harry Elliot, father of Brenda, who later married Fred Kirton, a contemporary of Maggie's brother, Ralph, was the manager of "Three Houses", a sugar plantation. He was also responsible for "Tony Bay Castle" (later, and today known as "Sam Lord's Castle"), and probably "Bushy Park" and "Borva". A number of young people, including ten college students organized a three-day picnic. They all had a good time but Braddy had to leave on Monday morning to catch the train at Bushey Park for Bathsheba or rather for a small bay house called Borva, just before Bathsheba on the rail line. Harry Elliot had sent a donkey cart to take Braddy to the station; however, he found this too slow, so he walked most of the distance. Braddy assumed we would wonder why he left the picnic early to go to Borva. Maggie and her mother were at Borva.

Being a bank holiday, the train of about six coaches, was packed. When they got to the steep decline at Consett's Bay, the trainman could

Picnic, 1915 Standing left to right: Arthur Bailey, Maggie's father, Malcolm, brother Noel. Sitting left to right: brother Ralph with Braddy's dog, Maggie's mother Bessie, Maggie and two family friends Lulu and Evelyn

not go to the brakes between each coach - the brakes were the old-fashioned type of a wheel and chain connected with the brake shoes. As a result, cutting the engine going down Consett's could not hold the train back and soon two coaches left the track, but did not turn over. People were jumping out on all sides. However, the engineer did stop the train just past College Station and Braddy had to walk the rest of the way to Borva.

"Grannie" (Bessie Greenidge) was very fond of little Borva and quite often rented it for a week or two. On one occasion Braddy remembered an amusing incident, although "Bessie", as everyone called her, did not think it was at all funny. There was a small verandah or porch overlooking the sea, and on this porch, there was an old square arm chair with no seat. She always told Braddy that he must not sit in that chair and he wondered why she would want to sit in a chair with no bottom in it. One day when Braddy was out back of the cottage Maggie called," Come quickly, Braddy, Mother has sat in that chair!" When Braddy arrived on the scene he noticed that indeed she had sat in the chair and her bottom was wedged in tightly a few inches off the floor. They had a time getting her out. Braddy recalled that he was rather handicapped because he was convulsed with laughter, much to Maggie's disgust. Lulu Outram, who was visiting at the time suggested that they light a fire under Bessie and that might cause her to jump out. What complicated matters was that her corsets were caught under the top rail in back of the chair. Finally, by turning her over on her knees and applying a little pressure to her rear, they managed to extricate her. After that, what should have been done long before, the chair was banished to a shed.

Declaration of War,... "Engaged", "Enlisted", "Tragedy"

Nothing much of consequence happened after that until the declaration of war on August 4, 1914. That night was a beautiful moonlight night and Braddy and Maggie were sitting on the low wall that surrounded the lawn in front of the house at Haynes Hill. That was the time and place that Braddy "popped the question" and Maggie accepted. After that he spent as much time as he could at Haynes Hill.

When the new term began about the middle of October, a citizen's committee was formed to be sent over to England, with all expenses paid, to enlist. There was already a West Indian Regiment but few seemed to want to join this. The majority of Codrington students went into Bridgetown for a medical, and if found fit, to offer themselves for enlistment in England. The medical was a very careful one as it was not wanted for anyone to be turned down in England and Barbados responsible for their return home. Braddy's eyesight eliminated him. Hodge had some lung trouble and was also turned down. Braddy did not know if Cashmore offered or not but he knows he did not go. He thought eight or nine students were accepted, among them were Cuthbert Peterkin, Stanley Reece - who was killed in action, Ash Everist- declared missing and believed killed, and Price, who was killed. Peterkin did well in the war and remained in Africa, probably Rhodesia. He was missed very much at Codrington because he was always so full of life and a ringleader in any "ragging" that went on at the college.

It was early in 1915 that Professor Wippell took a telegram to Braddy telling of his brother, Charlie's death in France. That was a very great blow to Braddy as they were very close.

Charles in Uniform

Braddy at Hayne's Hill

It was during the long vacation of 1915 that the Clark- Hunts wanted to spend the time at a bay house at Bath. They asked Bessie Greenidge if she would put Braddy up at Haynes Hill while they were away. She agreed which made Braddy very happy. Braddy went to parish visiting from there and would take the evening service on Sundays at St Gabriel's. The rector always came up from Bath to do the morning service. The vacation was a very pleasant time for Braddy; but he recalled one weird experience. One early evening, which was dark and rainy, he was reading in the gallery, when he heard the sound of a buggy driving up outside. He could hear the creak of the harness and the coachman stepping on the buggy bell when they stopped to announce their arrival. He called one of the servants to come and open the door and to his surprise, there was nothing there. When he later told Bessie about this she calmly said, "Oh! That was Sir Boucher Clark. He often drives up". Sir Boucher was supposed to be one of the early owners of Haynes Hill some one hundred years before.

Hayne's Hill Plantation House

Vacation Time and Back to the Books

The vacation of 1915 was more study-free, as the students awaited the results of their examinations from Durham. If they failed it would be a change of text books at the next term, so it would not be much use going over the old ones again. Braddy did spend some time going over the divinity part - the Bible and Book of Common Prayer - but much of the time was spent in parish visiting and getting in visits to Haynes Hill. When the new term opened, about the middle of October, as there was still no word of the exam results, the rector advised him that there did not seem much use going back to college only to hang around there with little to do.

About four days later Braddy received a letter from the principal saying that he wanted to see him promptly. Braddy went down to college and found the "old man" in his study and he promptly dropped a bomb. He had heard that an engagement existed between Braddy and Miss Greenidge. Braddy informed him that there was no formal engagement but that there was an understanding. The principal informed him that that was contrary to his contract with the Society for the Propagation of the Gospel (S.P.G.) which forbade such an arrangement. The contract that Braddy had with the Society was that he would not become engaged nor,

47

of course, married, during his college course; nor if he were sent into part of the mission field under the auspices of S.P.G., he would not get married for four years. This he pointed out to the principal but he still maintained that Braddy had violated the contract. At this point Braddy got, in his words, "rather hot under the collar and said one or two rather unpleasant things". Finally, the principal told him to go back to the rectory and write him a letter plainly stating the position of affairs between him and Miss Greenidge. If he were not satisfied he assured Braddy that he would notify the Society and ask permission to send him back to England. Braddy went back to the rectory with a heavy heart as he felt things looked rather gloomy. He talked the matter over with the rector and at his advice, wrote to the principal stating that the rumour that he had heard was entirely untrue, and that no engagement existed between him and Miss Greenidge. He soon got a letter back suggesting that he go back to college which he did that afternoon and arrived just before dinner. When he took his place at the table, and grace had been said, the principal welcomed him back and told him that with his presence the sun once more shone over Codrington.

Braddy heard afterward that he had placed the principal in a difficult position because he had known for sometime that Cashmore was more or less engaged to Margery Hutchinson and he did not want to take any notice of it because Cashmore, who had had architectural training, had been very useful to him in his various buildings and was engaged at the present in the building of the Codrington High School for Girls on the hill. He knew that if he fired Braddy he would also have to do something about Cashmore.

The day following Braddy's return to Codrington, the examinations results arrived. Hodgekins had passed but Braddy and Cashmore had only passed one part - divinity. They had failed the classical part so had to write that part again. Because of a change in textbooks, it would take them until the following May to bone up on it. The rule was then in English universities, that if a person failed in one subject, the whole exam had to be written again. That was rather annoying to Braddy because out of the four classical subjects he had been given distinction in one, done quite well in two and had not achieved a class mark in the fourth. He had to study the whole load again but did not find it too difficult because he had ten weeks to work on the four papers instead of the past year on eight.

Codrington magazine reports that:

After passing the B.A. Final, Braddy and Cashmore were admitted to the Diaconate by the Right Lord Bishop of Antigua at St. Mark's Cathedral on the Feast of St. Mark, April 25th, 1917. The first hymn was 'Round the Sacred City Gather'.

Canon Clark-Hunt delivered a forceful sermon on the words:

God is my witness; how I long after you in the tender mercies of Christ Jesus'
(Philippians, chapter 1, verse 8)

Was it any wonder it was "Love at First Sight"?
Beautiful Maggie, circa 1918

Appointments Afield

Soon after Christmas of 1916, the three Englishmen heard from the S.P.G. that Hodgekins was to go to India on completion of his college course. He left very soon after that; was ordained Deacon in England and went to India. Braddy was to go to the Diocese of Calgary; Cashmore was to go to India. Braddy wanted to be ordained Deacon in Barbados so that Maggie could be present and he asked the Diocesan Archbishop Swaby if he would do it. He was told that because he was going to Calgary that he must have permission from the Bishop there. Braddy obtained this permission but before he was ordered Deacon, Archbishop Swaby died. The Archbishop of the West Indies, Dr. Edward Hutson, took the service and Cashmore and Braddy were ordered Deacons on St. Mark's Day, April 25th 1917. As the service was to be at nine o'clock in the morning, Cashmore and Braddy went the evening before and stayed at St. Paul's vicarage with Father McConney who was vicar of St. Paul's at that time. (Four years later Braddy was acting for him at St. James.) After the service they went for lunch at the deanery with the Archbishop and others and returned to college that afternoon. Until his death, Braddy always remained very close to Archbishop Hutson. It was because of that relationship, that Dr. Hutson became Godfather of Charles whose second name Edward was the Archbishop's.

Before dinner that night at college an amusing little incident happened. It was the rule that all students be properly dressed for dinner with clerical collar or tie and gown. When Braddy started to dress for dinner, with not too much time to spare, he could not find his tie. He had forgotten that now he wore the clerical collar and had put his tie away. After a frantic search he saw his clerical collar and black bib and hurriedly put them on. He rushed to the dining room to find everyone waiting for him to say grace. He was representative student that term. The principal looked pretty "thundery" and especially so when Braddy stumbled in the Latin grace. However, he cheered up and became quite chatty during dinner, saying how delighted he was that Braddy had at last been ordained Deacon and glad that he could be present. In Braddy's words, "... when the old devil had nearly put a crimp in the whole business".

At the end of the term the students wrote their exams. Cashmore and Braddy had received word, by this time, from the S.P.G. that their passages had been booked for Calgary and India. They began their journeys in June not knowing whether they had passed their exams or not and not really caring at this point. Actually they both received word after they reached their destinations that they had passed.

The original arrangement was that at the end of their college courses they should have a leave home, but because of the war they were asked to postpone that leave until after the war's conclusion. This suited Braddy nicely because being in a diocese, under a diocesan bishop, he only had to get permission from him to marry and this he readily gave. (Married in Brooklyn, New York, January 18, 1919).

Off to Canada - Alberta Bound

Before Braddy left St. John's where he had been lay reader and for a few weeks deacon, he was given a parting gift from the congregation. It was a cheque for around $125.00 and was the largest sum that Braddy had ever had at one time. His expenses to Canada, with the exception of meals on the train, were all paid, so he felt quite rich. Early in June, Braddy boarded the R.M.S.P. for Saint John, New Brunswick. Maggie was at the dock to give him a loving send off.

With Braddy were Cashmore, who was booked for Calcutta via Vancouver, a young priest, Leonard Woolcott, who was going to England

On board Ship R.M.S.P. sailing for Canada, 1917. Left to right: Braddy,
a passenger Rose, Leonard Woolcott, wireless operator Hardy, Cashmore.

via Canada, and a young Barbarian, a wireless operator, whom Braddy thought was probably also going to England. They had a rather pleasant voyage taking about two weeks to St. John. There they boarded a train for Calgary. That was a four day trip. Braddy arrived there at two o'clock in the morning. In later years Cashmore insisted that he saw him off the train but Braddy's recollection was that Cashmore was snoring in the lower berth. There was no one there at the station to meet Braddy so he went to the nearby Palliser Hotel and got a room and finally got to bed around three a.m. He was awakened at seven o'clock with the information that the Bishop had called to tell him to transfer to the Yale Hotel where a room had been booked for him. Arriving at the Yale there was another message telling him to go the Cathedral of the Redeemer to assist at the eight o'clock service. As it was nearly eight when he got there the dean told him to stay in the congregation. After the service, Braddy saw Miss Pinkham, the Bishop's daughter, who told him that he had been appointed assistant to the Rev. H. H. Wilford, rector of Okotoks, but that he would be away for two weeks on holiday. In the meantime Braddy was to stop at the Yale and assist at the cathedral. After this Braddy took the service at the cathedral at eleven o'clock with his eyes somewhat propped up. After the service, the dean took Braddy to dinner at the deanery. Dean Pagett, a bachelor, was a dear old man. After lunch, the dean did the washing up and gave Braddy a towel to dry. That was the beginning of a long life of washing up and drying. During this drying up, Braddy's first, the dean informed him that he looked after himself. Braddy learned afterwards that some women of the congregation used to slip into the rectory occasionally and do some tidying up when they knew he was out of the way. The dean confided in Braddy that if he had an elderly keeper she would boss him. If he had a young one he would always be worrying about what she was doing when he was not watching her.

While Braddy was in Calgary, he used to go to a movie at night. One evening he dropped into a movie house; he thought it was called, The Princess. He found out afterwards that it was considered rather disreputable. Anyway when he went in a ticket was given to him with a number on it and he was told to keep it. Half way through the show a young man appeared on the stage and began to call out numbers and people went up and received various gifts/prizes-some quite valuable. Suddenly the number on Braddy's ticket was called. He didn't move as his gift was a very beautiful baby carriage. Somehow, he could not see himself - a shy young deacon - going out of the theatre pushing a baby carriage. Braddy tore up his ticket and poked it into the edge of the seat.

52

Soon one of the ushers came along, and wanted to see Braddy's ticket but could not find it so no one claimed the baby carriage.

After two weeks the Wilfords arrived back in Okotoks and Braddy went there and took up his work as curate. He found them a delightful couple. She was a little younger than Braddy; he was in his late fifties. For about two weeks Braddy lived with the Wilfords and then got a small apartment over the town clerk's office. For this he paid ten dollars per month for two rooms - a sitting room and a bedroom. After about two months, Ronald Knowles, the town clerk, would not charge him any more rent as he said it was too much trouble keeping accounts of it.

The parish of Okotoks, at that time, had three churches and two mission points. The churches were St. Peters's, Okotoks, All Saints, Nanton and Christ Church, Millarville.

Christ Church, Millarville   *St. Peter's, Okotoks*

The two places where they frequently took afternoon services were Aldersyde, ten miles south of Okotoks, and Midnapore ten miles north. With regard to the others, Nanton was fifty-five miles south, so they alternated going there every two weeks, generally by train on the Friday and stayed over the Sunday, so that they could get a little visiting. At Millarville, they took a monthly evening service and also monthly communion service. The church at Millarville was a beautiful little log structure, being rather different as it was built with upright logs. Some of the chancel furniture was also logs, peeled and polished. This church was right in the foothills of the Rockies - very beautiful countryside. The congregation came from scattered cattle ranchers. This church and rectory were built by an archdeacon from England who suffered from tuberculosis, and the doctors thought that the clear air of the Rockies would help him. He lived there about forty years in good health. It was indeed a beautiful spot and clear cleaner air, it would be hard to find anywhere. Sometimes the Wilfords would go there for a week or two in the summer. Generally Braddy spent a few days with them.

The only family near the rectory, a couple hundred yards away, was a Scots couple, named Cochran. A few years previous to Braddy's arrival in Okotoks, Wilford had had his trouble with Cochran who was apt to imbibe too much. In those days, there were open bars in Okotoks and on occasion, Cochran would go into town on business and remain to booze. One of these times when he had been away a couple of days his wife got anxious and asked Wilford if he would go into town and get Cochran to return home. Wilford did this and found Cochran well "soaked". He persuaded him to return to Millarville; then Cockran insisted they take a bottle with them for a fresh one on the way. So Wilford persuaded the barman to fill a bottle with water with just a little whiskey to colour it. Quite often they had to stop and take a swig at that bottle by the side of the road. On one such occasion when Wilford had the bottle to his mouth, a woman from Millarville drove by. She was one of those - to be found in all congregations - who loves a little bit of scandal and soon the whole district had heard how she had seen the rector tippling with that "salt", Cochran, on the roads coming out from town.

How Wilford loved that woman! Braddy was witness to a sign of this love. Mrs. Wilford, dear soul, was always trying to make friends with her, so one day while he was with them, she invited her to tea. He thought that it must have been in the early fall, as it was quite chilly outside and the windows had steamed up. At time for tea no visitors had arrived, so of all things, Wilford amused himself by writing on the mist in the window, "Mrs. So and So is a liar." Being Wilford he went away and forgot to wipe it off. You've guessed it. The woman arrived late and saw the inscription on the window. Braddy went for a hurried walk outside until things had quieted down somewhat

While relating things connected with Millarville, Braddy related a rather shivery experience he had. One very cold Sunday afternoon, he drove in the sleigh - there was quite deep snow - to take a service in the church. It was a moonlight night when he drove back. It was at least a two hour's drive, and he was looking forward to the end of the trip and the warmth of the house, when he became aware that he had company. There were shadowy forms trotting along the banks on either side of the road.

"My gosh", Braddy thought, "wolves," and when one let out a terrifying howl, he was sure of it, but comfort came to him, when he saw that Girlie, his pony, took no notice of them. They were coyotes.

Girlie

Braddy mentioned two little mission stations from Okotoks - Aldersyde and Midnapore, where they took afternoons services on Sundays. They were each of them about ten miles away; Aldersyde was on a good road and fairly straight but to Midnapore, the road swerved away from the village, but Braddy noticed that the rail line went as the crow flies. So Braddy asked the railway authorities if they would object to his cycling along it. They told him they could not give official permission, but if he wanted to take a chance, a blind eye would be turned in his direction. So when the weather was good, Braddy cycled to Midnapore along the tracks and saved at least a couple of miles. The road bed was quite smooth and when he came to a bridge over a gully, he walked the bike across to save mishap.

Wilford was what Braddy called accident prone. The incident in Millarville was one example. Another in which Braddy had a share, took place after he been appointed Rector of St. Mark's Church, Calgary. That was when Braddy began as Rector of Okotoks. They were visiting them in Calgary and Wilford and Braddy had been out rabbit shooting and when they returned home, he went down to put coal on the furnace. He had what is known as a hunting vest, that is, it had pockets for short gun cartridges. He'd hung this rather carelessly on a peg on a beam overhanging the coal pile. Braddy was sitting on the top step of the steps into the

Braddy, the Hunter

basement and they were carrying on a conversation about various incidents of the afternoon's hunt. Looking at Braddy, he was shovelling coal into the furnace, and unfortunately did not notice that the weskit of cartridges had dropped down onto the coal and he shovelled it into the furnace. Braddy let out a yell of warning, but too late. Also too late was his attempt to shut the furnace door. The result was that it sounded as if a miniature battle was going on in the basement. Every now and then, there would be some sharp pings, as stray shots hit furnace pipes. Wilford was flat on the floor, cautiously raising his head occasionally to see if the bombardment was over. Braddy thought that he was above the line of fire, but hastily retreated when a shot, fortunately somewhat spent, hit his trouser leg. Mrs. Wilford, getting supper, soon began to take an interest in the event and asked what had happened to "Deary" - she always called him that - and why was he making all that noise down in the cellar. Finally, the last shot was fired, and a very shaken parson came up out of his retreat in the cellar.

Braddy remembered so well several delightful families - in Okotoks - his first Canadian families. First and foremost, there was the Wyndom family. They consisted of old Mrs. Wyndom, a daughter and an army colonel, and their two children, Alec, a retired northwest policeman and a daughter. This daughter was probably then in her middle to late fifties, and she was younger than her brother. She was full of good works, not only in the church and community, but also wherever there was anything good to be done, you would be sure she was doing it. And the fourth member of the family was a cousin of old Mrs. Wyndom, a Miss Jane Seymore. She had been connected with political circles in Ottawa and was on Sir John A. McDonald's staff, (a secretary, Braddy thought). (Sometime after the Bradshaws left Alberta, she wrote a series for MacLeans, which Braddy always regretted not having kept.) Braddy was very close to this delightful family, and he could drop in at anytime and have a chat and often a meal. He kept his pony, Girlie, in the barn at the back where she got expert attention from Alec, who was an accomplished

56

horseman, and he also gave Braddy his first lessons in harnessing and caring for the horse. He warned Braddy that in very cold weather he must never put the bit in Girlie's mouth without first dipping it in a pail of water, so that it would ice over, and thus eliminate the risk of damaging the pony's tongue. Braddy and the archdeacon from Calgary often went partridge and rabbit hunting with Alec.

Another family that Braddy saw a lot of were the Knowles. He was from a wealthy English family, town-clerk, and owner of the rooms Braddy had over his office on Main Street. His wife came from Ontario; they had two children. The younger one married Kemp, who was one of Braddy's successors as Rector of Okotoks. He was afterwards Rector of George's Church, Montreal. Braddy spoke to her once on the phone while visiting his daughter, Beryl, who was living near Montreal at the time-probably during the 1970's.

On one occasion when Braddy paid an afternoon call on Mrs. Knowles and was sitting next to the piano, and without thinking, blew the dust off the top.

She, a very good housekeeper was shocked, but just said, "Well"! Braddy shrivelled.

During another afternoon drop-in call, he was asked by Mrs. Knowles to stay for dinner. While Braddy was saying grace, Ronald was mumbling something. His wife asked him what it was all about. He said, "I was only counting the pork chops to see whether they would go around. "

Another very fine family with two small daughters, was the Downeys. One of these girls called on the Bradshaws at the rectory in Yarmouth, during the war. She was married to an army officer stationed at the camp in Yarmouth at that time. Downey had the Jed's Furnishing in town.

Another couple was the Sam Hodsons. He was editor, publisher and compositor of the weekly one sheet town paper, *The Okotoks Review*. He was very proud of his literary accomplishments. He read largely, especially history. He seemed to have a warped sense of humour and once annoyed Maggie when they were at tea at the rectory. Maggie had some buttered thin slices of brown bread and Sam said, "Mrs. Bradshaw, I like my bread buttered around the edges." Maggie, in haste, had only buttered the slices in the middle.

There was one man in Okotoks, who did not like Braddy, mainly because he was Anglican. He was a rather bigoted Methodist. His name was Welsh. He thought he had Braddy on the spot. It was the last year of the war and he was chairman of the draft board. He told Mr. Wilford that he was calling Braddy before the Board to find out why he had not enlisted.

He could have gotten out of it without appearing before the Board but Braddy thought it would be rather fun to appear. Braddy did so and showed them his release from active service because of his defective eyesight. Also they were ignorant of the fact that clergymen were exempt anyway. They thought that a deacon, like in the Methodist church, was only a layman.

After Braddy's ordination on May 24, 1918 in St. Peter's church, Okotoks, he moved to Nanton to take charge of that parish, to which was added the town of Vulcan that had a growing congregation although they had no church. Vulcan was a small town about forty miles east of Nanton, on a C.P.R. Branch line.

For a time the parish of Nanton had been added to that of Okotoks. There had been a rector of Nanton, a priest called Hilchie. He was very similar to the late Gordon Lewis, whom Braddy met many years later in Yarmouth. He was quite a scholar but different from Father Lewis - not a good parish priest. His mind was more inclined to farming so when Bishop Pinkham got word from the S.P.G. he asked Wilford to take charge of Nanton with Braddy's help. So Hilchie retired from active ministry and settled with his wife on a small farm which he owned on the edge of town. They were a happy-go-lucky couple. They lived in the barn in a part divided from various livestock by a partition. These living quarters were divided into two by a curtain. One part was kitchen-come-sitting room and the other was the bedroom. Braddy used to drop in and see them quite frequently and he found their living habits quite crude. For each meal, part of the kitchen table was covered in newspapers. Mrs. Hilchie said that it saved a lot of laundry.

Bishop Pinkham

Braddy recalled their departing from Nanton shortly after Beryl was born. They had bought a small fruit farm in the Okanagan Valley in British Columbia. Braddy thought that he had some private means. To move his belongings, and they were a weird collection, he ordered from the C.P.R., a box-car. This car came and he was told that if he held it more that three days for loading, demurrage would be charged. The people of the community all thought that that should give them plenty of time; but,

58

they did not allow for some of his peculiarities. One was, that while like a pack-rat, he had gathered a weird collections of goods including hundreds of flattened out kerosene tins, also many more tins filled with cow manure, which he was taking to fertilize his new orchard, and also lots of other junk. When he started to load the box-car, he had help but he was never satisfied that he had utilized the space to the best advantage and pulled it all out and reloaded it differently. The result was that it took over a week to load and thus he had to pay heavy demurrage fees. The congregation and their friends in town were quite peeved about this as they had given the Hilchies quite a large cash present on their leaving. One man told Braddy that this was practically all used up for demurrage fees. How they did in B.C., Braddy did not know as he heard very little about them after they left.

Until Braddy's marriage, he boarded with a very nice couple called the Langstroffs. They were a delightful couple and made Braddy think of Jack Sprat and his wife. He was quite small and thin; she was very large and stout. He was the town engineer and she ran the boarding house. During Braddy's time with them, there were three permanent boarders. These were two teachers, besides Braddy, and also there were quite frequent occasional boarders. Generally they were commercial travellers and bank and government officials. Mrs. Langstroff charged Braddy $5 a week for his room and then there was a good scheme for meals. A meal card which cost $6 had 21 little divisions on it, which covered a week's meals, namely three meals a day. After each meal, one little division was marked. If one was not present for a meal it was not marked and that meant that Braddy's ticket generally lasted for at least two weeks, because he was frequently absent for one meal, and sometimes two a day, because he had invitations for many meals. Braddy's boarding was not expensive, for which he was glad, as his stipend was then only $75 per month, and he was saving for their marriage. The Langstroff's had one son, Charlie, who was with the Canadian Forces in France. His poor mother used to worry about him and at the time of the Armistice, November 11, she worried until she got a telegram telling her that he was safe.

Braddy remembered one morning, after he had eggs and bacon for breakfast, she asked him whether the eggs were good, and he replied, "Excellent". She then told him that they were over a year old. She had put them down in water glass a year before, when eggs were plentiful and cheap. They certainly kept wonderfully.

Fred Ings and his wife, lived on what was known as Mid-way ranch. It was supposed to be midway between Calgary and MacLeod near the

U.S. border. He was an uncle of Mrs. George Armstrong and was a typical, lusty, hard-swearing rancher. Mrs. Ings use to have a time keeping him partially subdued when Braddy was around. While Braddy was still travelling from Okotoks, one weekend he stayed with the Ings. They had a beautiful home. While with them, Braddy's pony, Girlie, roamed in the coral near the house. On Monday when he was leaving for Okotoks, Fred Ings said that he would catch and harness Girlie for him. Braddy told him that he might have trouble getting her to take the bit.

He replied, "Parson don't you teach a grandmother to suck eggs!" After a time as he did not appear, Braddy and Mrs. Ings looked out and there was Fred with his arms around Girlie's neck trying to get the bit into her mouth. As fast as he put it in, she grinned and spat it out. The ground and air were blue from his swearing and Mrs.Ings begged Braddy to stop his ears. Anyway, Braddy went out and Fred looked at him and he could see he dared him to say anything. Braddy didn't, but went to Girlie and she had a sort of grin on her mouth. Braddy took the bit and slipped it in and there it remained. He said goodbye to Mrs. Ings and thanked them both. Mr. Ings was still "blankety, blanking" when Braddy drove away.

Mrs. Ings used to have a time getting Fred to go to church, but at one evening service she did get him there. They had with them their small daughter, Mary - about five. All went well until during a pause in the prayers, Braddy heard Mary say in her shrill treble voice, "Daddy when are we going to have 'Tip'?" "Tip" was short for "It's a Long Way to Tipperary", her favourite song.

One other incident with regards to Fred Ings, the memory of which caused Braddy shivers for some time. Braddy had had midday dinner with them and Fred, during the afternoon, said that he had to go to a distant field on the ranch to look out some young steers, to see how they were fattening. He asked Braddy if he would like to go along and Braddy certainly did. Just as they were setting off, Mary who had just had her afternoon nap, appeared and demanded to go too. As her father could deny her nothing, he said, "Yes." She could sit on the parson's knee. Mrs. Ings was a bit doubtful, but agreed. Fred drove a buck-board with a pair of very sprightly young horses, so they set-off into the foothills where the steers were pastured, found them all right and returned home. When getting into what was known as the home pasture a flock of prairie chickens got up under the horse's feet and they promptly took fright and ran away. Fred told Braddy to hang on to Mary and he would soon have the team under control. As he spoke, one of the reins broke. Things did not look at all pleasant, because the only control on the tearing horses was one rein;

60

however, Fred, with that one rein, managed to steer them into a barbed fence, that circled the field. It was a masterly piece of driving and continually bumping into the fence on one side, slowed them down, and gradually they came to a stop. Braddy knew that the only one who enjoyed that incident was Mary, who seemed to think that the whole thing was put on for her entertainment. Sometimes over the sounds of Fred's swearing at the madly flying horses, Braddy got snatches from Mary of, you guessed it, "It's a Long Way to Tipperary." Personally it seemed to Braddy to be a very short trail.

Another note-worthy member of Nanton congregation was a Mrs. Jack Samson, who was often a thorn in the flesh in the Women's Guild, as she wanted to boss everything. Her husband, Jack, was a very pragmatic individual. He did not believe in saying two words when one would do. Sometimes he had difficulty in even getting in the one. He was a commercial traveller and was away from home a lot. Among other things, Mrs. Samson was a social climber, and in appearance was quite an attractive person. Her turn-out for social occasions was something to behold. One such occasions stuck in Braddy's mind. He was returning home one afternoon when he saw her dressed-up "to the nines", driving her cow up Main Street, to be ready for its evening milking. Cows in Nanton, during the day, were allowed to roam at will throughout the town and then were collected by their owners at night. Mrs. Samson had been on a women's social gathering and thought she would save time by taking the cow home with her.

Two doors away from the rectory were the Winsbys. Tom Winsby was an accountant, Braddy thought in the Bank of Commerce. His wife was younger than he was and rather "rattled-pated". They had one small son, about a year old, called John. They used to have quite fierce rows and on occasion, Braddy was called in to mediate. She was always threatening to leave him. One morning, Braddy was going down to the post office to get his mail, and Mrs. Winsby was coming out of their home with her suitcase, and announced cheerfully, "I'm leaving Tom."

Braddy replied, "Let's go to the restaurant and have a cup of coffee. You've got plenty of time before the train leaves for Calgary." So they did that, and after about thirty minutes, she said, "I'd better be getting home to see if John is awake yet."

Living was very casual in those days. One Nanton incident always remained in Braddy's mind. On the outskirts of town there lived a family called Whiteside who had a small farm. There were a number of children and the family sometimes found the going rather hard. He was a sort of man of all trades around the town. If anything wanted fixing, Whiteside was called to do it. Their youngest boy was called Sammy, and one winter night the alarm went out that Sammy was missing. He was about four. The last that had been seen of him, he was following an older brother out to the barn to milk the cows. Very soon the R.C.M.P. constable had organized a search party of men and women to search the neighbouring prairie and neighbourhood. It was a cold night, about twenty degrees below zero, and there was no snow on the ground, so there were no tracks. Braddy thought it was about three o'clock in the morning when they got word that Sammy had been found. At least in one sense, he had never been lost. It seemed he crawled out from under the sofa in the kitchen, where he had hidden to escape going to bed and had fallen asleep there. Braddy was very glad to get home and crawl into bed, not under it.

At Vulcan, the congregation was small was quite active. They had no church building. The Anglicans with the Roman Catholics, used the Oddfellow's hall on alternate Sunday mornings. A church warden, Howse, was a bank manager, who with his wife was very enthusiastic about building a church for the congregation and to do this they had to build up the congregation itself. Braddy believed that not long after he left, they accomplished their goal and eventually had a church.

They used all kinds of means of raising funds. One Braddy remembered in particular, as he had an active part in. There was in the town a fine covered rink for skating and it was arranged to have a skating carnival with prizes. Proceeds were to go toward the building of the new church. Braddy was asked whether he would go to Calgary to solicit from firms there, prizes for the carnival. Doubtfully he agreed; he did not look forward to being very successful in this. So one morning he set off by train and got into the city about ten o'clock. There were then, two daily newspapers published in Calgary, *The Herald* and *The Albertan* which had both morning and evening editions. Braddy saw both editors and got from each of them three morning and three evening gift subscriptions. That was twelve prizes right away. Then he saw Robin Hood Flourmills and got from them two ninety-eight pound bags of flour. Pat Burns & Company produced a couple of sides of bacon. Braddy went to the Hudson Bay company. The manager gladly gave him an easy chair. Going across the road to Eatons, there he was asked what the Bay had given and they would go one better. They gave a chair and a little end table. Then the thought struck Braddy that perhaps the photographers would come through, so he went to a couple and got from them, gladly, several orders for three and six cabinet photos. Incidentally, these caused him some trouble in Nanton by the local photographer who took a dim view of what might have been customers going to Calgary. Ironically, he got a prize; you guessed it - six cabinet photos from Calgary. The carnival was a great success and the proceeds quite large.

Braddy remembered two brothers who were very regular attendants at church services. Their name was Sings. They came from Ireland. Their older brother was Lord Sings. They farmed a half section of land, that is three hundred and twenty acres and lived in a small shack under primitive conditions. Once Braddy called to see them around midday dinner time. They begged him to sit in which he did. One of them wiped a tin plate on the seat of his overall pants and with a knife and fork Braddy was equipped. Like most bachelor homesteaders, they did not spend much time on housekeeping; but these two, although they lived in very primitive conditions were always immaculately dressed when they went into the church services in Vulcan. Early training in their home in an Irish castle had had results.

On Braddy's last Sunday at Nanton, the rector at High River, the neighbouring parish, wished to be away and asked if Braddy would act for him on that day. This Braddy gladly did at the eight o'clock communion service. He had present the Prince of Wales, afterwards Edward the Eighth and his staff, at that service. He was staying at his ranch about thirty miles into the foothills. Braddy mentioned this fact to Joe Clark, the newly elected leader of the Progressive Conservative Party when writing to him congratulating him on his election, as High River was his home town.

Braddy wrote back to the Codrington College magazine now and then and the first message from Okotoks, Alberta during the summer of 1918 in his own words is :

Well, I am here in this little prairie city twenty eight miles this side (south) of Calgary. I am under the Rev. H. Wilford, a Cambridge man. He was Father Wilford of Chesterfield in England. 'Nuff said'. We have a large district, which up to two years ago was administered by four priests. It consists of six little townships. So you will see that Sunday is a fairly busy day for us. We have to separate, and that to my sorrow, only gives me one celebration a month.

The visiting is quite a task too. I am getting a bike for the present, but I expect it will mean horses very soon.

The weather now is just awfully hot - 85, 90, 95 degrees in the shade. Then at night it freezes.

I have my own rooms - bedroom, sitting room and kitchen for which I pay four dollars a month unfurnished but inclusive of electric light. I do all my own work and go out for meals at the restaurant which costs me six dollars a week.

The people here are very kind. We get both tennis and bridge. The tennis court is an earth one and it took me quite a time to get used to it, but when I did I found I could almost shine.

This place is very much like an English village - awfully sleepy and gossipy. The church people in it are few. Our average congregation is 30. Dissent is very strong. In other places it is just the same and I don't know how they manage to find our combined salaries. There is no coin less than a five-cent piece and no copper coinage.

Just now one of the scourges of Canada is daily expected, that is, hail storms. One passed quite close the day before yesterday. The hail stones are generally about one and a half inches square and they destroy everything green about. One hundred square miles of wheat and oats were entirely destroyed by this storm that passed us by. All the windows on the western side of next town of High River were broken. This part of Canada is, I am glad say, intensely patriotic; the same cannot be said of the East, where they are anything but patriotic. It is the brutes of Liberals led by Laurier that are causing the trouble. People here are raving because every town and village has given its best and there is barely a family here in Okotoks that has not contributed one at least to the fighting line. Many have returned maimed for life and many will not return at all.

The local paper here is awfully funny. It even records the fact when I breathe extra hard. Such a thing as this came out of it. "The Rev. A.G. Bradshaw passed this office today on his way to church.

In his next letter he writes about one of his favourite things:

I am fairly busy now endeavouring to put the finances of the church on a firmer and more businesslike footing. We are trying a new scheme and it seems to be the only one; that is getting every one to promise a stated weekly subscription. I have seen a fair number of the Church people and so far have had promises amounting to 700 dollars yearly. We want to try and raise l,200 dollars and then we shall be self-supporting. At present we get a grant of 200 dollars from the diocese which is not satisfactory at all; and I told them on Sunday night that they ought to be ashamed to take it.

Braddy writes about his 1918 Lenten and Easter Services:

We have had a fairly busy Lent. I have taken a week service every Thursday at Nanton, another small town in our charge forty miles off by rail. On Ash Wednesday we had eleven people present, and there has been an increase of one each Thursday since then; last night there were fifteen. This will seem awfully small to you, but when you consider that it is half of our Sunday congregation it is not so bad after all. Next Thursday I go down to Nanton again and stop over Easter.

During Holy Week I am having a service every night there, and the usual Good Friday service on that day. I take the Easter Service there, and Mr. Wilford will motor down for a noon Celebration if the roads will allow him to do so. He will have to take the Celebration at 8 a.m. and then leave directly for Nanton, forty miles by road. This will be the only chance I shall have of making my Easter Communion. If the roads are in their present condition it will be impossible for him to make the trip. That is my present sorrow, that it is but rarely that I get a Celebration.

Braddy comments on his Lenten observations:

My Lent observances this year have been especially hard to keep. I have simply longed to smoke. On Sundays there is such a little time to spare; all one can do is to get a smoke on the trail between churches, and then after Evensong here I go to one of the Vestrymen's houses and we sit and discuss the doings of the week, and puff away until midnight.

And thoughts of his car:

Situated as we are in Okotoks we do get plenty of chances of going to Calgary. It is only about twenty-six miles of road, and there are always cars going into the city. There are some lovely cars out here. Big Powerful brutes which just eat up the road. The other evening I came from Calgary in just under forty-five minutes. Several times we touched fifty miles an hour. One of the Wardens at Nanton lives about five miles out. I was at his ranch on Sunday evening last, and made it rather late for Church. Evensong was at 7.30 and we left his house at 7.24 and got to the Church at half-past seven, doing the five miles in six minutes, not bad was it? He has a Mitchell, eight cylinder car, a beauty. It cost three thousand dollars. I am thinking seriously of trying to get a three-seator Overland very soon.

And in late 1918 Braddy writes with much less pleasant news:

I am sorry to say that there is sickness on all sides here. Half the town is down with something or other, and I am nearly run off my feet. There is so much to do when a whole family is down with the "flu", even if it is only feeding the cows and children, and drawing water for use in the house. All the doctors and nurses are so busy that every little bit helps in taking some of the work off them. I have had more funerals in the last month than I have had in all the rest of my time in Canada. I do hope that we will be open for Christmas time. The Church has now been closed seven weeks.

The weather remains very warn for the season of the year.

The Church is looking up and I believe that when we do open up again we shall go ahead fast. I am hoping that the people will build a new church for a peace memorial, and then we can turn the present building into a rectory.

... then much more pleasant news:

The following notice is appearing in certain papers in the Dominion of Canada -

Bradshaw - Greenidge

On Saturday 18th January a quiet wedding was celebrated at 9 a.m. between Rev. Alleyne George Bradshaw (Braddy), Incumbent of Christ Church, Nanton, and Margaret, only daughter of Mr. and Mrs. Malcolm Greenidge of Haynes Hill,

Barbados, B.W.I. The Rev. Heritage officiated.

That is the great news I have to tell you. I can hardly realize it myself yet. My Bishop is pleased, and my people are pleased, and I, well I won't mention my own feelings at all. We are leaving for home, i.e. England. for a short visit before we return to Nanton to settle down there.

And after the honeymoon Braddy writes:

We are fairly well settled down in Nanton again after a most pleasant trip to England. I was glad to see the old County again, and to renew old friendships, but I don't think that I could settle down there.

We have a nice little house here (temporary) until the Rectory is finished for us. It is a four roomed cottage, with a kitchen at the back. But it is quite sufficient for my wife to look after, as there are not the number of servants which Barbados boasts of here.

When we get our proper Rectory that will only be a five roomed bungalow, with a verandah. All being well we shall build our Church this year, that is if there is a good crop. It is to cost about 5,000 dollars, 3,000 of which are promised already. The people are very keen indeed, and I believe that a dignified House of God will stir up their enthusiasm more than the present little shanty has done.

And then Braddy tells about a very bad snow storm:

Last Friday and Saturday we had the worst snowstorm that has been known for fifty years, and many cattle and horses were lost. But the moisture did a lot of good to the ground and springing crops. The change in our climate is wonderful; on Saturday it was 10 degrees above zero, today 80 degrees in the shade and a beautiful May day. The snow which was two feet deep on the level and in drifts ten to twenty feet deep, has nearly all gone except where the drifts were very deep. By tomorrow there will be no sign of it at all.

And on his natal day (February 3rd) Braddy writes to his College

Magazine and expresses his thoughts about the Canadian Theological Colleges:

> From here nearly all our men go to the Canadian colleges, preferably St. Chads, Regina and also unfortunately to Whycliff, Toronto.

And again something about the weather:

> We have had a terrible cold winter so far, but I hope that the worse is over. We have not had as many warm waves as usual. Last week the thermometer hovered around 38 degrees below zero for several days.

More about the church and the church laymen:

> Of my two parishes Vulcan is the most encouraging. On Sunday it was bitterly cold and we had 38 in the morning at the Eucharist at 11 a.m. and 30 at Evensong - 20 men in the morning and 25 men at night. I only lack incense there of the 9 points now, and who knows I may get it soon, as a brother of one of the congregation there is on his way out from England, and she tells me that he used to "sling" the incense in St. Mathew's, Leicester, so perhaps he will "sling" it for me. On my vestry in Vulcan I have a Presbyterian Church Warden - my warden, a Methodist, another Presbyterian and two Theosophists; the two latter are by far the best Churchmen there. I do not know quite what to say with regard to the people here in Nanton. Two weeks ago, I had out for the day one person; it was a bitterly cold day, but still there would have been more if it had been a dance. We had some awfully inspiring interchurch services a few weeks ago. We had a service in a different Church every night; I took my own service as well and preached at the Methodist one on Friday. The Bishop here will not permit exchange of pulpit, but he does not mind the clergy preaching in other buildings belonging to other denominations. I had my church full on the Wednesday evening, one of the only times that I have it so.

6   MARRIAGE - A NEW EXPERIENCE

Off to New York and Marriage

(Braddy taped this on January 18, 1974, on his and his wife's fifty-fifth wedding anniversary).

A few days after the war ended Braddy had received a communication from the Bishop of Calgary, telling him that he heard from the S.P.G. and that he had been asked to release Braddy for his three month's leave which had been on hold because of the war, as soon as possible. Braddy was to reply so he wrote to the Bishop and asked him if it would be all right if he left at the beginning of the year. At this time, the influenza epidemic that took place late in 1918, was in full flood and both churches in Nanton and Okotoks were closed because of the 'flu'. Finally, it was agreed with the Bishop, that Braddy should take his leave at the beginning of 1919, and he also agreed with him that during that time he might be married. Braddy had to get his permission because that had been the arrangement with the S.P.G.

Early in January of 1919, Braddy started off for Brooklyn, New York. Maggie was already there. She had come up from Barbados and was staying with a Mrs. Polson. She was working in the office of the World Council of Churches. There they were to meet and there on January 18th they were to be married. Braddy went by train, from Calgary to Brooklyn.

A rather interesting thing happened on the way. It was a long journey - about four days. When they got into the United States, going along the side of the Hudson River, there was a gentleman in the same car with Braddy who came up and sat beside him and asked if this was his first trip. He told him yes, and he then asked Braddy if he would like him to explain about some of the places they were passing on the banks of the Hudson. He told Braddy that he was president of the Y.M.C.A. in Montreal for Canada, and also vice-president of an American company and that he was going on business to New York. They began talking and finally when they reached New York Central Station, he told him that this was the only station in the world where the station was level with the train. You stepped straight off on the level from the train and did not have to go down the usual steps to get to the platform. Braddy knew that every little wayside station in England had the same type of platform - level with the train. Anyway, he kindly asked Braddy to have lunch with him at the Yale club before he continued on to Brooklyn. So they went there to lunch and they had lunch with another friend of this man, Samuel Compers, who was then president or Labour Leader of one of the big unions. While at lunch, there were a number of young men who came into the lunch room and this man from the train identified one of these men as MacKenzie King, a very prominent political leader or would be a prominent Liberal leader in Canada. He smiled and said he thought he had been dodging the draft in the States. Braddy did not know anything about MacKenzie King, in those days, so he made no comment. After lunch, Braddy said that he must get out to Brooklyn. This man kindly offered to take him there and so they got onto the subway and went out to Brooklyn. There they separated and although they did correspondence once or twice after that they lost touch with each other and in later years Braddy could not remember his name.

Braddy arrived at Mrs. Polson's boarding house in Brooklyn. Maggie, her Aunt Ada and Clarice Bistrom, a friend of Maggie's, also from Barbados, were there to greet him. Braddy had already gotten bookings on one of the White Star liners for their trip to England. Quite early he got in touch with their office to confirm their reservations and check on departure time. He was told that they would keep in touch with them. Braddy did not want to make the wedding arrangements until he knew about the reservations. In several days he was notified that the ship had arrived but that it would take a little while for it to be put into condition to make the return trip to England, as it had brought back American troops and was in a pretty shabby state; but they promised to keep Braddy informed on when they could sail, and to go ahead with their wedding so they would be ready when they got the call. So, they arranged for their wedding. They found there were several things that had to be done before they were married. One was they had to apply for permission to get married from a Bureau in Brooklyn and their names had to appear in the paper for three days stating that they wished to be married. To get this permission they both had to go to the Bureau Hall. They went off, and to Braddy's horror (He admitted he was rather a retiring young man in those days.), he discovered there were about sixty couples lined up going into the Bureau to get their marriage licenses. He was quite peeved and going up the steps he said to Maggie that if he were ever married again it would not be in Brooklyn. There was an old Irish policeman on the steps to the Hall controlling the procession going in and he laughed so much, Braddy thought he might shake his helmet off. When they got into the hall the clerk who attended Braddy, said, "Dr. (In the States they called every parson, doctor.), will you swear or affirm. Braddy answered that he would

70

affirm because he had been swearing violently for the last fifteen minutes. The clerk said that he was afraid that Braddy was not taking this matter seriously. Braddy let that go by. Finally they got the permission for the license, or permission for their statement to be put in the paper that they wished to be married on January 18th. Then as it got close to the eighteenth, they made arrangements with the acting priest in charge of the church of All Saints. The rector was away and there was a man called Heritage, who was in charge. He didn't appeal to Braddy at all; he discovered that he was an Ulster Protestant and was he ever Protestant! When they told him that they wanted a Communion Service at the time of the marriage, he said that he had never heard of such a thing and asked why they wanted that. Braddy told him that it was very customary, even if he didn't know it and that they wanted one. So after that the priest agreed that they would have a Communion Service.

The night of the 17th, Braddy was stopping at Mrs. Polson's visiting with Maggie, Clarice and Aunt Ada. Braddy decided to have a good hot bath. So he got the water in the bath - good and warm - just as he liked it; then, he went into the bedroom to undress and he put on his dressing gown, fortunately. When he got back to the bathroom, he found Maggie, Clarice, Aunt Ada and Mrs. Polson all in the bathroom testing the water and they all agreed that he had gotten it too hot. They didn't think that Braddy should get into water as warm as that. He told them if they didn't get out, he was going to take off his dressing gown and get into the water. They all fled.

The next day, at nine o'clock they went to the church. They had intended to have a quiet wedding. Braddy's idea was that Maggie, with Clarice, as her attendant, would be present and he told them that the rector would probably find another witness, so that they would have the two necessary witnesses. To Braddy's surprise, when they went into the church, there were about one hundred people present. He found out afterward that nearly all of them were Barbadians. Maggie's Uncle John was present, father of Graham Clark, and a lot of others including a great friend, Ellie. Rev. Heritage asked who the best man was, and Braddy told him he had not gotten anyone. Braddy asked him to find another witness, so he looked out over the congregation and called out a young man and Braddy didn't know who he was; but he found out afterwards that it was Ellie's husband. (Not too long after that Ellie and her husband were divorced.) Rev. Heritage was so unhappy about the Communion Service that he made them go down to the bottom of the church and sign the register before he would go on with the Communion Service. He wanted to make sure that the

Communion Service was separate from the marriage service itself. Finally, they were quite happily married. As they left the church there were newspaper signs up everywhere, the greatest day in the history of the world. Braddy thought that was probably so. He was feeling pretty on top of things himself. He turned to Maggie and said, "Who told them we were getting married?" He discovered after that it was the day of the first meeting of the Peace Conference, after the closure of the war on November 11, 1918.

They had the usual festivities when they got home, including a cake, and Braddy met people he had never seen before. They had quite a good time. Braddy kept phoning the steamship company and they kept telling him that no other boats had come in and they didn't have any that were fit and ready to make a return trip. It was toward the middle of February and they were getting anxious, when they were finally told there was a ship for them so they got off to England. Unfortunately, their stay in England would be now only about six weeks because they had to be back by the end of March when his leave expired.

Back to Nanton

Wedding Picture of Maggie and Braddy, 1919

The newly weds got back to Nanton after the expiration of Braddy's leave and found that the churches were still closed because of a continuation of the 'flu' epidemic

Beryl, their first child, was born in Nanton. The rectory was rather on the tiny side, consisting of four small rooms-dining room, sitting room, two bedrooms and a lean-to kitchen. The night that Beryl was born - April 6th, 1920 - there was a late severe spring blizzard. However, both nurse and doctor, who did not live far away, struggled through the

Nanton Rectory, 1919

blinding snow and arrived on time. Dr. Keen was typical of many a prairie doctor of those days - somewhat rough and ready - but ever faithful in attendance wherever and whenever he was needed. In the Spanish 'flu' epidemic of 1918, he was not home for ten days. He travelled from patient to patient and got what sleep he could between visits, in his car.

When he arrived at the rectory to deliver Katherine Beryl that snowy night, the first thing he asked for was a can. Braddy found him one, wondering what he wanted that for. He soon found out. The doctor placed it in the living room which was off the bedroom where Maggie was. All this was a help to Braddy, who was very jittery, like most expectant fathers, and he kept wondering what he was going to do with the can. He wanted it to "spit" in. He was chewing tobacco and he never missed that can once. His working over Maggie in bringing Beryl into the world was accompanied by frequent "pings" as he hit his mark - the can. Braddy was so fascinated by this performance that he almost forgot to be worried about the safe arrival of his first-born.

Preparing to Leave Canada

Early in 1921 Braddy had been in touch with Bishop Berkeley in Barbados and he assured Braddy that he would be welcome back there, first acting for the rector of St. James, who wished to go on holiday out of the island for six months, and after that the Bishop had no doubt that a parish would be available for him. So Braddy tendered his resignation to Bishop Pinkham of Calgary diocese and toward the end of April, 1921 they prepared to leave.

The Bradshaws packed their limited amount of clothes, books and other belongings at Okotoks which had been their permanent home for the past year. Incidentally, Braddy used for his books, the very strong wooden box that his brother, Jim, had made for him when he left home for Codrington College, Barbados in 1913. This box, Braddy recalled, got to Musquodoboit Harbour in 1928 but he did not recall how much longer it served him.

They spent a few days with the Wilfords (He was then rector of St. Mark's in Calgary.) and then they started on their four-day train journey across Canada to Halifax to reach the boat for Barbados. Knowing very little about the railway system in those days, Braddy, Maggie and Beryl took the C.P. which landed them in St. John, New Brunswick where they had to disembark and cross on the ferry to Digby and thence to Halifax. If Braddy had known, they should have travelled by C.N. which would have taken them into Halifax without the wear and tear of crossing the Bay of Fundy. Of course, Braddy little knew then how familiar in years to come that ferry would be, how it would be used by the Bradshaws frequently and, of course, all that knowledge was a good deal to do with their offspring who were then still in the womb of time.

During the long train trip they found that the dining car attendants were always ready to supply hot water for Beryl's frequent feeds. Braddy and Maggie had been worrying about this but as so frequently happens there was no need at all for worry. They stayed at the Queen Hotel, Halifax, and received very kind treatment while waiting for the ship to Barbados. The ship eventually sailed with them on board for the two week's voyage. Also on board was Canon Malone, his first wife and their son, Edward. He was returning to his cure at St. Pauls, Bay Street, Bridgetown, Barbados, after having acted for the encumbent at St.Peters Cathedral in Charlottetown, P.E.I.

In early 1921 Braddy writes to the Barbados Magazine of the coming return to Barbados:

> *I suppose that you have heard by the time you get this letter that we are returning to Barbados in May. I am acting as Locum for Mr. McConney for six months and after that the Bishop thinks that he can find me work.*

Before he leaves the west, Braddy has an interesting comment:

The majority of persons one meets here are seared with the spirit of the West, which is hurry and indifference; not one in fifty reads, and the one that does perhaps you hear accused of being lazy because he had had to neglect his work.

Tragedy

A tragic incident concerned a young R.C.M.P. officer who was a regular attendant at Braddy's services. He was probably a member of the church Vestry, Braddy thought. After the Bradshaws left Alberta he moved to a small town south of Nanton with his wife and child. There happened then a bad bank hold-up in Calgary and two of those responsible - a man and a woman - fled south evidently trying to get to the United States border. On their way they stopped at the R.C.M.P. officer's house and on their knock a small daughter came to the door. They told her they wanted to see her daddy. When he came, they both fired their guns and shot him dead - yet another violent tragedy of the west. They were both caught and tried. The constable was only hit by one bullet but they had both fired and both were found guilty and hanged. Those were before the days when Canadians exerted every means to avoid the death penalty for such merciless murderers. All this happened within a year of the Bradshaws leaving but Braddy got full accounts of it.

BARBADOS MINISTRY

Barbados- 1921 to 1928

On his return to Barbados, Braddy, his wife, Maggie and their young daughter, Beryl, were enthusiastically welcomed back:

> *It has been a great pleasure to welcome back to Barbados the Rev. A. G. Bradshaw (Braddy) who since 1917 has been working in the Diocese of Calgary, West Canada. Mr. Bradshaw is going to act as Rector of St. James in this island for six months and then hopes to take up permanent work in the diocese.*

St. James Church, Barbados

Braddy and family took up residence in the Rectory of St. James for six months at the beginning of June, when the McConneys left on their holiday to the United States. For transportation Braddy bought from Father McConney his pony and buggy. This he sold when he obtained a car.

The most important thing that happened at St. James was the birth of Joan, their second daughter. It was Sunday, the 28th of August. Braddy went to church and took the eight o'clock service and afterwards went to Dr. Massiah and told him that he did not think it would be long before they had a son or daughter. He laughed at him and told him not to be in such a hurry. However, when Braddy got back to the rectory the nurse told him that the arrival might be any time. So back he drove to the doctor. Again, he did not seem very impressed but said that he would be there by the time Braddy got back home again. When he arrived at the rectory, things were happening and Joan was soon in the world. One of the servants had Braddy sitting on a larder in the passage - the hallway that went from the dining room to the kitchen - and when he heard Joan give a cry upstairs he looked around and said, "Puss! Puss! Puss!" It was not the only time that Joan had this experience relating to a cat. Rhue Holmes-Watson, of Edgehill, once said that Joan reminded her of "the cat that walks alone," a quotation the source of which Braddy could not remember. In passing Braddy commented that Maggie never lost much time bringing her offspring into the world; and they all had the distinction of being born at home.

In August of that year, Braddy got his second car. In Alberta he had a Model T Ford. This new one was a MacLaughlan Buick.

When Clyde Greenidge, Maggie's brother, came back from the war, Bessie, his mother, had given him this car. It was a two-seater, a six-cylinder car and a very nice one at that. About now, Clyde and his wife, Elise, decided to go to New Jersey to farm and the car was passed over to Braddy.

Clyde and his wife, Elise, were living at Bird River on a road going seaward, somewhere near St. Stephen Church and the Mental Asylum. One day Clyde went to St. James and Braddy went back with him to Bird River and there he handed the car over to Braddy. Braddy had never driven a geared car so to get back to St. James he was on his own to sort out all the intricacies of the strange controls. Coming out of the Bird River Road, Braddy nearly had his first mishap by just missing the street car from Bridgetown. Braddy admitted that his course was a rather wobbly one back to the rectory. By the time he reached home, he had begun to master the various changes of gear. After that he never had any difficulties with the car.

It was probably about the middle of their term at St. James, that Braddy was having lunch at the Women's Self Help in Bridgetown when he was joined by the Rev. Buris Watson, rector of St. Lucy. He introduced himself and told Braddy he had been wanting to see him. The cure of St. Clements was about to become vacant and Rev. Watson asked Braddy if he would like it when his stint at St. James was over. Braddy said that he would talk it over with Maggie and let him know. This happened and they accepted that cure to go to St. Clements at the beginning of December.

One of the four appointments made to Braddy in Barbados was announced as follows:

> *The Rev. A. G. Bradshaw, who has been acting Priest in Charge at St. James. Barbados, has been nominated to the Vicarage of St. Clements and St. Swithens in the Parish of St. Lucy, Barbados. He took up his duties on December 1st.*

Now they were forced with the furnishing problem of the rectory; but as so often happened during Braddy's life, the unexpected happened here to solve this difficulty.

Miss Lottie Parr lived in the small house close to the rectory. One day Braddy dropped in for a chat and she told him that as she was getting on in years, she was moving to Bridgetown, he thought to be with a relative. He asked if she would be disposing of her furniture and she replied that she was getting rid of everything. He told her about their upcoming move to St. Clements and of their need. She then told him she would let them have anything - furniture, towels, bed linen - all the household effects for fifty pounds; that in dollars at the time was two hundred and forty dollars. Braddy did not hesitate at this great bargain and closed the deal right away. As far as he remembered, he only saw Miss Parr once more after they moved to St. Clements and that was after their third child, Dorothy, was born. Miss Parr asked him what they called the three girls. Braddy said facetiously, "Battle, Murder, and Sudden Death."

She was rather deaf and replied, "Faith, Hope, and Charity; that is lovely." She gave each of the three girls a small broach of the three virtues.

The Parish of St. Clements

The Bradshaws entered into residence at the beginning of December. The rectory was just a house - adequate, but nothing to get excited about. It stood on a small piece of land which had very little soil above the rock. The outlook consisted of a few sugar cane fields and a rocky savannah - over Mills Seacoast.

Attached to St. Clements was St. Swithens, about three miles away, not far from St. Lucy's parish church. There were one or two plantations near it. Both churches were clean and well kept but architecturally weren't very exciting.

St. Clements did have one very beautiful stained glass window. It depicted the crucified Lord and was in the east end over the altar. This

St. Clements Church, Barbados

window had a rather peculiar history. It had been given during the time of Braddy's predecessor, Canon Johnson. Its donor was a former parishioner, named King, who had gone to live in the United States. Apparently, he paid a deposit on the window and had sent money to defray the cost of installation and then had paid no more. During Braddy's time in the cure, there were frequent letters from the firm that supplied the windows, for payment. They could get nothing more from Mr. King. Braddy passed these letters over to the diocesan authorities but they refused to pay anything. King died and as far as Braddy knew, the window was never paid for. Before King's death and before the question of payment for the window arose, he sent Braddy a small censer for the use at St. Clements. Braddy wrote to the Bishop requesting permission to use incense in the services. Bishop Berkeley's response was typical of him. He gave permission under one condition; namely, that he was to be present at its first use and that he dedicate it himself. This would safeguard Braddy as to any objections as to its use. Incidentally the Bishop was present and Braddy instructed the thurifer to see that there were plenty of hot coals in the censer when the Bishop put in the incense. They were such hot coals that when the incense was put in the smoke puffed up and his lordship sneezed and scattered hot coals around. One burnt a small hole in Braddy's

Bishop Berkeley

surplice. He was glad that the censer was a small one.

Braddy considered the family lucky, while at St. Clements, to have as parochial medical officer Dr. Hallam Massiah. He was most capable and faithful in attendance when needed and they did need him badly when Beryl was about three years old. She had very bad convulsions. The doctor instructed Braddy and Maggie, when they occurred, to put her in a bath of warm water with a cold cloth on her head. They did this for about three days and she seemed to get much worse; in fact, so much so that the doctor called in his son, Dr. Graham Massiah, who had brought Joan into the world. Neither doctor thought Beryl had much chance of survival; but towards morning the chance came and Beryl's temperature went down and she was not long in getting back to health.

Then Joan acted up. Braddy thought it was possible that she was rather annoyed with all the attention Beryl had been getting. One night she wouldn't go to sleep. She just simply grumbled about this and that and finally Braddy smacked her on the rear end. She gave one shout of murder and then grumbling a bit she decided she had better go to sleep.

Another thing happened with regard to Joan while the Bradshaws were at St. Clements. There was a dressing table in the bedroom and in this table there was a little metal pig out of a Christmas fire cracker. One day after the maid had cleaned off the table, this pig was missing and the girl said that she thought that Miss Joan had swallowed it. They called the doctor, who told them that if she began to cry, he would get her to the hospital at once for X-rays. She did begin to yell one morning and off to the hospital she was taken. There was shown the pig, apparently walking around her large intestine. The doctor assured them that it had passed the danger point and that she would soon discharge it. This happened, Braddy thought, at Haynes Hill, because Grannie Bessie cherished that little pig. Braddy didn't know what eventually happened to it.

Dr. Massiah always inquired after the young lady who could swallow a whole pig. Really, he did not believe she had swallowed it until the X-ray revealed its presence.

Many times in Braddy's ministry, he had, at least one dear old lady in the parish and that was true at St. Clements, in the person of Miss Edith Seal, who lived alone in a very small stone house over in a place called Conneltown - no real town - but for the most part just small shacks. Miss Seal often helped out at the rectory, especially with Joan, and became very fond of her.

Mrs. Grahm, who was known by the Bradshaws and whom they always called Grahmie, was Miss Edith Seal's sister. She lived in a small house up a lane near the cathedral. In fact, it was from that house that Braddy left to come up to Nova Scotia in 1928.

At St. Clements Braddy became very fond of a man named Willowby. He had lived in the United States for some years and had gone back to his old home quite close to the church. He was a very accomplished cabinet maker and did some beautiful work, generally in mahogany.

Braddy got him to do some furniture for the sanctuary at the church. One was a reredos for the altar. Also, he made Braddy a large mahogany tray.

Braddy and Willowby used to go shooting together. There were a number of hares in the cane fields and sweet potatoes patches. On one occasion, when they were out together, Braddy was on one interval between the canes and he on another - not in each other's sight. Braddy heard him fire twice and thought he had missed the first time, but did not think he could miss the second as he was a very good shot. He was surprised when they met to find Willowby had two hares. He gave one to Braddy. They did not do any more hunting that evening.

Not far from the rectory, on the main road in the parish church district was Pickerings, where lived a couple, of whom Braddy and Maggie were very fond. The Queen Mother had a small cottage there that she visited some winters. She was another dear old lady. One day Braddy got a message from her telling him that her nephew David Bower Lyons was visiting her and asked if Braddy would go and have some tennis with him.

Pickerings was also the home of the Mount Gay distillery and once a year, Jim Bovell used to bottle off rum that was matured, When he was doing this he would call Braddy to take over his demijohn for a supply. It cost $1.20 per gallon nearly 100 over proof, so Braddy used to get two gallons to which, before he bottled it, he would add two gallons of water which made it a good drinkable quality and would last about a year. Once when he went over to get his rum he found it ready for him; but he asked Mrs. Bowell where Jim was. She told him to go into the bedroom and there he found Jim drunk to the world. He was surprised because he knew that Jim rarely took a drink but his wife told him that he always got drunk when he drew off the rum. It was the fumes that did it without him drinking a drop.

At one time there was a cane fire in the field next to the rectory. It was a weekday evening, Braddy thought during lent, because he was in the church taking a service. He stopped off talking to a woman in the vestry which was on the side away from the rectory. They did not see the fire until they got on the road leading to the rectory. His heart was in his mouth as he could not see how the rectory could escape. He did not lose much time in getting back to the rectory, about a quarter of a mile away. He found some from the service on the roof of the rectory keeping it damp with buckets of water. Afterwards when all the danger was past, Braddy's yearly supply of rum came in for an awful beating.

Very rarely in parochial life do things go on entirely smoothly. Something may crop up at any time which has a disrupting force. So it was at St. Clements. The headmistress of the girl's school, because of age, retired and the appointment of a new one was in Braddy's hands after consultation with the local school trustees. The second mistress of the school was a young lady, Leonie Griffith, in her early twenties but exceedingly capable. The Griffith family lived about a hundred yards away from the rectory. The father was Superintendent of Lowlands Plantation. Leonie had two young sisters, Coralee and Doris. When the resignation of the headmistress came about, Braddy advertised in the press for applications for the post. He had a number of these and after talking it over with the other trustees and the assistant inspector of schools, Nat Greenhage, who incidentally was married to the youngest daughter, Aggie, of the Clark-Hunts, they all agreed that Leonie Griffith should get the post. She was a very capable teacher, a good disciplinarian and was liked by the children. Greenhage said that he could see some squawks coming from some of the applicants senior to her and Braddy said he certainly got them soon after he had written to the Education Board for the endorsement of Leonie as Headmistress. He had a letter from the board secretary, saying there had been a number of complaints from teachers senior to Miss Griffith and the Board asked Braddy to give the appointment further consideration. He consulted with the chief inspector of schools together with Nat Greenhage and they both agreed with Braddy that Miss Griffith was the logical appointment. He so informed the Board. The next thing that happened was Braddy received a letter from the secretary of the governor telling him that His Excellency had had complaints about

82

the appointment and asked that Braddy go and see him. He was the successor to Sir Leslie Probyn, governor in Braddy's college days. Braddy had a long discussion with him and he decided that it was the best appointment considering the fact that Miss Griffith knew the girls and was liked by them and there would be less disruption of the school if she were appointed head. So it was and she continued in the post until she retired in the early fifties.

(When Braddy and Maggie visited Barbados following his retirement in 1959, Leonie and Coralee used to visit them.)

A comic incident happened while at St. Clements. Near to the entrance to the rectory was a small house, on a high bank, and one day a small pig came down the bank right in front of Braddy's car. He could not stop and turned the pig into pork. The woman who owned it agreed that it was not Braddy's fault. She philosophically thought she could cut it up and save the cost of killing it.

A short time after this as Braddy approached the same spot a donkey rushed out. Fortunately Braddy stopped in time without hitting it. The woman hearing the screech of his breaks, came out and said, "Hey, the reverend killed me pig and now he nearly killed me donkey."

Another important event - Dorothy's entry into the world - happened while the Bradshaws were at St. Clements. Maggie went to Haynes Hill for the birth as she wanted to have her uncle, Dr. Briggs Clark attend her.

Dorothy arrived on May 13, 1923. Braddy, of course, had to remain at St. Clements to look after the services but he went to Haynes Hill as often as possible.

The Parish of St. Jude

In 1924, Braddy was offered the cure by the rector of St. Jude in the parish of St. George. He thought the rector's name was Rev. Howell, a brother-in-law of Bishop Berkeley. They were sorry to leave St. Clements as they had many friends there, but St. Jude was more central and, most of all, because it was nearer to Haynes Hill. Belle Farm, owned by Maggie's family, was also in the district. There was only one church to look after. This was the only time in Braddy's ministry when he had only one, except for a short period in Yarmouth, Nova Scotia, when he only had Holy Trinity, until he took over Tusket on the death of Gordon Lewis.

There was no rectory at St. Jude. They lived in a rented house belonging to a near-by planter, Gordon Gale. The small church was an attractive one within an easy walk from the rectory. There were two very

St. Jude Church, Barbados

active members of the congregation. One was Captain Norse who owned Ashbury Plantation, with a house on the same road as the church. He was an Englishman and as a young man had been thurifer at one of the London churches, All Saints, Margaret Street. Braddy admitted he had never seen anyone more proficient with a censer. In processions, he had a little black boy, who carried the incense, and walked just in front of him. Norse used to swing the censer so it went on one side of the boy's head and back on the other. For a time, Braddy expected and dreaded to hear it smack into the boy's skull but it never did. It spoke well for the boy's steadiness of pace beside the evenness of the swing. The Norses had one son, John, with whom he used to play.

The other very helpful member in everything concerning the church was a shopkeeper, called McConney. He had a small shop near the rectory and often dropped in for a chat.

Before Braddy left St. Clements, he exchanged the heavy Buick car for a light four-cylinder one, an overland by the same firm. In the exchange no money changed hands; so for what it is worth, this was the third car without cost to them. The first car he bought in Alberta for $500 and sold it for the same amount when he left. The second was Maggie's brother, Clyde's, and now no cost in cash.

(When Braddy retired in 1959 and ended his car-owning days, he had had twelve cars with a net cash deficit of around $2,000 for purchase.)

While on the topic of cars, Braddy recalled, a comic incident that happened at St. Jude. One day Braddy was returning from a jaunt somewhere with Joan sitting in the seat beside him, when a little black boy came tearing out from an interval right across the road in front of the car. He quickly swerved into the cane field at the side. He went up the bank and back into the road. He then looked for Joan, but all he could see were her panties. She was up-ended in the bottom of the car. To his relief she slowly climbed back onto the seat and said, "Never do that again, Daddy." The boy was yelling somewhere and he appeared with his mother apparently more scared than hurt. His mother said, "Don't ye worry about that one, Reverend. He tough. He was always following de last Reverend before you and one day he was on the top of de steps behind de Reverend when he opened de church door. The door flew back and the knob caught that young one in de head, and knocked he right down de steps." She then showed Braddy a bump on the top of his head.

In 1925, Charles was born at St. Jude, on August 3. Dr. Briggs- Clark was in attendance. He was the first Bradshaw son.

While at St. Jude, Maggie, who had always enjoyed having "stock" could only have here a couple of goats and a few hens, as there was a very small amount of land. There was one hen with a brood of chicks. As Braddy went into the study one morning, the hen was on the other side of the house from the study. To Braddy's surprise, while he was at the desk, he heard a clucking outside the window. Thinking that the old biddy had soon travelled with her brood around the house, he looked out and to his surprise, he saw a mongoose sitting up and clucking for all it was worth. That was one time that the accomplishment did not have results as he went out and chased Mr. Mongoose away and put the hen and her family in a coop.

Another item of interest while at St. Jude was the parochial mission. Bishop Berkeley obtained from England, three missionaries to take an island-wide teaching mission. They were headed by Canon Burton, Father Simpson from Belfast and the Rev. Hon. Stephen Fillmore, son of Lord Fillmore, a well-known ecclesiastical lawyer in England. St. George's and St. Augustine's parish shared Father Fillmore, each having him three days a week. He was a brawny type, full of fun and a very good speaker and they had a full church at all the services. After the first three days,

Braddy took him over to St. Augustine where Father Sisnett was the vicar.

Fillmore had one phobia - an absolute hatred of cats. He could not stand them. Braddy wondered how he would get on with the Sisnetts as they had several very beautiful Persian cats. When they arrived at the rectory, they were invited to lunch. At that meal, it happened! In the midst of a very cheerful conversation, one of the cats jumped up on the table right next to Fillmore's plate. He never hesitated, but took one swipe at it and knocked it right out of the window into a bunch of bushes. Coming together were the howls from the cat, with this unexpected treatment and the shriek from Mrs. Sisnett. Poor Fillmore had gone very white, and Braddy felt sorry for him. He did not think that this would be a very happy beginning to his mission at St. Augustine, but he found out that Fillmore explained and made his peace with the Sisnetts, who afterwards kept their cats out of his way, as they did not appreciate him playing handball with them.

Many had hoped that Fillmore would succeed Bishop Berkeley when he resigned a few years later, but the majority wanted Bishop Bentley, who was at the time, Assistant Bishop of Jamaica, or Rev. H.B. Gooding. If Fillmore would have become Bishop of Barbados, Braddy felt it was probable that they would never have left the diocese. He wondered in later years what kind of difference that would have made in the lives of the whole Bradshaw family; he knew it would have been considerable.

Braddy said that he firmly believed there is a Divinity that shapes our ends. So many times in his life, courses had taken an entirely different one than what he expected. He felt this was true of all people.

It was while the family was at St. Jude, and were visiting Haynes Hill that Grandfather Mac, Maggie's father, got Braddy to look at a little pimple inside of one nostril. It did not look like much to Braddy, but he shortly afterwards got Dr. Briggs-Clark to look at it. The result was that a smear was sent to the hospital and the verdict came that it was malignant. So it was decided that he should go to New York for treatment. He asked Braddy while he was away to look after his beloved shooting pasture, Coles. He told Braddy he had there a very reliable man, called, Yank. At Coles there were about forty sheep and a small garden in which Grandfather grew shallots, lettuce, herbs, small potatoes and other vegetables. He had instructed Yank to go Haynes Hill every Saturday for his wages and to take with him any money he had gotten from the sale of the produce in the garden. Braddy was to meet him there. The first Saturday Yank did this and also told Braddy that two sheep had died. He didn't think too much about this as the sheep lived a precarious life and they existed only on the barren pasture at Coles. The next Saturday Yank reported that three more had died. Braddy then began to have his doubts which were strengthened when the following Saturday two more had died so he told Yank that he would take a trip to Coles and that if any more sheep died he wanted to see their bodies. Yank flew into a rage and said that he would quit. Braddy told him to do so and he did. Braddy then went to Coles and put it into the care of Jimmy, a small lad, who had been helping Yank. Jimmy was not very "smart" but Braddy believed him to be honest.

When Grandfather returned from New York, he was most annoyed with Braddy for having dismissed Yank. Incidentally, when Braddy had visited Coles he found that there were twelve less sheep than there should have been. He thought that Yank had a good thing going by selling them.

The Parish of St. Mark's

It was late 1925 that the Rector of St. John's, Dr. H.B. Goering, offered him the cure of St. Mark's with St. Catherines, which he gladly accepted. It was the most pleasant spot the Bradshaws had ever lived. The view up the east coast from the verandah in front of the rectory was superb and then there was quite a bit of glebe land. Maggie now had plenty of scope to keep "stock". There was also a tennis lawn near the entrance to the property. It had not been used for sometime and was just a

St. Mark's Church, Barbados

lawn so it remained unused while the Bradshaws were there, except that it made a good grazing spot for the sheep and goats. There was also a good orchard.

The church was back of the rectory on a large rocky mound with steps going up to it. Under it was a hurricane cellar.

There were two lovable capable men at St. Mark's that stood out in Braddy's memory as two real Christian characters. John Taylor was the sexton of the church and he looked like a character out of the Bible with his long brown beard. John Weeks looked after the glebe land and the "stock". They grew a little cotton, yams, edoes, peanuts and the like. John used to sell what the family did not need. Sometimes he made quite a bit, especially from having the cotton picked and sold on the market. Also they had spare fruit from the orchard. Keeping account, at the end of the year, Braddy determined they had about broken even - just a little on the black side of the ledger; but they always had enough in vegetables and fruit for their own needs. The two Johns were indeed treasures.

St. Catherines was about four miles away. There were large congregations at both churches. At Festivals there were between four and five hundred communicants. It meant that at Christmas, Braddy started at midnight and went steadily through until one o'clock in the afternoon on Christmas day. Only once did he get any help - his last Easter in 1928 - when he managed to pry the Archdeacon loose from the Cathedral to help out.

Under the cliff in front of the rectory was the line of the Barbados light railway which ran from Bridgetown to St. Andrews, now long defunct, as its rolling stock wore out. Braddy always felt that if it had been kept going, it would have been a great attraction to tourists, especially that section of it that ran along the beautiful east shore from Bath to St. Andrews. The incline from Consett's Bay to the level of the savannah was a very steep one and a long line of freight cars taxed the limited capabilities of a small engine to its limits. In fact, sometimes it had to back down and make another run at the incline.

One day Braddy saw a strange thing happen. He heard the engine labouring up the last few yards and suddenly gave the final gasp of relief that once again it had triumphed. Looking down the line toward Bath Station, Braddy saw, to his surprise, an engineless train going backwards with the apparently frantic efforts on the part of the brakeman to stop it. Looking over to the savannah, Braddy saw that the engine had only a piece of one freight car attached to it. In its endeavour to make the grade, it had pulled the end out of the freight car.

Railway at Bathsheba on East Shore

The old railway had many derailments and other mishaps but Braddy did not remember that it ever had a fatality. On one occasion when approaching a long decline into the terminal at Bridgetown the engineer discovered that his brakes were not functioning. The only thing that he could do was get the whistle going. In Bridgetown they heard the shrieking and kept the line clear and the foreman down on the wharf got his labourers busy piling bags of sugar across the line to prevent the whole train from going into the harbour. This was successful and stopped the still rapidly moving train. What a relieved engineer!

On another occasion at the top of this incline there had been a derailment and a gang was busy clearing up the mess. Like labourers everywhere they wanted to do this in the easiest way possible so they lifted a pair of very large wheels, put them on the track and gave them a shove to start them on their way. They forgot that they were on the incline and the wheels gathering speed got away from them. The gateman at the point where the line crossed Constitution Road, saw the wheels coming and thought he would stop them by closing the gate. In fact, he delayed them slightly and diverted their course. They smashed through the gate and swerved across the road where there was a small rum shop with a girl sitting on the counter. The wheels took the counter from under her and continued on through the back wall of the shop and finished up in a pig pen turning the occupants into pork.

To get back to the rectory home, Braddy said that the orchard was John Week's pride and joy. Most of the trees were worn out but they did get many apples, soursop, guava and papayas. Also Weeks had squash and pumpkin vines. One day he went to Braddy and told him that a squash that was nearly ripe had been stolen and handed him a Bible saying he had found it on the spot. They discovered that the Bible belonged to a go-preacher - the name given then to the Pentecostals. They used to have a meeting down on the side of Consett's Bay. Braddy saw the preacher one day and handed him his Bible and told him where it had been found. He was not at all disconcerted but said, "Praise the Lord!" He am returned to me His Holy Word. It was He who led me to a lot of squash. The good Lord said, "He will provide. Praise the Lord!" Braddy told him that the Bible also said, "Thou shalt not steal". That old fellow looked surprised and said, "Good dear, Reverend! Dat ain't stealin'. That's only taking what the good Lord provided." He went on his way with a fat chuckle.

One night a small dog began to bark. Braddy thought that he saw a light in the orchard so he got his shot gun and fired one barrel into the air. Hearing nothing more he went to bed. The next morning when he went up to the church for the daily service, he thought that John looked rather out of sorts and he asked him what was the matter. He said, "Reverend, the old woman and me did not get much rest last night. When you fired that shot it fell on our roof and we sat on the edge of the bed waiting for you to fire the other barrel."

Maggie was delighted that at St. Mark's she could have a larger number of "stock", so they had several goats, sheep and a cow - generally called the wild cow because of its objection to being milked. This objection often took the form of the milker being kicked off the milking stool. To prevent this, one of her back legs was tied. In the vernacular, "She foot was tied."

There was a very bad tempered old sow who objected to any invasion of her pen and any chicken that trespassed was often gobbled up.

They also had a flock of hens, some ducks and turkeys. Charles, about three at the time, was at continual warfare with an old turkey cock. It was a frequent sight to see Charles and the turkey in a fierce scrap, with a flurry of chubby limbs and flying feathers. One day Charles was missing and a wide unsuccessful search was made for him. At last, in passing a chicken coop on the lawn, Braddy saw Charles peering out through the bars. He had crawled into it and the trap door had fallen down and imprisoned him. When Braddy extracted him, he asked him whatever was he doing in the coop. He pointed a fat finger at Mr.Turkey, who was drowsing nearby, and said, "Him."

The last, but not least, among the accumulation of live stock was a flock of guinea birds. In those days nearly every plantation had a flock of these useful birds. They were excellent watchmen. Should a stranger

90

appear they would give out a shrill cackle. They were also excellent table (eating) birds. They never really became domesticated. They would feed with the other fowl but liked to roost at night in trees and lay their eggs in weird places, in bushes and tufts of grass. To take out the eggs when nests were found, one had to use a long-handled spoon. Otherwise, if the scent of one's hand was left, the guinea bird would not go back to the same nest. To hatch the eggs, they were put under one of the domestic hens.

One hilarious episode which Braddy called, "Operation Guinea Bird", follows:

One early evening after visiting in one of the tenantries, Braddy was relaxing before dinner on the verandah, enjoying, as he always did the beautiful view up the East Coast. Maggie came and asked him to get a pair of guinea birds for dinner the next evening, as they were expecting company. The only way to achieve this was by shooting them and this had to be carefully arranged as a flock generally took flight together.

One planter told Braddy that he sent out his bookkeeper to get a pair and he came back with seven at one shot.

Braddy got the twelve gauge shotgun and went guinea bird hunting. He found them in the back yard and they rose in flight together; but to his delight one settled on the top of the barn. Casually he noticed the back of Weeks in the doorway of the barn milking the wild cow. He had told Braddy that he had her trained and did not have "to tie she leg". Anyway, without delay, Braddy fired at the guinea bird on the barn roof. Two things happened simultaneously. The bird dropped into the pig pen and Weeks and the milk pail erupted violently out into the yard. Braddy did not stop to discuss the reason for this with him but dashed around the barn to rescue his bird as he knew that the old sow would soon make a meal of it. In fact, when he got there, the sow was just sniffing at it. Braddy did not hesitate. He vaulted over the sty wall right onto her back and grabbed hold of her ears. Naturally she objected most noisily to this treatment. Her howls brought Beryl and peering through the bars of the gate to the sty, she enquired, "What you doing sitting on the old pig's back, Daddy?"

Braddy did not go into any discussion on the matter but told Beryl to get John at once. They had a yard boy, John Goslin, a reliable worker but not overpowering in brain matter. In a few minutes, Beryl came back and said, "John, has fallen into the cistern, Daddy."

It seems that John was watering the garden from a large cistern they had that gathered rain water from the roof. It was covered and had a hole in the side from which water was drawn up with a bucket and a rope. The water level being low through lack of rain, John had been leaning into the cistern and when Braddy fired the shot, he overbalanced and went into the drink. Fortunately there were only about two feet of water including a considerable amount of slush mud. However, feeling that John and his troubles would have to wait until Braddy extricated himself from the his by-no-means pleasant perch on the old sow's back he leaped off and in one moment, grabbed the guinea bird and leaped over the wall again, just a snippet ahead of some vicious teeth. The old provider of pork was plainly annoyed at the treatment she had suffered.

With a rather bedraggled guinea bird corpse, Braddy tried to sort out the other results of his shooting expedition. First he extricated a rather wet John Goslin from the tank and then tried to pacify John Weeks who was recovering from his exit from the barn. He explained sorrowfully, "You know Reverend, I tol' you we did not now have to tie she foot; and then ye come and fire the gun. Bam! She up with she one foot and she kicked me and the milk into the yard. What the mistress say, when she find the milk throw away?". Braddy could not remember how or when or ever he got the other bird.

Following this rather harrowing experience, Braddy sat down to relax for a few minutes on the verandah and heard Maggie's voice in the dining room talking to the young black girl who helped with the children.

"Clemmie", she said, "there's an awful smell around here. Whatever can it be?"

Braddy heard Clemmie giggle and then say, "Mistress, I guess that it's the Master."

"What! said Maggie. "Whatever do you mean?"

"Well," said Clemmie, "He's been struggling with de ole sow in de pigpen and I guess that some of the stink has come off on he."

This statement caused Braddy to sit up and take notice. He had been conscious for some time of an odour, but had been so close to the sow, who did not exactly smell like violets, he had not taken much notice of it. He realized that a shower was in order but before he could do anything about it, he heard a car coming up the driveway. It was a local planter, Jones, and his wife coming to make an afternoon call. They got out of the car and Braddy went down the steps to greet them very conscious of "de stink". Mrs. Jones came forward to greet Braddy with outstretched hand.

"Vicar," she said, "how very nice to find you at home. Sniff! Sniff! Whatever is that dreadful smell?"

As he grasped her hand with his covered with the smell of Madam

92

Sow, all he could say was, "When the wind is in this direction we do get sniffs of the pigpen."

Jones who knew where the pigpen was and that the wind was in the opposite direction looked at Braddy rather strangely. Braddy feared the story would get around the community that he smelled, so he tried to back away from them. Maggie saved the day by appearing and after greeting the guests she asked Braddy to go see what the children were doing. Mrs. Jones spoiled his exit by saying that she had just seen them on the tennis lawn as they drove up. However, Weeks came around the corner than and asked to speak to Braddy. He excused himself, talked to Weeks, then went off for that most necessary shower before returning to his guests.

So ended "Operation Guinea Bird"

It was during Braddy's second year at St. Mark's that the Vestry decided to repair and paint the rectory inside and out. This meant that for nearly six weeks they took up their abode in a Bay house at Bath. This was a delightful time for the children and they enjoyed every day in the small pools in the sea. The bathing at Bath is certainly not the best in the island but for small children it is safe as long as they keep out of the deep pools. Those deep pools may be inhabited by conger eels.

Braddy had to go up to St. Mark's frequently, not only for the Sunday services but also for some weekday ones. He generally went up on Saturdays, stayed over Sunday and after the service on Monday morning he returned to Bath until Wednesday when he took another morning service and repeated this on Friday.

At the usual weekday morning services Braddy generally had a number of interviews after the service at which he had to sort out various family difficulties, among which was sometimes the chastisement of unruly children. This meant switching their legs with small switches gathered from the trees in the graveyard. Howls of objection began before he started the punishment which was never severe. He did have one peculiar case. A mother brought her small daughter to him and told him that she "could do nothing with she", so Braddy applied a very small switching. Later that day the father went to see Braddy and accused him of brutalizing his daughter and was going "to have the law on him". He showed him some very bad bruises and welts on the child's legs. What puzzled Braddy was that some of these were on the child's thighs which he had never touched. All his lashes, as they called them in Barbados, were below the knees.

Next morning Braddy called the mother and she told him that it was the father who had beaten the child after Braddy's mild chastisement, so that ended that.

While at Bath, in the evening, Braddy would often climb the hill at the back of the house with his gun to see whether he could get a hare. There was a sweet potato patch surrounded by canes at the top of the hill. One evening when he crept through the canes he saw a hare feeding at the other side of the field. He managed to get it after some manoeuvring through the canes.

On one occasion Braddy had a weird experience at trying to shoot a hare at Haynes Hill. One day when he was there the watchman told him that he had seen hares feeding in a potato patch toward Society Chapel so one evening Braddy went out early and took a seat on the edge of the field in some canes. When it was getting near to dark and Braddy was about to give up he heard a rustle near him and there at his side was Mr. Hare. Braddy could have touched it. It was sitting up and surveying the potato patch. Braddy kept very still and gradually it hopped around him. His gun was lying across his knees and finally Mr. Hare was in front of the barrel, about three feet away. As far as Braddy could gage he was well in line so Braddy pulled the trigger and the hare went straight up in the air and soon disappeared over the horizon. Braddy thought he must have fired over its head. He remembered throughout his life how he was soaked with sweat through the tension of those few moments while the hare was hopping around him, all the time within grabbing reach.

After about six weeks the work at the rectory was nearing completion. Many repairs had been made and the house had been painted inside and out. One day Braddy was up from Bath and Mr. Richard Haynes, the parish church warden, was looking over the work. They were talking together in the dining room. There were two men outside the window painting. The warden said, "Well, Vicar, the job is nearly done and you will be able to move back home very soon."

Braddy replied, "I will have a special teazeum when that happens."

One of the men outside hearing that said to the other, "I hope that he gives us a drop."

So the family moved up from Bath. Braddy thought that even the children had become bored and were glad to be home.

Grandfather Mac

It was either August or September of 1926 that Grandfather Mac died. He had been fairly well since his nose operation in New York in 1926. He had followed his usual way of life - driving his car, going to Coles during the shooting season. He often had his old cronies there, sometimes for a day or even for a few days - Harry and Nellie Innis; Clarence Greaves from New Castle; Roland Taylor, the grandfather of Ronnie Taylor, curator of the museum during the 1980's; an old fellow, a retired planter, Dunlop Smith; Maurice Armstrong; Philip Greenidge.

Malcolm Greenidge - A Mark Twain Look-a-like

When they were at Coles one shooting season, some birds came into the swamp and Grandfather Mac and Harry Innis, too lazy to move, told Braddy to go and get them. He walked out on the path in the middle of the swamp and the birds got between him and the hut. He swung around with the gun on them and saw the astounding sight of Harry and Grandfather trying to get through the door of the hut together. They were wedged in the door - Harry, short and fat; and Grandfather, tall and lean. They both kept shouting, "Don't shoot! Braddy! Don't shoot!." They thought that Braddy would fire into the hut but he was really aiming and holding his fire until the birds were over the roof of the hut. "How these incidents come back to one," mused Braddy.

An old fellow, Dunlop Smith, was rather at a loose end and with not much means so he was glad to be at Coles for quite a long stay. He paid for it by being the butt of Grandfather Mac's frequent jokes. On one occasion Grandfather had cooked a lot of eggs for breakfast, at least nine or ten. Braddy did not want more than two and Grandfather had three leaving the rest. Poor old Dunlop stopped at three and Grandfather insisted that he eat the rest. When he objected Granddad took him by the neck and fed the rest to him forcibly. Braddy felt for the poor old fellow but with Mac one had sometimes to put up with a lot.

One late afternoon, Jimmy, who had replaced the beloved Yank and in whom Grandfather had at last put trust - finding him a good worker and thoroughly trustworthy (He was also a good whistler to bring in the birds.) came to the vicarage with the message that the captain did not feel very well and asked that Braddy go and spend the night with him. So Braddy put a few things in a bag and drove to Coles. He found Mac quite weak and he had a troubled night. The next morning Braddy got a message to Maggie who communicated with her mother at Haynes Hill who then got in touch with Dr. Briggs-Clark. Grandmother Bessie and the doctor soon arrived at Coles. Mac seemed rather easier but Braddy could see that the doctor did not think much of him and he tried to get him to go back to Haynes Hill. He would not and said that with the southerly wind the birds would soon be flying. However, he was certainly too weak to go out to the hut near the swamp. The doctor who had his gun with him did get a few birds. In the afternoon the doctor and Grannie Bessie left for Haynes Hill. Braddy wanted them to take Mac with them but he would not go so the doctor told Braddy to get him to Haynes Hill telling him that he would probably die in the car on the way - nice cheering thought. Getting along toward dusk, Mac finally decided to call it a day and it was his last. He seemed stronger and when they passed through Ruby Yard, where Uncle Frank lived, he got out of the car and filled and lighted his pipe and talked to some of the people in the yard. Braddy eventually got him home and he was put to sleep on a cot in the gallery. In the early morning, Braddy and Maggie had a message from Bessie saying that her

96

husband had died in the night. Next morning Braddy went to Haynes Hill as the funeral was to be that afternoon.

There was a rather bizarre incident that took place before the funeral. At Haynes Hill there were two friends who often visited - Maurice Armstrong and Philip Greenidge, Maggie's cousin. The latter was the usual Greenidge prankster. The undertaker had nearly finished soldering up the copper lining of the casket and turned away to reheat his soldering iron leaving a very small hole unsoldered. Into this hole Philip slipped in a pair of wire cutters with the remark, "That will help Mac to get out."

The funeral was held that afternoon from St. John's Church. In the absence of the rector, it was conducted by Father Briggs from St, Margaret's and Braddy. The burial was in the church cemetery.

Grandmother Bessie, began a search for a will the day after the funeral. She found one dated some years before which left everything to her. Then going through some old papers she found one from an exercise book that was evidently a draft for another will. It was undated and unsigned. She called Braddy to tell him about it. He went to Haynes Hill and at once recognized the paper. It may have been a year or more before this that Mac had called Braddy to his little room upstairs and he was writing on a piece of paper. He read to Braddy what he had written which was the draft of another will. In this one he had divided his estate into twelfths, three of which were to go to Maggie, three to Uncle Clyde, two to Uncle Ralph and four to Uncle Noel. He explained this by stating that Ralph had had a considerable amount spent on his college education and thus was to get less than Noel. Noel had wanted very badly to go to Codrington but his father would not hear of it. It was Braddy's personal opinion that a few years at Codrington mixing with other young men of his own age might have saved Noel mentally. Braddy did not think that he would have accomplished very much in a scholastic way but who knows? However, it was not to be!

When Grandmother Bessie showed this paper to George Evelyn, then head of Cottle, Catford and Company (law firm), he said that it would need to go to the Chief Justice for his decision. The Chief Justice called Bessie in to certify that it was her husband's writing. Braddy was not called for which he was thankful, although he could have sworn to the fact that he had seen it written. Although it was not dated or signed the Chief Justice ruled that it was the last will and testament of Malcolm F. Greenidge. It was written after the other. He stated the fact that in the other will Maggie was referred to as Margaret Greenidge but in this one as the wife of the Rev. A. G. Bradshaw. So that will was probated and the provisions over Noel's share became a matter of controversy up until the 1980's. Bessie was satisfied with the new will as she was to receive the income from the estate as long as she lived.

One further incident occurred at that time that rather upset the idea that news in Barbados spreads very quickly via grapevine. It was several days after the funeral before Braddy could go to Coles; he found out how Jimmy was getting along and everything was in order. There was not much to do. All the sheep had been sold; the garden was no longer in existence and it was only a case of keeping trespassers off the place. Jimmy surprised Braddy however when he asked Braddy, "How's the Captain?" He had not heard of Mac's death and he was shocked when he heard that he had died and had been buried.

Another incident with regards to Coles which Braddy was sorry Grandfather Mac had not lived to see. He had always wanted to have a shot at ducks which were rare visitors to the swamps and he did not think Mac had ever had a shot at them; if so, it was only rarely. One morning Jimmy arrived at the vicarage early and told Braddy that there were five ducks in the swamp. Having nothing very particular to do that morning, Braddy took Jimmy and drove to Coles. They soon located the ducks which were still there. Braddy crawled round behind one of the hedges behind the pool where they were. When the ducks flew up he got two of them. The three of them flew around but did not leave and settled in another pool. Braddy stalked them again and got another. The remaining two still did not leave but flew into another pool. Braddy got another and finally got the fifth one. They were teal and quite small but with the children with good appetites the whole family enjoyed them. They did have somewhat of a revenge on Braddy though. When he left Coles he had them on the floor of the back seat. On his way home he had to go to the parochial treasury office in St. John's to pay some taxes. When he stopped there he had some irritating itching on the back of his neck and found his neck covered with lice which apparently had left the ducks and climbed up the back seat and found a home on Braddy. When Braddy got back to the vicarage he had to take a shower and some soaping to get rid of the little pests. Braddy recalled that this reminded him of the time his son-in-law, Randy Day, had climbed up into the palms to collect coconuts and had a similar experience with ants.

The following is a letter written by Grandfather Mac to his look-alike, Samuel Clements (Mark Twain), 1908:

SAMUEL CLEMENS Alias Mark Twain

Dear Sir, take I the liberty of writing to you in verse
That in your humorist moments you may with laughter burst,
To think, that I unknown to you, and yet, so much resemble you
That throughout Canada, New York, I'm taken here and there for thee.
I've played a trick or two, "Dear Sir" of course you know I'm vain
In impersonating such a man as humorist Mark Twain,
But Dame Nature has made us both almost fac simile,
Herewith my photo I enclose, please send yours back to me.
No joke or trick on you I play, this is my heart's desire
To place your photograph with mine, your humorist jokes inspire.
But should this liberty to you be annoyance, put away,
For I'll apologize to you, and to age all homage pay.
I am not of your nation, oh how I wish I were!
I think I'd better naturalize and work your credit here.
Now you know I'm joking, now you know I'm vain
For in reality the world has only One Mark Twain.

faithfully yours,
Malcolm Fiddis Greenidge (Barbados, B. W. I.)

A reply with thanks came to Barbados on October 1, 1908.

Mark Twain

Bishop Bentley

In 1927, Bishop Berkeley, having reached the age of sixty-five, had to retire. The church was then under the government with regard to stipend, age of retirements, and the like. When Bishop Berkeley notified the Archbishop of Canterbury the reason for his retirement, his Grace of Canterbury replied that, in his opinion, a bishop was not much use until he had reached sixty-five. Bishop Bentley, assistant Bishop of Jamaica, succeeded Bishop Berkeley and for Braddy, at least, the change was not helpful. Braddy worked under ten bishops during his ministry and Bentley was the only one with whom he had any disagreement. When he went to act at St. James in 1921, knowing that many Canadian Bishops had certain rules with regard to the age of confirmation candidates, he asked Bishop Berkeley if he had any. The Bishop gave his usual chuckle and said he did not want to know either their weight nor height as he considered these were of little importance as to their spiritual preparation. Incidentally, Braddy always thought that the generally accepted idea of a fit age, namely around fourteen, was a bad time because that is the age at which many physical changes take place and to have a vital spiritual experience at the same time as this is liable to have a bad effect. Surely the spiritual experience should come earlier, then it will help a passing of the physical. Soon after Bishop Bentley's took office as Diocesan Bishop, Braddy had a class ready for confirmation; he recalled that it was about eighteen in number. He filled in the required government form with regard to age, sex, marital status and the like and sent it to the bishop. When he arrived for the confirmation he objected to what he called the immature age of some of the candidates. Many were ten and eleven. One particularly bright girl was only nine. To save argument Braddy got the Bishop to question her, and he had to admit that she knew all the answers. In those days preparatory classes for confirmation were generally about nine months in length. In fact, Braddy often began a new class soon after one confirmation was finished. Bishop Bentley accepted that class as Braddy had presented it but stated that in the future, he would require a minimum age of twelve for black candidates and fourteen for white, the difference in age was because the black children matured earlier than the white.

Braddy's next clash with the Bishop was at the St. Mark's Patronal Festival beginning with St. Mark's Day, April 25th, 1928. Braddy invited His Lordship to visit them during the Festival which lasted eight days. He came on St. Mark's Day and pontificated and preached at Evensong. He did not much like the incense but he survived it. The trouble was in the procession; to the north of the altar at the head of the aisle there was a beautiful statue of the Blessed Virgin Mary and Child. It had always been Bishop Berkeley's custom to turn and bow as he passed it. Braddy had provided, as customary, Bishop Bentley with two small accolades to hold the edges of his cope. It seems, although Braddy did not see it as he walked ahead of him, these two small boys, accustomed to Bishop Berkeley when they reached the statue, swung the Bishop around to bow and made elaborate bows themselves. The Bishop was not amused and stated so to Braddy afterwards. The strange thing about it was that aside from their differences with regard to church practices, Braddy always found Bishop Bentley most affable and friendly. He always remembered one story that the Bishop told him while they were having a friendly chat in Braddy's study. He said that as a boy he'd always thought that in the story of the prodigal son that where it was said, "He wasted his living with harlots, it meant that he had spoiled his father, living with harlots".

After Bentley's retirement he continued living in Barbados. He was a great friend of the Emptijers, Braddy's daughter in law's (Peggy, Charlie's wife) sister Graeme and her family. Braddy recalled that he did not expect that Charles would ever forget the elaborate high tea that they were invited to that the Emptijers gave to entertain Bishop Bentley. That was the last time that Braddy saw him. Bishop Bentley always dressed in full episcopal rig - probably the last Bajan Bishop to do so - leggings, apron, the full works, and he confided to Braddy how embarrassed he was when his Grace, Archbishop Worrell from Nova Scotia, visited him and and wore full tourist outfit - baggy pants, a red tie and a white floppy cap. He said as they went together down Broad Street and he had to introduce him to various persons that they met, he didn't know which way to look when they looked so surprised, when he said to them, "I would like you to meet the Archbishop of Nova Scotia and the Primate of all Canada."

One other incident that happened in Barbados that Braddy vividly recalled involved his daughter, Beryl. She attempted to get clammy cherries that hung over the cow pen into which she fell. Fortunately she was not hurt but she emerged smelling not like a rose. Maggie and the nurse-girl, Stewart, had quite a job getting her hair clean.

Fire at Codrington College

It was at Whitsuntide in 1926 that there was the disastrous fire at Codrington College which entirely destroyed the interior of the college and the chapel. As far as Braddy could recall on Whitsunday, he has taken an afternoon Evensong at St. Catherine's and was taking a nap in his bedroom when one of the servants went in to tell him that Codrington College was on fire. Braddy, at once, collected his walking stick to ward off dogs on the way across country to the college, where when he came into sight of the college the flames made an impressive sight. As he neared it he could see that it could not be saved. The whole roof was burning. When he reached it he found students and others busily trying to save as much as possible of the tutor's goods and chattels. Father Lee, his wife and children, lived in the southern wing of the college. Braddy started in to help and they got out practically everything. Braddy put down his walking stick in one of the landings and never saw it again. He was sorry because it was a favourite. After that he was asked to help on the roof of the principal's lodge to keep it wet and extinguish any sparks that might

Fire at Codrington, 1926

light upon it. They succeeded in saving that building. On the roof with Braddy, until about two o'clock in the morning, was Professor Dunlop. Braddy discovered that he had forgotten his cigarettes and Dunlop handed Braddy his gold case full, warning him not to set fire to the Lodge with a carelessly deposited cigarette. The Bridgetown Fire Brigade arrived with a flourish when it was impossible to do anything.

One incident remained in Braddy's memory and that was the sight of one of the fireman perched on the roof on a spot where the fire had passed and trying to cut through one of the massive beams with his small axe. What good would have emerged if he had succeeded was doubtful. Anyway he was cheered by the large crowd that had assembled. At about three o'clock in the morning as the fire had about burned itself out, Braddy started back to the vicarage taking with him one of the students who had come from one of the other islands and had lost all his possessions in the fire. He remained with the Bradshaws until the teacher's quarters, which had been built on the edge of the football field, had been made ready to accommodate the college students.

Before Braddy went to bed he emptied his pockets and found that he still had Dunlop's cigarette case which he took back to him later that day. There had been a good deal of looting of things salvaged from the fire. One man was caught with three pairs of Lee's trousers on and several others were caught with various things which they claimed that "the Lawd had provided". Beryl heard the servants talking about various things that the people had obtained and she proudly announced that her Daddy had gotten a gold cigarette case.

It spoke well for the strength and workmanship on the walls of the college that practically no repairs had to be made to them when the college was rebuilt. They are now as they were and have been through the centuries. The biggest loss was the beautiful chapel with its organ and worst of all the destruction of the lovely glass mosaic which had been over the altar depicting the Good Shepherd. Thousands of small pieces of glass were gathered up but experts in England said it would be next to impossible to reassemble them and anyway tremendously expensive. He did not know if the pieces of glass had been preserved. The present chapel is quite beautiful but it is not the chapel that Braddy knew and loved. The pipe organ has never been replaced. They use now a small harmonium for the chapel services.

In the spring of 1928, Maggie and Braddy discussed the possibility of Braddy going on leave to Canada to investigate the possibility of getting a parish in Nova Scotia. They both felt that the children, especially the girls, would have a better chance for employment when their school days were over, as things were then in Barbados, with its limited opportunities, especially for girls.

However, there was one parish in Barbados that Braddy had always wanted. That was St. Joseph's. The rector, Tom Hutchinson, was on the point of resignation as he had reached the age limit for retirement. The Bradshaws had always been very friendly with the Hutchisons. Joan, especially had spent a good deal of time there with them. She had a great friend in Dorothy Cashmore, the eldest daughter of Tom and Marjorie Cashmore, who were at that time in India and had left Dorothy, with her grandparents, the Hutchisons, at St. Joseph's. In Braddy's opinion the rectory there was one of the nicest in the Island. It has a glorious view over the Bathsheba Coast and then attached to the parish was the little chapel on the coast, St. Aiden's, with his accompanying nice seaside residence. Hutchinson had collected quite a sum which he had hoped, with investment, would provide an income sufficient to pay the curate. The Bishop had the nomination right for vacant parishes and the committee, consisting of representatives from the parish, the Island legislature and the diocese accepted or rejected the nomination. The Bishop nominated the Rev. Dudley Moore. It seemed that his Lordship had been very friendly with Mrs. Moore's parents, while he was assistant Bishop of Jamaica.

Freddie Stanton, rector of St. Phillip's told Braddy that there was some surprise at this nomination as Braddy was much senior to Moore, but it was accepted. So the wheels of fate turned and Braddy, at once, applied for leave out of the Island for three months, which was due to him.

St. Joseph's Church

Beryl Remembers

The following was left on tape by the oldest daughter, Beryl, and appears here as she preserved her thoughts. Any changes were structural or for clarification, as assisted by Braddy's notes and other members of the family.

Memory is a strange function of the brain. One would suppose that in the newborn child, the memory bank is like an unused tape or uncut record, awaiting the depressing of the on switch of awareness to start recording. Each early impression would be indelibly engraved, clear and sharp, ready for instant replay. Unfortunately, I find that memory does not work this way. I push the rewind button and my mind obediently zips back to April 6, 1920, but when I switch to replay, there is only silence. Could I have forgotten to push the button to record? I hear no first outraged bellow of a healthy

Beryl Katherine

newborn girl child. There is no remembrance of the gruff tobacco-chewing doctor who was present at my birth. No memory of every day life in that small square frame house, in Nanton, in the foothills of the Canadian Rockies where I was born; and most frustrating, no memory at all of the pretty dark-haired young woman who was my mother, nor of my shy handsome parson father. I wish I could say with the poet:

I remember, I remember the house where I was born,
The little window where the sun came peeping in at dawn;

but try as I may, I have no memory of the sights and sounds of that first year of my life. Would that I could remember the icicles dripping into spring, the prairie roads dusty with summer, the shimmering wheat fields awaiting the harvest home, and the silence of snowflakes drifting down to blanket the golden stubble.

At the end of that first year, 1920, the tape is still quite blank. I recall none of the plans, the joy and excitement of the journey homeward to the warmth of a tropical island. Most of all, I wish I could remember my first sight of Barbados, which was to be my home for many of the lovely days of childhood, the green cane fields blowing in the sweet wind, the stately royal palms reaching to the drifting snowy clouds, the married-hued flowers and on every side the deep blue sea. I wish I could remember the welcoming greetings - and yes - even the adoration of a first spoiled grandchild, blond and beautiful, no doubt, but whose unique status was to be short lived. I wish I could remember the rectory at St. James, and the first glimpse of the baby sister who was born there and who came bounding into the world, roaring like a lion, instead of purring like the kitten for which I mistook her. She should have been a boy, John Cecil. Never mind, as Joan Cecilia, she did quite nicely and soon left me far behind.

In recent years, I have stood and gazed at the rectory - typical Barbadian house, four square with hooded windows and well-kept grounds and coconut trees on the edge of the sea. I try to recall too the little girls who played there, watched over by a nurse, who no doubt called us Miss Beryl and Miss Joan, or unaccountably "man". One was so fair and slight, the other dark-haired and fat and self-reliant. I try to remember the feel of cool sand between little bare toes. Moses spoke God's word of the morning doves, the shiny-coated black birds in the big bay tree, and the sun dropping with a green flash into the azure sea at dusk. I would like to say I recall the moonlit nights and sun-filled days, but all I really remember is the unending happiness of that long ago childhood.

The life of a parson's family is a movable feast and ours was no exception. We seldom stayed put long enough to take root or "hatch" as they say in Barbados. Our birth certificates read like travel logs as we moved from parish to parish, clockwise around the island; but I remember none of these very early homes, or even the arrival of my second sister, Dorothy, or "Dogflea", as Joan and I called her.

Each time I try to recall my earliest memory, the picture is always the same. I would like to say that some momentous event set the tape in motion - a hurricane, an earthquake, a comet streaking across the heavens or even an unforgettable memory of the glorious rainbows, which follow every lovely rain in Barbados. Incredible as it may seem, all I can manage to dredge up from the dim past, is a picture of two small chairs side by side on a lawn. I suppose they belonged to Joan and me, but in my memory no one sits in them. The over all impression is one of coolness - cool grass and green ferns, the kind of ferns which grow on every wall on which we later pressed against our small arms, to see the delicate feathery tracings. Where were these little chairs? St. Clement's, St. Lucy's, St. Jude's, St. Swithen's? Suddenly there is a second recollection, and now it is of a cane fire. The time was Sunday evening because Dad was at Evensong. I have no actual memory of the fire, only of being taken down a long gap between fields of cane, at what seemed to be the middle of the night and later the acrid sooty ashes which covered everything.

Once triggered, the memories come thick and fast, tumbling head over heels as clearly as though it were yesterday, and for some reason, they begin at St. Mark's, where we went to live when I was about five years old. I don't remember the actual move, but moving days have much in common and there were many. I do remember the vicarage and grounds, the old church on the cliffs, the long view over the hills, and undulating green canes to Society chapel, and down across the Savannah to Consetts Bay, along the creamy coastline, to distant misty Pekotenoriph.

The approach to St. Mark's was by a narrow winding road which branched to the right of the entrance to the church, then again to the right up a winding mahogany-lined lane, past the grass grown field on the left that was once a tennis court. At the top of the lane, on the right, just below the church was the fruit orchard. I remember guavas and limes, but no doubt there were others. At the top of the incline, the lane divided and became a driveway in front of the house encircling a large tree-lined lawn. The house itself was long and low. Cement steps flanked by stone pillars led to the raised-gallery, which ran along the front of the building. At each end of the gallery was a door, one leading to the drawing room, the other to the dining room. These two rooms opened into one large area. The east windows in the drawing room looked out on a water cistern and the remnants of a wall garden.

I remember very little of the furniture, but it probably was the bare necessities - mahogany chairs and tables, a few pictures, and oddments. The door at the back of the drawing room led to Dad's study, which also faced east. There was a desk in the center of the room, a narrow folding canvas cot, and his pet lizards darting along the walls. The door off the dining room opened into a passage, on the left of which was a storage room, which had slats for ventilation, and which was kept locked, and smelled deliciously of raw sugar and over-ripe bananas. On the right this passage led past the walls of the nursery wing, to the kitchen area. A door at the far end of Dad's room led into a small entrance, which opened onto the back yard.

Another door led to Mom's bedroom. From her room could be glimpsed the brass cross atop the church on the cliff glistening in the endless sunlight. Her room contained a large wardrobe, her bed and a high-sided cradle over which hung a circular mosquito net. The cradle was for the St. Mark's baby - Charles Edward, the long-awaited brother who was born in 1925, when I was six years old. The far door of Mom's bedroom opened into yet another small passage, leading on the right to the front of the house and opening onto the backyard on the left. Off this passage were the shower and toilet rooms, the latter complete with stinging red ants.

Across the passage opposite Mom's room was the nursery, where Joan, Dorothy, and I slept with the nurse, or a succession of them, none of whom I remember. On the left against the wall was a wardrobe for our clothes. Our beds were lined-up along the wall on the right, under windows which opened onto the passage leading to the kitchen area. The side windows of the nursery also opened onto the back yard, and the door at the far end led into a passage and the stairs to the second story. This top floor contained only two rooms-a small one on the left overlooking the garage roof and orchards, and on the right a very large room with a glorious view and a large cupboard, where Mum once raised some piglets.

The kitchen area contained two rooms. One was a type of breakfast room with a large table and the only activity I remember here was knives being cleaned with Bricksome-blanco. A door from this room led to the garage. The other room contained a stove, and a cook who gathered wood to stoke it.

At the back of the vicarage, guinea hens roosted in the almond trees; chickens scratched in the dusty yard; a cow or two was tethered under the clammy cherry tree; and for a short time, a baby donkey - a neddy - came to live with us. Old John looked after the livestock with the help of a yard boy named Heustis. John also acted as sexton at the church.

I suppose we had the usual assortment of games, books, and toys. I remember only a cherished doll's tea set - silver and deep mauve, which Grannie gave me one Christmas, and two small hard-covered books, entitled, *Once in Royal David's City* and *All Things Bright and Beautiful* - illustrated in reds and gold and blues.

While life for us children was simple, it was not so for our parents, for in those days the vicar not only cared for the souls in his keeping but for most of the bodies as well - hiring and firing school teachers, settling arguments, providing for the poor, the sick and the lost. Each day started when Old John rang the bell for the six o'clock service and Dad walked up

108

the hill to the church in his long black cassock and jaunty berretta. Going to church was a matter of course for us. I remember the smell of incense and the melodious singing of the white-clad congregation; and at the Easter service, the eggs which we took to present at the altar. The rest of the week was forever. Clad in pinneys and panties and barefoot, we played on the grounds or in our nursery, climbed trees, went for walks with our nurse down the chalky hills to the sea and paddled in the clear pools.

Jenny was my special friend, perhaps I should say my only friend. She was Old John's granddaughter. Her mother was in England, her father who-knows-where. She went off to the local school each day with small squares of cloth pinned to her slip which seemed much more elegant that the rough toilet paper that we used. Now and then we were taken to spend time with friends, usually for a day. I only remember the Kirtons at Kendal - Gordon, Graham and Ralph, for even at that age people made less impression on me than places. Sometimes we went to Haynes Hill where Grannie, Grandfather and Uncle Noel lived.

I have two memories of Grandfather. The first was of sheer terror that he might take off his false nose; the second was of the dresses that he brought us from America and which we always called our Grandfather dresses. He died when I was six years old. After that we went to Stuart's Hill to visit Grannie. Once she took me to meet Mr. Thorn who grew delicious cucumbers.

Much of the time Joan lived at the rectory at St. Joseph's with the Hutchisons, as company for Dorothy Cashmore. I didn't envy her being away from home, only the tricycle which she and Dorothy Cashmore had. Now and then we all went to St. Joseph's for tea with the rectory family, the Hutchisons, and we saw the monkeys playing in the gullies.

Aunt Mim, Aunt Winnie and Aunt Doris played tennis with various young men. Aunt Doris wore step-ins, this being the Scott-Fitzgerald flapper age of the mid-twenties.

Now and then we went to a band concert on the rocks at Hastings or to a bazaar - the latter usually at Christmas. We were dressed in our starched going-out dresses with strapped Buster Brown sandals and white socks. At the bazaar we had lucky dips in the fishpond. I still have one of my prizes, a tiny blue enamel charm. Once I went to stay with Grannie in Hastings when she was with Aunt Wo and Aunt Aggie. The visit didn't last any longer than I could help and Uncle Noel soon took me home on the train.

Our meals were simple with none of today's variety - rice, sweet potatoes, breadfruit, yam and cocoa with chicken or fish. We drank cocoa or ovaltine and for dessert we had some of the fruit which was usually ripening in the drawers of the dining room buffet - mamey apples, sugar apples, mangoes, or perhaps guavas stewed with milk. Sometimes we had green pawpaws boiled at the factory to a delicious stickiness. When the crop was being cut we were given a calabash filled with peeled sugar cane to suck, or, as a special treat, Dad brought us English apples when he went to town. Our candy was golden barley sugar sticks which we were given after meals, and at Easter we had huge marshmallow and chocolate Easter eggs from Grannie.

When holidays came we went to the sea - Bath or Bathsheba- both visible down the coast from St. Mark's but an Arabian Night's journey nevertheless. We stayed in a bay house and were visited by relatives - Grannie, the Kirton cousins and the Bailey Annes. Once I remember arriving at Bath just before dark and we all played hide and seek in the long grass. Once Jenny went with us until she became homesick for her coffeetea. We were taken for baths in the clear pools under the big rocks and wore navy blue cotton bath suits and took our pink water wings which didn't stay inflated very long. When our nails turned blue from cold, we sat on the beach with our heads wrapped in towels and ate spiney salted golden apples or hunted for puppy dog eggs or sea egg shells to paint. The grown-ups gathered moss to bleach for jelly. Once while at the seaside we were invited to a birthday party where we played games. When it was my turn to hide, I ran away down the beach, past the grape bushes and the old men tending their nets, safe home.

At Christmas time we had a cherry tree instead of the North American fir or pine. This was either in the drawing room or in the large upstairs room at the vicarage. Of course, we also had stockings filled by Father Christmas, in whom I believed forever. We always received lots of books and gifts from Dad's relatives in England, also crocheted dresses and hats.

We knew nothing of the Easter bunny, St. Valentines or Halloween, but on the Fourth of July, Guy Fawkes Day, we had fire crackers, sparklers and catherine wheels. Sometimes we even had the sparklers as a special treat when Dad and Mum had to leave us with the nurse in the evening and sometimes we had a sip of rum swizzle. The swizzle stick was angostura pink and smelt of rum punches long past.

Now and then relatives and friends came to stay with us to help Mum with four active young children. One of these was Lulu Outram, tall and unkempt and noisy she was, but lots of fun. On one of her visits we built a bonfire at the entrance to the cave under the church and roasted corn. Mr. Rhodes-Cooper was another visitor. He specialized in making sticky suet puddings.

I only remember two parties - Charlie's christening when we had our first ice cream and a party at St. Mark's just before we left there. Nor do I remember ever being very sick. I do remember once I stomped my toe when we were at St. Mark's and I had a very sore infected toe for a long time. Another time, I remember I must have had what was intestinal 'flu' because I was taken somewhere to tea (we seemed to go in a car), and I was quite sick on the trip.

I remember once Dad had two boils, one on the back of his hand and another on the back of his neck which had to be lanced. Once he got an ant in his ear and to get it out Mum had to float oil in his ear. I asked him what it felt like, what the ant felt like walking around in his ear, and he said it felt like an elephant.

For a short while we had a governess, Miss Gray, who used the small bedroom upstairs. Dad bought us a school set - pencils and paper, crayons and cutouts. My first educational attempt was cut short when I fell from a wall into the cow pen trying to pick clammy cherries for glue to use in school. Only my pride was much hurt but Mum had the unpleasant task of cleaning my long blond hair. After this I was enrolled in the kindergarten class at High School, the memory of which strikes terror to my heart even today. Joan was soon brought home from St. Joseph's to lend me moral support. Although she was barely five years old nothing phased her. On Speaks Day that year we were dressed in brown outfits - she as the brown bear, while I, incomprehensibly, was the good bear. Good and scared was all I was that day!

Dad used to drive us to school in his little English Midget car which always stopped half way up Gun Hill. We got out and looked at the cement lions on the hillside and hoped the car wouldn't start again, but somehow it always did and off we would go with our bookbags and lunch pails and thermos bottles. The Winter boys, who were in the class with us, engraved themselves for all time on our memories for the gay abandon with which they regularly broke their thermos bottles.

School days in Barbados were short-lived. When I was eight years old Dad went to Canada. We stayed on at the vicarage at St. Mark's with a young curate taking the services,

Beryl with husband, Randy, 1961

but I missed the walks with Dad down the coast, over the railway trestles, where I always closed my eyes and clung tightly to his hand as we went over the high parts, and sitting in his long chair with him on the verandah at bedtime when he told me stories of Miss Mouse and I watched the ships disappearing over the edge of the sea and wondered where they were going. Soon I would wish I didn't know!

Charles and His Memories

Charles Edward

Charles came to Canada with his parents, and three sisters in 1929, when his father was rector of Musquodoboit Harbour. Charles recalls very little of Barbados before this time as he would have been a small boy of three - almost four years old.

He remembered at St Mark's one Sunday his uncle Noel (Mother's brother) walked up over the pasture in front of the vicarage. He remembered what he looked like and that he had a shot gun with him. He thought that soon after that Uncle Noel was placed in the Psychiatric Hospital, where it turned out that he spent the rest of his life.

When Charles returned to Barbados in 1935, he spoke to Lulu Outram, who happened to be at St. Mark's when this happened and although the image was so vivid in Charles' memory, he wanted to verify whether or not this incident actually happened. Mrs. Outram assured him that was exactly as she remembered it at that time. She asked Charles to describe to her what Uncle Noel looked like at that time and he did so and then she showed him a picture of him which was very close to the description he had told her.

Other than that, Charles could remember nothing of Barbados at that time. He presumed that the family must have moved to Stuart's Hill after his father left Barbados, because he left in 1928 and the family did not follow until a year later. Granny Greenidge (Bessie) would have been living there at that time as Uncle Clyde must have taken over the sugar plantation of Haynes Hill in 1928. Charles thought also that the family took their black servant with them when they came to Canada and

112

Musquodoboit Harbour in 1929. He does not recall the trip to Canada at all, and cannot recall life at Musquodoboit at all.

Charles did remember Hubbards (Braddy's second parish in Canada) very vividly. He remembered the rectory and the big barn to the left of the rectory, and that you walked down the road and down a track to the harbour and there was a little island right out in front. There was a tremendous big sawdust pile on the left of the Harbour which at one time must have been the sight of a lumber mill. Further down the road there was a garage and across the road was a little shop that sold candy and other goods. He thought the wife of the man who ran the garage ran the store.

Charles remembered going to school, for the first time, in Hubbards. A road led to the school but the Bradshaw children walked through the woods and across a brook. He would have been accompanied by his three sisters, Beryl, Joan and Dot.

To the right of the rectory were two Dorey families, farmers or fishermen. The second family had two sons, Tommy and Herbie, with whom Charlie played, and he thought they also had a girl. Further down

Hubbards, Grades 1-5, Spring 1934
Left to Right, first row: Herbert Dorey, Bernard Dauphinee, Benny Johnson, Charles Bradshaw, Eldon MacLean, Brenton Shakel, Laurie Shakel;
second row: Shirley Dauphinee, Marjorie MacLean, Dorothy Bradshaw, Evelyn Maclean, Nancy Miller, Katherine Dorey, Mary Dauphinee, Jean Dauphinee;
third row: Lawrence Winters, Murdock Miller, Eric Jollimore, Seeley MacLean, Blair Jollimore, Bernard Schwartz, Donald Dauphinee.

113

the road there was a general store and Charles recalls that he and Tommy collected bottles which they would swap for money to buy ice cream at the store.

Charles remembered when his youngest brother, Malcolm, was born in 1931. When his mother showed the new baby to the youngest sister, Dot, her comments were not too complimentary, Charles recalls. He thought she was probably thinking that the new baby would take her place as she was the youngest of the girls, and felt threatened by this new "red …" whatever.

Charles assumed, in later years when he thought about it, that it was probably during a visit by Canon Whippell that the idea was hatched for Charles to go back to Barbados. Canon Whippell, after living in Barbados, probably thought that the conditions under which the Bradshaws were living were quite primitive and that the poverty was quite prevalent. Charles thought all of this might have stirred him up a bit and offered to do something to help the situation by deciding to take Charles, when he got a bit older, under his support in Barbados.

Charles did not remember packing or moving to Upper Kennetcook. He did recall how Beryl cried for days and days when the family left Hubbards to go to the Maitland Parish and live in Upper Kennetcook. She was very saddened to have to leave her friends.

Charles recalled the rectory in Upper Kennetcook. It was a comparatively new house with a wooden board walk up to the front but the landscaping was not complete at all. Out in the back, he remembered a garage and a barn with a loft. All the firewood used to be cut and stored in the barn. To the right of the rectory was a fenced-in field for keeping the cow or animals. Behind the rectory was a hill with woods. Charles recalled setting rabbit snares that winter and he used to take David with him while he set the snares. He remembered having a sleigh (sled) for coasting (sliding) and that he also had skates with double runners.

Further on to the right of the rectory was the Harold Clarke family. He remembered them because they had a girl that was about Charles' age. That would have been Gwen. He remembered the river near the rectory. The school was across the road and not too far away. He could remember the General Store that was run by the Clarkes and he remembered visiting the store with his father and mother. He also recalled going out to Maitland with his father that winter in a sleigh drawn by a horse. Some one was driving the sleigh and Charles and his father were passengers sitting on the front seat all wrapped up in blankets. He also remembered the hayrides the Sunday School children went on.

114

Charles cannot remember leaving Upper Kennetcook to begin his journey to Barbados. He remembered his father accompanying him as far as Boston where he was put on a ship, probably the Lady Drake. He remembered when his father left him on the boat with the captain but he assumed that he was probably quite upset at leaving the rest of the family in Canada and that all memory of the departure from Upper Kennetcook has been blocked out. On the boat Charles was in a cabin with two men and he had an upper berth. He ate all his meals at the captain's table. There were no other children aboard the boat, but there were about twelve people at the Captain's table. Charles did not have a tie, which he had to wear at the captain's table, so one of the men gave him one. Charles could not tie the tie so each evening he used to go to the saloon door and the chief steward would meet him and tie his tie for him and then he would take his place at the captain's table.

The boat stopped at many of the islands on the way to Barbados and someone would take him ashore on each island. He recalled that the actual trip on the boat was very enjoyable. Uncle Clyde met Charles on the boat when it docked in Barbados and he told Charles that he was his Uncle Boy Blue. Maggie, Charles' mother, had always called her brother Boy Blue so he assumed that when she had told Charles about him she would have referred to him as Boy Blue, but she had not. They went from the boat to Haynes Hill and Charles recalled that Granny's sister, Aunt Maimie Bailey was staying there. She was an old lady with grey hair, and not particularly well groomed and Charles was told to go and kiss her. Charles thought she was the maid and could not understand why he would be asked to kiss the maid.

Charles' life in Barbados continued as other Barbadian children and although he returned to Canada he realized after a short while that he was not a Canadian and was a Barbadian and all that he knew and all his friends were in Barbados so he went back to continue life and happiness as a Barbadian.

During Charles' boyhood he had very little contact with his family in Canada. His parents did go to visit after Charles and Peggy were married, and they had two children (Valerie and Lynda) probably around 1957. A third child (Michelle) was born in 1958. They stayed with them at Brierly and then they went to Bayview at Bath and spent a month there. Rev. Pemberton had come to Canada to take over the Yarmouth parish so they could have a Barbadian holiday. Charles remembered a special incident at this time. In those days you could not go into a supermarket and buy a chicken. You bought a live chicken and the cook would kill it. Charles had taken a big rooster down to Bath for the cook to kill for Sunday dinner and it got away and went up over one of the big tall hills. Braddy and Peggy, who was about eight months pregnant at the time, chased it up the hill but they never did catch it. Braddy thought that Peggy would lose the baby running up the hill. Charles also remembered that when they got to Bayview that Maggie went from room to room and checked all the beds and she said, "This is the best, and this room is mine." Braddy admitted that he had slept on the floor the night before at Brierly as it was softer than the mattress. On that visit Valerie threw a rock at a lizard in a tree and Braddy was sitting under the tree drinking a beer and the rock missed the lizard but dropped straight into his glass of beer. When they were at Brierly Braddy did not have a lot of love for Doris' husband and when Doris and her husband came to see Braddy and Maggie, Braddy would go sit in the car and played with the children until they left.

After their retirement, Braddy was very particular about his meal times. It was very embarrassing when they went to stay with Charles and family at Airy Hill as his routine would be upset. He would have his routine one beer before supper and then he would get up and look at the clock and watch it and walk around.

One time when they visited in Barbados they stayed at a place Charles owned called Snug Harbour. Braddy told about mixing cocktails in the late afternoon and Maggie had two and then tripped over the step going into the house and fell. Later Braddy told several people this story. Finally Maggie got a little fed up and said," You know, Braddy, I have heard that story four or five times. It seems to be very popular with you. And, I've said nothing, but it's time now for me to say something. You had two cocktails, as I did, and in all of the years that we have been married that was the first evening that we ever had a meal that you did not say Grace."

Another trip they made down they stayed at the Aquatic Club. (Mac and Shirley spent Christmas of 1963 there with them.) Later they stayed at a place called Pavilion Court. (Mac and Shirley also spent one Christmas with them there in 1967.) Later they used to stay with their cousin Doris. (David, Shirley and children, Catherine and Brenda, visited them while they were there.)

On another occasion when Braddy and Maggie were visiting Charles and family when they lived at New Castle, Peggy drove them back to Doris' and he was to go to town with her. He had to go into Doris' to get something and then was to rejoin her and continue on to town. Peggy dropped him at Doris' and forgetting the plan she kept on going. She did not remember that she was supposed to take him to town until she got

116

part way there and she turned back and caught him at a bus stop near Doris'. So he got in again and they continued on to town.

One time Braddy visited Barbados by himself and stayed with his daughter, Beryl, at her villa at Sunset Crest. As Braddy and Maggie got older they found it difficult to travel because they were quite deaf and they could not hear announcements in airports. Then they were not shown electronically as they are today.

While visiting Barbados, Braddy very rarely assisted at church services. He did baptize Charles Cox and also Charles' fourth child, the first Bradshaw grandson, Peter.

Charles remembered the time in Hubbards, Nova Scotia when his father had Pink Eye and he passed out during the sermon. Someone drove each of them home separately.

Charles and Family, 1973
Left to right: Valerie, Charles, Peter,
Michelle, wife Peggy, Lynda

Cars, Barbados and Back to Canada

Braddy's car purchases create a saga in themselves. Soon after going to St. Mark's, the overland Ford began to show signs and repairs became more and more necessary and expensive, so he looked around for a replacement. Grandfather Mac had a very close friend, Harry Innis, who with his wife were often guests at Coles during the shooting season. Harry had a garage on Constitution Street, just east of the Cathedral. Grandfather always went there for his car needs and Braddy did also. Harry had a little English car, an all day's onion midget. Braddy always admired this car. It only had two cylinders, was a two-seater and wonderfully made. Braddy thought it dated back to the early nineteen hundreds. It also had a sliding gear shift, that is four gears in a line. From neutral one pulled back for reverse and then forward for first and on through second for high. It had a gas tank that when filled had less than five gallons but as it did forty five miles to a gallon, this gas lasted a long time. However in one front fender there was an extra small tank that held about a gallon of gasoline for emergency purposes. A light flashed when the main tank was getting low. This car had all kinds of gadgets too numerous to mention. One unique feature was that the two seats lifted out if repairs were needed to the drive shaft, and other parts, giving easy access to the under gear. Its top speed was about thirty miles per hour.

Harry told Braddy that he was selling this car by auction. When this happened Braddy went to bid on it. He found more opposition that he expected and got it eventually for something over two hundred dollars. Braddy certainly did a lot of travelling in it especially taking Beryl and Joan each day up to the high school and getting them home again in the afternoon.

Braddy told one funny story about this midget car. It had a horn something like the quack of a duck. While Harry still had it, one day he drove through Speighstown. Barton Skinner, who then managed Plantations Limited, told Braddy that one day he was in the store and heard what he thought was a loud quack of a duck and went to the door onto the road. All he could see was a cloud of dust going toward Bridgetown. His foreman looked over his shoulder and said, "Captain, that was a hell of a large duck."

While Braddy had this car he felt the need for something a trifle larger and Dean Shanklon had a Model T Ford for sale which Braddy bought for two hundred dollars, so he had two cars. He thought of the famous comedian, Dan Leno, of his early days whom he heard once say that if he ever got rich he would buy two cars and run between them.

It was in 1927 that Braddy bought a Singer that had just arrived from England. Mr. Taylor of Taylor and Redman in the Cathedral yard took it out to St. Mark's to show Braddy. Braddy forgot its price but he thought it was around nine hundred dollars. He managed to sell his two other cars for a little more than he had paid for them and Grandmother Bessie advanced the balance for the Singer. This Braddy used until he left for Canada in September of 1928. Taylor and Redman bought back the Singer paying the good price of about two hundred less than Braddy paid for it, a tribute to the care he had taken of it. That car would go up District Hill without changing gear, very differently from the little old midget that had its work cut out to make the hill at all on low gear.

Codrington Magazine Reports

After seven years in four parishes in Barbados Braddy's ministry there comes to an end and the Codrington Magazine reports it as follows:

The Rev. A.G. Bradshaw, Vicar of St. Mark's, Barbados, was granted a few months leave last September. He has been helping the Rev. Canon Malone in Prince Edward Island, Canada. A cable arrived towards the end of November, stating that he has accepted a cure in Nova Scotia. We are very sorry indeed that we shall lose him as a near neighbour. We owe him a debt of gratitude for being one of the small band of helpers that saved the Principal's Lodge from destruction during the fire of 1926, and for having sent us within a fortnight of the disaster the large sum of L50 from his poor district, for our restoration fund.

The clergyman who was mainly responsible for Braddy's return to Canada was Rev. Edwin Malone, later Canon Malone. The Codrington College Magazine reports in 1943:

Canon Malone obtained his B.A. at Codrington in 1904. After serving in the Diocese of Antigua for the next six years of his ministry, he spent the next ten years in Barbados, being successively Vicar of St. Saviour's, Assistant Curate of the Cathedral and Vicar of St. Paul's. He has held his present post at St. Peter's Cathedral in P.E.I. since 1922.

In September Braddy sailed in one of the C.N. ships for Saint John, New Brunswick. He wrote to Canon Malone in Prince Edward Island accepting an invitation to visit him if ever on leave in Canada. The day that Braddy was to leave Barbados, Maggie, Beryl and Joan went with him to Graeme's house near the Cathedral and in the afternoon they went down to the wharf and Braddy took a small boat out to the Canadian National ship anchored in the bay. He thought that it was the S.S. Exporter. These passenger freighters were used before the beautiful lady boats that were put into use on the West Indies run by the Canadian National.

Braddy remembered an incident that was rather humorous but also could have been tragic. Harry Innis, a great friend of Grandfather Mac, went to meet an aunt coming from England. He engaged a small boat and went out to the anchored liner. He collected his aunt on board with her trunk and small baggage. Incidentally he was rather startled by the size and floral decorations of his aunt's hat. He went down the gangway ladder to the boat below followed by his aunt and a porter with her trunk on his head. In the boat Harry bent down to put the small baggage under the seat. He heard a "Oh, Loss" from the boatman and when he looked up there was no aunt, no porter, nor trunk only a flower garden of a hat floating on the sea. In a few seconds his aunt bobbed up from the water at the same time as the porter, and of course no trunk, which by this time rested on the bottom of Carlyle Bay. It seems that the ladder gangway had collapsed and deposited them all in the drink. No hurt nor injury fortunately occurred and the steamship company paid a generous amount for damages and loss.

Braddy had a very pleasant trip to Nova Scotia. The first week they were island hopping through the West Indian Islands and the second week was straight sailing for Saint John most of which was through calm seas. The captain on the ship was Captain Coffin from, he thought, Dayspring - a typical Nova Scotian sea dog. The doctor was Dr. Gow from the Annapolis Valley and the purser's name was Frith from Bermuda. In the latter part of the voyage as his duties were very light, Braddy became very friendly with him. He was an Anglican with a great love for his church. It was their custom to meet before dinner at the bar for cocktails. They each had two - that was each one treating the other. One evening

120

when they had completed this daily custom, the captain made an unexpected visit to the smoking room and called on the bar keeper to serve drinks to all present. Braddy begged off as after his experience with the strength of Barbados rum during his early days at Codrington, he was very temperate in its use. The captain said, "Padre, on board ship the captain's word is law." So, on that he had to take the third cocktail. He was, to say the least, feeling the effect when he went into the dining room. His table was to the right of the captain's and when he saw Braddy a little wavery he winked, so Braddy took up his glass of water and ironically toasted him with it. Unfortunately when he went to put it down, he missed the table and put it on the floor. The captain grinned and called the steward and said, "Steward, the padre's eyesight seems to be rather out of kilter. You had better sop up that mess!" To say that Braddy was mad was putting it mildly as his mishap was all his confounded fault. However, for the balance of the voyage they were quite friendly.

On the last day from port, which was Sunday, they entered the Bay of Fundy. Braddy asked permission from the captain to have a Communion Service at eight o'clock in the saloon. He granted it and asked whether he might receive Communion. He said that he was a Presbyterian and could rarely receive it in his own church. Braddy gladly granted this. They had a good turnout at the service but Braddy never took a service under such conditions ever again. As often happens, the sea in the Bay was quite rough and Braddy had great difficulty keeping his balance and he also had to fight against the fact that he felt extremely ill. However, spirit triumphed over matter and he got through successfully. A doctor who was present and had been watching him, directly the service was over, got him outside in a deck chair and administered some seasick remedies. He was actually never sick but it was touch-and-go. Braddy remembered Coffin, Gow and Frith throughout his life.

They landed in Saint John, New Brunswick and Braddy got through customs with one little hitch. He was carrying his handbag and his shot gun which was in a canvas case, in two parts - stock and barrel. Just as the officer was going to chalk it through he asked casually what it was. He cheerfully told him a shot gun. He looked surprised and asked Braddy if he had a permit to bring it into Canada. Of course, he hadn't, as that was the first that he had heard about the need for a permit. So then the officer asked him where he was going and Braddy told him Charlottetown, and gave him Malone's address. He told him that when he got to Charlottetown to apply for a permit, and the gun would be delivered to him, which it was.

Braddy then went into Halifax and put up at the Queen Hotel. When he came up from Barbados in September of the previous year, he stayed overnight at the Queen before going on to Charlottetown. He knew the hotel because he and Maggie had come through from Alberta, in 1921, on their way to Barbados and they had stayed overnight there. On going to the desk to register in September of 1928 the clerk greeted him with," Hello! Mr. Bradshaw; glad to see you again." Braddy must have shown surprise because the clerk continued," Didn't you and your wife stay with us in 1921 on your way to the West Indies?" What a memory! To be able to speak to Braddy by name after all the hundreds that he had greeted in the several year's lapse between the visits was quite remarkable. Whether the hotel company knew it or not they had a treasure in that clerk.

Another strange thing happened that evening in that hotel. Braddy had been feeling very much a stranger in a strange land. The clerk's greeting had cheered him somewhat and he was sitting in the lounge, when a hand was laid on his shoulder from behind and someone said," What are you doing here?" On turning round he discovered that it was a Mr. James Niblock, a prominent merchant from Barbados, who was on a business trip to Canada. This further warmed Braddy and made him feel less a stranger.

Braddy telephoned Malone and told him that he would be with him the next day. He thought that he might find out something of job opportunities in the diocese and went to the Diocesan Office and saw Archdeacon Watson who was then diocesan secretary. He told Braddy that Archbishop Worrell and Bishop Hackenley were both out of town and he suggested that Braddy write to the Archbishop. So he set off for Prince Edward Island. Malone met him and told him of his arrangements. Braddy knew that his wife had died and he told Braddy that he was now boarding in his own rectory. He had given it over to a young couple, Rollie and Isabel Diamond. When Braddy saw Isabel she agreed to board Braddy for seven dollars a week. Braddy wrote to the Archbishop and in the meantime helped Malone at the Cathedral during the week. There was a daily Eucharist and Braddy took some of these. One of Braddy's servers at these services was one who later became Lieutenant Governor of the Island. He was a Heindman. On Sundays Braddy took services in the vacant parishes in Georgetown and Cherry Valley. He got enough from this work to cover his board bill. He also wrote Bishop Richardson of Fredericton about a vacancy there. He asked Braddy to visit the diocese one weekend as there was a vacant parish - Kingston. Braddy did this and the Bishop took him to visit the parish and meet with the Vestry. He left him and he went on further to look into the matter. The Bishop was taking a Confirmation at another parish. Kingston was on the Kennebecasis River and was a very delightful spot. The rectory with fine grounds going down to the river was a very fine old building. Braddy took four services that day at the four churches, talked to wardens and some Vestry members, and they thought that he would suit them and they would let him know.

There was a sad incident with regard to this visit to Kingston. Braddy had a meal at one house where he met a very delightful lady. They had a farm. Sometime after this, in Charlottetown, they saw in the paper that she had been drowned. She was trying to save her small son who had fallen into the river.

It was sometime before Braddy heard from the Kingston wardens telling him that they would not be able to take him as a son of the parish had returned from ministry in the Arctic and wanted a parish so they were engaging him.

There was still no word from the Archbishop so Malone phoned him and told him that Braddy would soon have to return to Barbados, if he had no work for him. Malone, as only Malone could, said "And you need not offer him Neil's Harbour." Neil's Harbour incidentally is at the most northerly tip of Cape Breton.

All the Archbishop replied was, "Send Bradshaw to me."

Braddy went rather diffidently to Halifax. He was a trifle scared of "the old man", although Malone certainly was not. He always referred to him as Ponto; Braddy supposed that this was short for pontificator. However, Braddy found the Archbishop to be very pleasant and with the heartening news that there was a parish - Musquodoboit Harbour - that had become vacant, unexpectedly, and thought that parish might suit Braddy. The one that was leaving Musquodoboit Harbour was John Furlong and the Archbishop was very annoyed with him. Furlong had been an actor before he entered the ministry and the Archbishop had shortened the time of his diaconate, under the condition that he remain at Musquodoboit Harbour for two years. In little less than a year St. Mark's in Halifax became vacant and Furlong applied for it. As he had a very fine voice and good presence, St. Mark's wanted him to take the parish. In those days a self-supporting parish had almost entire control as to whom was appointed as their parish priest. The Archbishop did not like the appointment but reluctantly agreed to it. He had a considerable amount of sardonic humour and said to Braddy, "He (Furlong) went there and preached and sang" and then his Grace looked thoughtful and added, "I guess he also danced a little."

Braddy always got on very well with his Grace after this. He got used to his bruskness. He reminded Braddy very much of a former Archbishop of Canterbury, Dr. Temple, of whom the story was told at the time of the Titanic sinking that a young priest talking to his Grace said, "My aunt nearly sailed on the Titanic but at the last minute was prevented. Does not your Grace consider that was providential?"

The Archbishop replied, "Cannot say. Didn't know your aunt!"

Braddy went back to Charlottetown until the end of November and then gathering together his goods and chattels he left for Musquodoboit Harbour and another new phase of life began.

First Nova Scotia Parish — Musquodoboit Harbour (1928-1931)

The first time Braddy heard the name of this small village on the Eastern Shore of Nova Scotia was from the lips of the Most Rev. Clare L. Worrell, Archbishop of Nova Scotia, Metropolitan of the Ecclesiastical Province of Canada and in 1931 he became Primate of all Canada. They were in his study at Bishop's Lodge in Halifax and the Archbishop had asked Braddy if he would like to go and see the Parish of Musquodoboit Harbour, and interview the church wardens with the idea of his taking charge of the cure.

At that time Braddy was still vicar of St. Mark's church in Barbados and was in the Maritimes on leave. Before leaving Barbados in September of the year 1928, Maggie and Braddy had talked the matter over and had agreed that if there were a suitable parish in the Canadian diocese offered to him that he should take it. They had enjoyed their work together in the beautiful little island (Barbados) diocese, but the time had come to look to the future, especially that of their growing family. There was at that time little prospect for young people, especially girls, to find suitable occupations in the island. At that time they were the proud parents of three daughters - Beryl 8; Joan 7; Dorothy 5; and one small son, Charles 3. So they decided that if they were contemplating a move to a larger country it would be well to do so while the children were still small, so that they might grow up in that country where, in later life, they would find occupation.

On arrival in Canada, Braddy had spent two months with Canon Edwin Malone, who was Incumbent of St. Peter's Cathedral in Charlottetown, Prince Edward Island. They were both graduates of Durham University, having taken their college courses at Codrington College in Barbados, which through provision of its founder, Sir

Christopher, was attached to the English University of Durham. While with Malone, helping out in various small churches in the Island, Braddy had had an opportunity of experiencing church-life in Canada, with its scattered congregations - often small in numbers - very different to those that he had been used to in Barbados with its large numbers in small areas.

This all led up to Braddy's interview with the Archbishop in November in Halifax and his suggestion that he might find a happy sphere of work in the parish of Musquodoboit Harbour which was shortly to become vacant.

The Most Reverend Worrell was in his late seventies but showed little signs of his age. Physically, he was tall and erect of carriage. He wore a close-clipped beard and was somewhat severe of countenance, but his rather infrequent smile lit up his whole face and one had a glimpse of the spiritual love which he had for his people and which endeared him to them. He was scholarly, a good preacher, and a very wise and able administrator. This was demonstrated and anyone could appreciate this ability when he chaired the annual synod. He saw that speakers did not wander from the point being

Most Rev. Clare L. Worrell

discussed, which is "the sign of a clear-thinking chairman". Until his death in 1933, Braddy said, "He was always to me a true Father-in-God and a kind friend."

Following the interview Braddy had with Archbishop Worrell, the latter telephoned Mr. Percy Weary, one of the church wardens of Musquodoboit Harbour, and arranged for Braddy to go there by train the following afternoon.

Being a stranger in Halifax the Archbishop thought Braddy might like to see something of the old seaport city, so he called up one of the young clergy, Rev. A. E. Gabriel, at that time assistant priest at St. George's Church, and requested him to show Braddy some of the interesting sights of the city. On their tour they visited St. Paul's Church, the oldest Anglican church in Canada, with its mementos of the tragic explosion of the munition ship in the Narrows of the Halifax Harbour on December 6th, 1917. This explosion devastated a large part of the city and St. Paul's church was no exception. Over the south door, embedded in the wall, was a length of steel girder, which had been hurled, no one knew how far, by the explosion. Another relic of that tragic day was the silhouette in one of the shattered windows, of a man's head. This has been preserved perfectly, by a sheet of glass placed on either side of it.

Their tour took them to Citadel Hill from which, in the old days, the approach of hostile ships was noted. They also saw Bedford Basin, with its superb anchorage for ships and in which the convoys were to gather during the Second World War, before setting out on their dangerous voyage to cross the submarine infested North Atlantic. Halifax, whose history is so vividly told by Thomas Raddall in his book, *Halifax Warden of the North*, is very rich in memories of the early days of the northern part of this continent, "which we know and love as Canada."

That evening Braddy spent at Bishop's Lodge, Luckknow Street, with the Archbishop and Mrs. Worrell, and on going to bed, found by his bedside a glass of milk and some cookies, placed there by Mrs. Worrell, a dear soul, who continually mothered all the clergy, especially the younger ones.

Next morning at breakfast the Archbishop uttered one of his infrequent jokes when they had lighted cigarettes," What is better than a cigarette after breakfast?" When Braddy did not reply, considering it a statement rather that a question needing an answer, he answered himself, "Two!"

That morning Braddy visited the secretary of the synod at the synod office on Barrington Street. He had a very intimate knowledge of all the parishes in the Diocese and gave Braddy some statistical and other details of the parish which Braddy was to visit that afternoon. In the course of the conversation, he said, "Oh! By the way, when you get your ticket at the station, ask for one to the Harbour; don't mention Musquodoboit as they will take you either to Middle Musquodoboit or Upper Musquodoboit which are thirty-five and seventy miles further on." This information was very useful to one who was travelling over the line for the first time. Braddy soon realized that reducing the name of the village to "The Harbour" was a sore point with the people who lived in that area. After various protests, their railway depot was given the full name of Musquodoboit Harbour. This name is one of the many Indian place names to be found scattered across Canada and means "The Stoney Crossing". Musquodoboit Harbour is at the mouth of the Musquodoboit River and at the head of a long, island-sprinkled bay. The river winds away for six miles until it reaches the Atlantic Ocean.

Although Musquodoboit Harbour is only twenty-five miles by road from Halifax, the distance by train seemed to be longer, as the train could be classed among those things mentioned in Genesis, - "... the creeping things of the earth". Eventually Braddy arrived there and was met by the church warden, Mr. Percy Weary, and was taken to his attractive home.

Braddy acclaimed "the tremendous work done over the years in the Diocese of Nova Scotia by Mr. Weary, ably assisted by Mrs. Weary". The work of the church, over the years he knew them, was one of the chief, if not the chief, interests of their lives. Over the years there were few committees of the diocese on which Mr. Weary did not find a place, and all benefited from his wise counsel and advise, gained by his many years in the service of the church as a faithful layman. Braddy was received into their hospitable home that November evening in 1929 for the first time, but it was to be the precursor of many happy hours spent there. After supper, Mr. Weary took him to see various members of the congregation, including the other church warden, Mr. O. P. Mosher, who was to become, throughout the years, a firm and true friend. The outcome of these visits was that Braddy was asked to take charge of the parish, providing the Archbishop gave his consent at a date to be arranged with him.

Braddy returned to Halifax the next morning and reported to His Grace the result of his visit and he promptly appointed Braddy the Rector of the Parish of Musquodoboit Harbour, to come into effect December 1st.

On returning to Prince Edward Island, Braddy wrote to the Bishop of Barbados tendering his resignation as Vicar of St. Mark's and wrote to his wife suggesting that she and the family not join him until the following spring. He felt that they might find it rather hard to be dumped into the midst of a Canadian winter after the warmth of the tropics.

Braddy duly arrived in his new parish December 1st, 1928 and stayed with the Wearys for about ten days while he tried to find a comfortable place to board until the family arrived the following spring. This he did in the pleasant home of Mrs. McKerracher. She had quite a large house and at the time had plenty of room as her husband was away working with the Ford Company in Quebec. She only had one small daughter, Jean.

The parish was entirely a rural one. Most of the people were occupied in lumbering and fishing. There were four churches. The parish church of St. Thomas was situated in Smith Settlement, about a mile from the village of Musquodoboit Harbour. The rectory was half a mile beyond that on the main road. Two miles further on was the Church of St. James, at the Head of Jeddore. On a branch road which ran for five miles down the side of the Harbour, was St. George's Church at a fishing village called Ostrea

Lake. In the other direction past Musquodoboit Harbour, about five miles on Petpeswick Inlet, at the mouth thereof, was Holy Trinity Church. From this it will be seen that Braddy would have a fair amount of driving to do. The parish church had a service every Sunday - occasionally two - morning and evening. and the other churches had a service every other Sunday. Each church had a Communion Service at least once a month.

St. Thomas

St. James

St. Georges

Holy Trinity

Churches of the Parish of Musquodoboit Harbour

During Braddy's first few weeks in the parish, he did his visiting on foot and some of the men of the congregation drove him to the outlying churches for the Sunday services. It was evident that he would have to get a car of his own if the parochial work was to be done satisfactorily. For this purpose, he obtained a loan of $250. from the diocese, to be repaid in quarterly instalments of $50. each. He was fortunate in getting a very good 1928 model Chevrolet from Teasdale and Foote in Dartmouth, for $850. It had seen less than a year's service and had been well taken care of. To pay for it, he also had to obtain a loan from the bank.

Very soon after obtaining the car in January of 1929, Braddy had a very disturbing experience. Along the shore line of Nova Scotia, during the winter, there is generally not as much snow as in the interior of the province, owing probably to the greater amount of salt in the air from the sea. However, there are frequently very icy roads. Braddy had no experience driving over roads in this condition. Between Smith's Settlement and the Head of Jeddore Harbour, there was a two mile stretch of road through the woods and this was frequently very icy in the winter as the sun could not reach it to thaw the ice.

One morning Braddy was driving to Jeddore, and the road was one sheet of clear ice. It was a gravel road and was apt to be quite rough. Although he did not realize it, it was dangerously smooth with the icy surface. He was bowling comfortably along at thirty-five miles an hour, when the car skidded. He tried to straighten it out, being ignorant of skids and how to deal with them, he turned the wheel the wrong way. Soon he was the unwilling participant in a merry whirl. One minute the car was facing one way and the next the other. He said later that he could not say that all the misdemeanours of his past life passed before him, as he was too busy looking for a soft spot to land. The inevitable happened. Tired of the road the car made a dive for the woods. It gaily leaped over a rock, about three feet high, at the edge of the road, with an awful scraping sound from under the carriage and settled down comfortably in a nest of smaller rocks just beyond. He surveyed the unpromising situation and decided that he must walk back to the nearest telephone and summon help from the garage. Jim Myers, the garage man, soon arrived with his tow truck. He looked at Braddy; looked at the car; took off his cap and scratched his head; and said, "How the — — — — did you put that car there?"

Braddy meekly replied that he had not put it there; it had put itself there. This did not seem to help. With an appeal to the Deity, he wanted to know how Braddy thought he was going to get it out; then he added a few words of comfort, "I wouldn't give you ten cents for the undercarriage of that car now." However, with some clever manipulation of his truck he did manage to get the car back onto the road. He then towed Braddy back to the garage where he hoisted the car up and proceeded to estimate the damage. He came out from underneath shaking his head, and said," You lucky, Son-of-a-gun; you must have lived right. The damage is a broken strut to the running board." Braddy added that after that experience when he got on icy roads it was hard to tell whether he was moving at all, as his average speed was about three miles an hour.

During Braddy's first winter in the parish he got to know a number of families in the congregations in the various churches. The other Church warden, Mr. O.P. Mosher was a lumberman in a very large business, and on the side he did a little fishing and farming. He was one who thoroughly loved his church and was always willing to help in its work in every way possible. Braddy always remembered his quiet unassuming friendship and the continual support which he always gave to Braddy in the work of the parish. To a newcomer, and in many ways a stranger to Canadian life, the support was indeed of great worth. His family, of four boys and four girls, was a delightful one. Mrs. Mosher suffered greatly from arthritis, but was always cheerful and gave ample support to her husband in bringing up the family in the knowledge and love of God. They lived in a pleasant old farm house not far from the beginning of the road that led to Ostrea Lake. This road was a branch off from the main Eastern Shore road, the turn being just beyond the rectory. To travel that road was, for a time for Braddy, a rather unpleasant experience. It was very narrow, winding up hill and down dale, and very rough. It skirted the harbour for all its five mile length. There had to be continual watchfulness, for visibility on the road ahead was never more than a few yards, and often one could not pass another car.

On one occasion, Braddy had gone up a very sharp hill and around a hairpin bend when he discovered ahead of him a very large bull moose. All he could do was stop promptly, and he meant promptly, about ten feet from it. It did not budge. Braddy dared not blow the horn for fear of startling it. One never knows what a startled moose will do. It turned around and looked at Braddy. It probably could not see the car clearly as moose are reputed to have poor eyesight. Then it lowered its head and snorted. Braddy admitted that he was nearly petrified with fright as he wondered if it was going to charge. He crouched down behind the wheel. The moose pawed the ground, snorted again, and then turned and trotted into the woods. Braddy says he collected his heart from somewhere in the region of his boots and proceeded rather meekly on his way.

130

On another occasion, Braddy was travelling the same road and had Canon Malone with him. They came upon a cow in the road. It was at a spot with a steep bank on one side and a drop to the water on the other. The cow seemed to be quite placid and unconcerned so Braddy thought that he could edge past it. Just as he got level with it, the foolish thing began to climb the bank, which was practically vertical. Malone saw what was happening and yelled, "Braddy! Step on it!" He did, and Madam Cow landed on her back, in the road just behind the car. She was not hurt, except for her bovine feelings, but the car would not have benefited by a very large cow landing in the middle of it.

Because of the many possibilities of mishaps on this road, the Moshers, whose house Braddy mentioned was at the beginning of this road, used to note his passing on the way to Ostrea Lake; if he did not return in a reasonable time, they would send out a search party. On at least two occasions, they pulled him out of the ditch.

The two chapel wardens at St. George's Church, during Braddy's time as Rector, were George Bowser and Stanley Williams, two stalwart churchmen. St. George's was a pretty little church with a very loyal congregation. There was no other denomination that had a church in that village. About a mile before reaching Ostrea Lake, there was a settlement known as William's Settlement. Nearly all the families there had the surname of Williams. The men were practically all engaged as seamen, many of them rising to Masters in the Merchant Marine.

The first winter, when taking a midweek Lenten service at St. George's, Braddy would stay the night with the Stan Williams' family. The evening meal was generally stewed black duck. During the late fall and early winter, these wild ducks flocked, by the thousands, in the coves of the harbour, and many of them fell to the guns of the men, who were, for the most part, experienced and accurate "gunners". The women were expert in canning the ducks so that in the closed season, there was still a plentiful supply for the table.

Braddy looked back, with pleasure, to the evenings he spent at Stan William's home and at other homes in the settlement too. Those were the days before even radios were common, so the evenings were spent with his hosts telling him many tales of the forest and the sea. Some were of the rather "tall" variety, as the one told very gleefully of the local hunter who crawled into a cave after a black bear. The entrance to the cave was very narrow and went through the roots of a very large fir tree. When the man was half way in, the bear, that had not quite settled down for his winter's sleep, decided that enough was enough and began to do something

131

about it by charging. The force of this charge thrust the hunter's head up into the roots of the fir. He had been pushing his gun barrel foremost before him. The barrel, in the charge of the bear, went into its mouth, and as it emerged from the cave the trigger caught, fired the shot through the bear's head, and killed it. Others had to extricate the hunter's head from the fir roots. It was quite a story!

Throughout his life, Braddy treasured in his mind the names of many local church people who were parishioners in his first parish in the Diocese of Nova Scotia. Most of the families in Smith's Settlement, where the rectory was, were Smiths. Travellers in Nova Scotia and, in fact, in all of Canada will find many such small settlements that have taken their names from the families who were the first settlers there. East of the rectory were three Smith brothers - Reubin, Lee and Milam. All of them usually worked in Halifax and Dartmouth on construction work. Reubin, who was a widower rarely came home but stayed in Dartmouth. The other two were generally home for the weekends. Mrs. Lee Smith, a very dear soul, was the settlement postmistress. On the Musquodoboit Harbour side of the rectory were the Donald Smiths and the Thomas Smiths. Then came the Bonns, the Faulkners, Mrs. McKerracher (where Braddy boarded those first few months), and Mrs. Stevens and her son, Howard, who were the telephone operators for the district. Howard was crippled, having no use of his legs, but was very expert at the Exchange. He did not allow his disability to keep him away from the church services. He was always there, when he could get someone to act for him at the Exchange. Years later Braddy could visualize him, being carried into church, by his stalwart nephew, Bert.

Most of the telephones in the district were on party lines. Howard was very sharp on people "listening in" and checked this pernicious habit whenever he could. When Braddy and family moved into the rectory, their number was 23, that meant they would get two long rings and three short ones. Once, Braddy lifted the receiver when 22 was being called and was quickly told," Calling 22 not 23; replace your receiver please." On one occasion, the rectory party line was out for two days. There was a "short" on it somewhere, which could not be located. The linesmen checked all the insulators and the telephones in the houses and finally the trouble was located. An old man had laid his steel rimmed spectacles on top of the telephone box and had shorted the connection there. He had been looking everywhere for his glasses and was delighted to find them, but he never understood how much it cost the telephone company to find them for him.

132

In common with all small rural communities, Smith Settlement had its general store, This store was kept by a retired sea captain, Dennis Williams. He was, like many others in the district, a very strong churchman. For many years, in fact until he was in his eighties, he was a lay delegate to synod. He was also a municipal councillor and a Justice of the Peace. Many an evening, before the arrival of the family, Braddy spent at this home, talking over current events, and most frequently, the doings of the church. Captain Williams had a wide knowledge of the history of the church and was conversant of its work throughout the world and a firm believer of the catholicity of the Anglican branch of it. They had no children of their own, but had an adopted daughter, Gertrude, who together with Mrs. Weary, had charge of the organ in the church. Both were accomplished musicians.

Also during those days, when Braddy was a "grass widow", he spent many a pleasant evening with the Wearys. It was about one and a half miles from the rectory in Smith Settlement. Mr. Weary was, at that time, manager of Robin, Jones and Whitman's General Store in the village. The firm, originated in the Channel Islands but had their head office in Halifax and many branch stores scattered throughout the Maritimes and on the Gaspe Shore of Quebec. There were two such stores in the district; the other one was at Oyster Pond, several miles further down the Eastern Shore. Mr. Weary was manager of both of them and had an assistant at Oyster Pond. Some years after this when the firm was disposing of some of their stores, Mr. Weary acquired both of these.

The Wearys had two sons, Bert and John. When Braddy was there they were both typical boys around the ages of ten and twelve, and were filled with vim and vigour. One occasion when Braddy called there just after lunch, he was greeted by Mrs. Weary with, "My word! It is a good thing you did not come a little sooner. The language around here has been such that it turned the air blue." Braddy asked what had happened and was told by Mrs. Weary that the boys had been out fishing and afterwards had hung the fishing rod over the stairs going down to the basement, with a portion of the line with the hook on it, hanging down. Her husband, Percy, was dashing around getting things done before he went back to the store, and ran down the cellar steps to see to the furnace. The hanging hook caught him just under the eyebrow. Fortunately, he was going at such a speed that it pulled loose. The boys heard the roar from their father and although they did not know then what had happened, they guessed they were in it somewhere and took to the roof, with Percy after them. She thought the boys were still there but Percy had gone back to the store.

Percy was always a very enthusiastic type, who went into everything that he did with all the energy possible. One winter he took up skiing. He practiced on the hill behind the house, sweeping down around the house, down the driveway and onto the road. One afternoon when his wife was entertaining the ladies of the Parish Guild at tea, he called them out to the veranda to witness his skill. He swooped down beautifully from behind the house before the admiring ladies, and then made the mistake of nonchalantly waving to them. The result was disastrous. Their next view was a pair of violently waving skis, sticking out of the hedge.

What he (Mr. Weary) could do on the run he did. So typical of him, was an incident which Braddy witnessed. The women of the church. were having a tea and social evening in the I.O.O.F. hall at Musquodoboit Harbour. Mrs. Weary asked her husband when he came along to bring some small doughnuts with him, which she had left ready in a basket. These were little round brown balls, which were made from the center of the traditional doughnuts. Mr. Weary had to stop at the store to get something, and dashing up the steps of the store, he slipped and spilled the doughnuts. It was in the winter and the ground was frozen hard. Sometime earlier, a horse, waiting outside the store, had, as horses will, left a deposit. Mr. Weary, frantically picking up the doughnuts, also picked up among them some little brown balls - not very much unlike the doughnuts - a contribution from the horse. Fortunately, Bert and Braddy saw this and rectified the mistake before embarrassment would ensue in the hall. Incidentally, neither Bert nor Braddy accepted doughnuts when they were passed to them.

During the late winter and early spring, Braddy was busy collecting furniture for the rectory in anticipation of the arrival of the family from Barbados in May. By attending auction sales, not too frequent in those days, and by visiting second hand stores in Halifax, he managed to have the rectory fairly fully and comfortably equipped with most of the necessities by the time he heard from Maggie that they were sailing by the C.N.S. Lady Nelson early in May. This boat docked in Saint John, New Brunswick, so Braddy drove to Halifax, left the car there and went on to Saint John by train.

The Lady Nelson was in on time and he soon gathered the family, got them through the Customs and they returned to Halifax by train. There Braddy engaged a room for the night at the old Queen Hotel on Hollis Street. In those days this hotel was about the most popular one in the port city.

Braddy got them safely to their new home in the new parish and they soon were exploring the rectory and its surroundings. With the usual aptitude of children, they soon accepted the differences of climate and living conditions, so different from what they had been used to in the West Indies.

The three oldest Bradshaw children soon started school. The school which the children from Smith's Settlement had to attend was not very satisfactory. The one room school house for that school section was about a mile and a half from the settlement, away in the woods on the Ostrea Lake Road. When Braddy enquired about its location being so far from the homes of the majority of the children, he was told that when it was built, some many years before, there were houses beyond it and it was then in the middle of the school section. Now these homes were no longer there, but the school had never been moved. During the summer months the daily trek to and from the school was rather enjoyed by the children, but in the winter, it was by no means pleasant and was exceedingly hard on the smaller ones.

About this time, Braddy was in Halifax and met in the lounge of the Queen Hotel, the Hon. Albert Parsons, who was, he thought, the Speaker of the Provincial Legislature. Knowing Braddy was a newcomer to the province, he asked him what his impressions were of Nova Scotia. Among other things, Braddy spoke to him about the inequality of the educational provisions for the children in the province, quoting as a sample, their own situation in Smith Settlement. In the settlement, the rate payers were few and none of them well off, so therefore all they had was a single room with one teacher who had to teach all grades up to ten. The neighbouring school section, Musquodoboit Harbour, was better off with a fine school and two rooms with two teachers. The reason given was that their tax roll was higher and thus they were able to provide for better educational facilities. Mr. Parsons agreed with Braddy and said that equalizing the educational provisions was one of the matters engaging the attention of government at that time. However, it was many years after that conversation that any endeavour was made to see that all children in the province were given an equal chance in education. You cannot satisfy all the people all the time; and there are quite a number who regret the passing of "the little red school house" and complain that their children have to leave home so early to "catch the bus" that conveys them daily to the large consolidated schools.

Charles, who was still at home, and like all small boys in search of amusement, often caused his parents embarrassment. On one occasion he wandered into the sitting room where his mother was entertaining a party of the church women, among whom was one who had very strong opinions as to what constituted and what did not constitute legitimate amusement. One of her aversions was card playing. Charles came in gaily shuffling a pack of cards and stated, "We like these. Mom says that Mrs. So and So says they are the devil's play things!" There was dead silence in the room and then a hurried renewal of the conversation with Mrs. "So and So" looking as though she had swallowed a particularly hard pickle. Braddy did realize that the lady in question never held it against them.

On another occasion, Charles entered a similar gathering with a grass snake curled around his arm. This caused much consternation.

To get Charles out from under his mother's feet, Braddy took him for a walk one day in the woods that came close to the rectory. He pointed out to him a hornet's nest, which looked like a large football hanging from the low branch of a fir tree just a few inches off the ground. He tried to explain to his son how wonderfully it was built, and with what skill and patience its little occupants had put it together. This did not impress Charles. Suddenly before Braddy could stop him, he took a kick at the nest and lifted if off the branch about three feet. Braddy said he never acted so quickly in his life. He grabbed up his small son and ran for the house, which fortunately was not far off. They were pursued by an angry and indignant cloud of hornets. They just made it in time to shut them outside the door.

During this preschool time, Braddy often took Charles with him in the car when he was making parochial visits. On one such occasion, he was visiting an old lady, who was renowned for never pulling her punches. She looked at Charles and then at his father and said, "My, his mother must have been good-looking!"

During these early days in Musquodoboit Harbour, Braddy had a most remarkable escape from falling into the clutches of the law, with a capital "L". A man, who was one of the village "ne'er-do-wells", went to Braddy, and asked him to visit his wife who was sick. In doing so Braddy left his car at the side of the road and walked to the little two-roomed shack a short distance in the woods. While visiting the sick woman in the bedroom, two men walked in. Braddy was saying a prayer at the time. They muttered an apology and left. Braddy returned home after the visit and the next morning, he, his wife, and three lady parishioners, left on a shopping expedition to Halifax, twenty-five miles away. In one place the road took a sharp bend around the head of what was known as Echo Lake. Just around the bend there was an R.C.M.P. block across the road. Two constables were stopping all cars searching for contraband liquor.

There was a good deal of boot-legging going on at the time. One constable went to the door of Braddy's car, but when he saw his collar, he said,"All right, Padre. We won't hold you up," and waved him on. They spent the whole day in Halifax and returned home quite late that night where he found the sick woman's husband waiting for him. He thought that probably she was worse, but he had another trouble. Rather sheepishly, he said," Them were Revenue officers that were in the house yesterday while you was visitin' the Missus. I had a bottle of rum and I put it behind the back seat of your car and I could not get it before you drove away." Then he dived his hand behind the cushion in the back seat and came up with the bottle and made off with it. Braddy's mouth was still hanging open when the man disappeared. What if he had not worn his clerical collar on their trip to Halifax? What explanation could he have given for the presence of the rum? And horrors of horrors, he suddenly remembered that Mrs. So and So, of the stern morals, had been sitting on the rum all the way. At the recollection, a slow grin always came to Braddy's face.

During Braddy's incumbency of the parish, there were two sad tragedies in the congregation of St. Thomas, the parish church. One was in the home of the O.P. Mosher family. Of their eight fine children, one, the eldest son was married and had a home of his own. Hazel, the oldest daughter, was working in the States. At home were Melvin, who had finished school and Oswald, Anna, Ruth, Ruby and Keith, who was about a year older than their Charles. They were all attending school. Ruth and Ruby were identical twins and Braddy could never tell them apart. Both were very pretty with sweet dispositions. They were both confirmed at Braddy's first confirmation in the parish. Ruby had an appointment with the dentist in Dartmouth for an extraction. The day following the dental work, infection set in. Braddy thought later that it was probably there before notice was taken of it. When she became worse, the doctor was called in but his best was not able to save her and she slipped away a few days later. It was a great blow to the close-knit family. The whole community mourned with them. Her burial service was one of the most harrowing Braddy felt he had ever taken. Many, many years later he still felt the poignancy of it. Their only comfort at the time was the knowledge that although that beautiful young body was laid aside in the stillness of death, her fervent young soul had gone forward into closer association with her dear Friend and Master, the Lord Jesus.

The next sad bereavement came in the home of the Lee Smith's, who lived two doors from the rectory. Mrs. Smith, or as she was affectionately known by all, "Aunt Kate", was the postmistress and her husband, a carpenter, worked in Dartmouth but came home for the weekends. One Sunday evening as Braddy was leaving for the evening service at St. James Church, at the Head of Jeddore, Lee Smith was just leaving his home to return to Dartmouth. He called out to him," See you next weekend!'

Shortly after Braddy's return from St. James, the telephone rang and the impersonal voice of the operator said, "Ringing from Dartmouth. Will you go in and tell Mrs. Lee Smith that her husband has been killed in a car accident on the Preston Road?" Although, Braddy asked, the operator could give him no further details. He felt at a loss for a few minutes then told his wife. Because she could not leave the children alone, Braddy went by himself on the sad errand. He remembered then that Lee's brother, Reubin, was on one of his rare visits to his house, which was between the rectory and Lee's, so he called there to tell him. He fell forward into Braddy's arms on receiving the news, which Braddy gave him as gently as possible. Fortunately, he soon recovered. The two of them then went on together to tell Mrs. Smith. Braddy always recalled how her bright smile of greeting faded when they broke the news to her. How very great is often the fortitude of women when faced with sudden sorrow! She quickly recovered from the initial shock. Kate Smith was one, Braddy always believed, who had a tremendous and vital spiritual strength. Her faith in God was very real and it was this faith that upheld her in this time of sudden bereavement. Later that night, her daughter, Elise, who was a nurse at the Victoria General Hospital in Halifax, came out and was with her. Braddy stayed until her arrival. Once more the community was plunged into mourning. Lee Smith, a gentleman in the fullest sense of the word, was loved and respected by all. His sudden passing was a sad loss to the congregation of St. Thomas and to the community as a whole. He loved his church and gave himself without stint in its service. Braddy often thought when such a person passes to higher service, "How great grows our store in heaven!"

On Maggie's first birthday in Nova Scotia, November 18, 1929, they were treated to the weirdest mixture of weather it is possible to imagine. The day started with some wet snow which quickly changed to rain mixed with ice pellets. This developed into a thunderstorm, and the grand finale was an earthquake tremor. When this took place Braddy was in his study and when there was a rumble accompanied by a shaking of the house, he thought that it was caused by a heavy truck passing. When he looked out and couldn't see any sign of a truck, he thought then that it must be the furnace acting up. They were burning coal which would sometimes give

138

off a gas which would form over the fuel bed and cause a small explosion when ignited. However on this occasion, he found that the furnace was going about its business of heating the house in a quiet and proficient manner. He then went outside to see if anything there would give a clue to the rumble. The first thing he saw was a man on the roof of the next house, the home of the Donald Smith's, pouring water down the chimney from a bucket. It might be thought that to carry a bucket of water up a sloping roof would be quite a feat. So it would be, if there were not the short ladders that were affixed to most roofs to help in the case of chimney fires, which were quite common owing to the creosote which formed in the chimneys from the burning of soft woods. As Braddy stood wondering about the rumble, a passer-by informed him that there had been a slight earth tremor. Mrs. Donald Smith told him sometime afterward that she had thought that the chimney was on fire and had sent her son up on the roof with the water to extinguish a nonexistent fire. It was only afterward that they remembered that there had been no fire in the stove to cause a fire in the chimney. People sometimes do strange things in a moment of excitement.

There was, indeed, a strange effect from this tremor, which was not discovered until the following spring. One of the Moirs Ltd. (Candy Company) travellers, Ross Day, had a small camp on the lake near Salmon River, which he used when on fishing trips. There was a small wharf attached to it. When Mr. Day visited his camp in the spring, he found that a large rock had appeared at the end of the wharf, with its top only about a foot below the water, in a place where there generally were eight to ten feet of water. The conclusion was that it had been pushed up from the lake bottom by the earthquake of the previous fall. There was nowhere else from which it could have come.

On March 26, 1930, the second Bradshaw son, David, was born. Like his brother and sisters before him, he did not dally in his entrance into the world. Braddy had arranged with an elderly woman, Mrs. Evans, who had had a great deal of experience ushering babies into this mundane sphere, to be with Maggie. She went to them about a week before the expected arrival. The local doctor, Dr. Rowlings, also had charge of the case. However, the night that David was born, the doctor had another call about four miles down the shore. He told Braddy later that when he passed the rectory, it was in darkness, so he guessed that there would be nothing doing there that night. How wrong he was! When the nurse called Braddy, he telephoned the doctor's house and was told of his absence, but that he had left the number of the place where he had gone and they would call him at once. He arrived about forty-five minutes later, but David was already present to greet him. Dear Mrs. Evans embarrassed Braddy beyond words by calling from the top of the stairs, "Don't let the doctor in; he will only charge you $25. and there is nothing that he can do." Braddy admitted that this remark left him and the doctor with red faces.

The doctor apologized for being late and explained the circumstances and said, "I won't come in if you don't want me to."

Braddy said, "Of course, we want you, Doctor." So the doctor entered and checked Maggie and the baby and found everything satisfactory.

Braddy explained that the fear of Mrs. Evans about the fee was entirely unwarranted as no doctor in Nova Scotia, and rarely elsewhere, had or did later ever charge him for medical services. It appeared that it was medical ethics to treat clergy and their families free of charge. It was a kind service for which the "cloth" were extremely grateful.

A rather strange coincidence happened with regard to David's "naming". They had at first thought of the names of John Mark for him, but changed them to David Bernard afterwards. Later Braddy learned that there was another boy born across the harbour at about the same time that David was born. Some time after, Braddy saw the father of this other boy and they commented on the fact of their births being so close together, and Braddy asked him what they had called their son. The reply was," David Wilford". The strange part about this was that neither of them had known previous to their meeting of the other's choice of name. Braddy wondered, "Was there some inexplicable thought transference? Who knows?"

Braddy found in Musquodoboit Harbour many interesting members of the congregation, especially among the older people. He always remembered, vividly, one old man, Benny Day. He was somewhere in his eighties and lived with his granddaughter in a little house by the side of the river. Mr. Day spent a great deal of his time sitting on the river bank, fishing, that is of course, during the open season. Not for him was the elaborate rod and equipment, without which the present day fisherman is lost. He used an alder pole, with a piece of string tied on the end, with a hook and sinker. His bait was generally a worm. His catch of trout was considerable with this primitive equipment. "Not sporting," you say? Benny was not interested in that; he fished entirely for the table.

One day Braddy had a call from Benny's granddaughter telling him that Grandad was not at all well and she asked Braddy if he would call and see him. On doing so, he found the old man in a very weak state and he could not help but think that his days on the river were finished. He

140

went to see him again the next day and as he could not find his granddaughter, he walked upstairs to the bedroom. To his surprise, Benny was not there and the bed was made. Puzzled, Braddy wondered if he had been taken to hospital, or could it be that he had died? He could hardly believe this as surely he would have been notified. While cogitating he happened to glance out the window and there was Benny, sitting on a rock, busily cutting firewood. Incidentally, he was in his high nineties, very close to one hundred, when he died.

Benny Day always made Braddy think of the story which he had heard in his youth in England. It was during what was known as the "Silly Season" in the newspaper world; it is the time when there is very little important news. One reporter heard of a village where people were reputed to live to a great age. Thinking that he might get a story out of it, he visited the village and saw an old man leaning over a gate. He began to talk to him, about his age and experiences in life. Finally the old man said, "I have to go in now; Pa will be calling me."

The reporter was amazed and said, "You mean to say that your father is still living? What is he doing?"

"Oh!" came the reply, "He's putting Grandpappy to bed."

Another old "character" was a retired seaman, Captain Freeman Faulkner. Braddy said he never saw him without thinking of the old pirates of the Spanish Main. He had a big black bushy beard and generally wore a red kerchief around his neck. He lived on Jeddore Harbour and represented St. James Church on the parish vestry. He always resented interference from outside the parish by the diocesan authorities. At one vestry meeting some matter under discussion was doubted to be according to canon law. One member said, "Canon law will not permit us to do that."

Captain Faulkner at once growled, "Who the h... is this Canon Law? I suppose one of those interfering fellows in Halifax. Let him come down here and we'll tell him where he gets off."

Old Captain Faulkner had a woodlot across the lake from his house and he used to cut his firewood in the winter and sled it across the frozen lake on a sled drawn by a pair of oxen. Icicles would hang from his beard and also from the oxen's beard. It was almost impossible to tell from a little distance which was Captain Faulkner and which were the oxen.

Another well-known character was Mr. Will Mosher, the brother of the church warden, but not quite of the same stirling character. He was often suspected of bootlegging - engaging in the contraband liquor business. The story goes that on one occasion he was busy burying some kegs of rum in the churchyard, when one of the vestry men came along having some business in the church. This did not phase Will at all. He managed to sit on a small keg and cover it, and lighting his pipe, said, "I like to sit up here and enjoy the view." He always seemed to have plenty of money, but the only apparent work that he did was occasionally to take out a party of fisherman on the harbour. He had lost one leg which had been replaced by a cork one and one of his favourite little tricks, when he had fishermen out, was to take out his plug of tobacco, pare some off and while he was filling his pipe, he would stick the knife in his cork leg. To those who did not know that it was cork, this was rather an alarming procedure.

A few years before Braddy went to Musquodoboit Harbour, there had been, in 1925, a union of the three Protestant bodies - the Methodists, Presbyterians and Congregationalists. This union was rather spoilt by a minority of the Presbyterians staying out of what was to be known as the United Church. At the beginning, there was great bitterness between the continuing Presbyterians and the members of the United Church. Braddy found this particularly so in Musquodoboit Harbour. Previous to the union there had been two church buildings, Presbyterian and Methodist, the former having the much better building. At the union the new United Church took over the Presbyterian building and told the continuing Presbyterians that they could have the old Methodist building. This, as was to be expected, did not please them at all and having some quite well-off members built another church for themselves. This brought about much bitterness between the two bodies, so much so, that neither would enter the other's church, not even for a funeral. They would sit outside in their cars. The Presbyterians, as their numbers were small, did not have a resident minister, but would have one come from Halifax for Sunday services and the occasional funeral. A boy from one of the Presbyterian families was drowned in the river. The minister, not knowing the circumstances of the death, chose one of the hymns at the funeral, "Shall We Gather at the River?"!

The annual Harvest Thanksgiving Service was held in most churches in the Diocese of Nova Scotia on the first or second Sunday in October, and it was customary in the rural churches to give, for the use of the rectory family, the fruit, vegetables and other harvest, used in decorating the church for the festival. This was very much appreciated by the clergy, and it provided vegetables for the winter. Few of the clergy ever had time to put in a garden, even if there were sufficient land around the rectory for

142

that purpose.

At Braddy's first Thanksgiving service in the parish, he found that the little Holy Trinity Church at Petpeswick had been decorated with dried salt fish - principally cod and pollock. That church was in the midst of a village down on the shore and the entire population was engaged in fishing, so it was the harvest of the sea for which they gave thanks, principally. There must have been several hundred pounds of fish strung around the church when Braddy arrived for the service. Fishing nets were also draped in the ceiling. In front of the pulpit was a huge dried pollock, weighing at least thirty pounds. After the service Braddy congratulated the chapel warden on the good effect of the church decorations and asked him what they were going to do with all the fish. Braddy was rather appalled when the warden said, "Not what are we going to do with them parson; it is all yours."

When Braddy went to carry it away, he had nearly a car full. The pollock alone lasted the whole winter, and he added, "Did we ever get tired of it!." Later in life he could always hear the children saying, "Oh! Not that again!" as it made its regular appearance on the table.

During that winter Braddy had a business trip to Halifax and took Beryl with him. He had to call at the synod office on Barrington Street and met Mrs. Worrell there. She said, "Do bring your little daughter to the house for lunch. We will expect you." Beryl was wildly excited at the idea and wondered what they would get for lunch. Braddy admired her restraint and good manners when she bravely tackled the lunch - salt fish and rice pudding, both of which she abominated. It was Friday!

Braddy and Beryl shared together in another experience which was not too pleasant. Beryl belonged to a girl's club which Mrs. Weary held in her home. One evening Braddy took her to the meeting and when they returned home later, drove the car into the garage (It was a converted barn with the hayloft still up a flight of stairs at one side.) and turned the engine and lights off. They heard a tremendous clatter up above their heads in the loft. Beryl, who had gotten out of the car on the other side, gave one scream and came dashing around the car and grabbed her father by the legs. At the same time, a rather large animal rushed down the steps with an appalling noise and it was only as it went through the door and Braddy saw its antlers, that he knew what was the cause of their fright. He said "ours" because he was scared too. It was a big buck deer. Evidently it had gone up into the loft after some dry hay which had been left since the time a former rector had kept a horse.

In 1930, from The Rectory, Smiths Settlement, Musquodoboit

Harbour, his first parish in the Diocese of Nova Scotia, Braddy wrote to the Codrington Magazine:

> *We are looking very Christmas-like here under a blanket of snow. The weather however so far has not been too cold. Things are going fairly well, sometimes I wish that I was back in Bimshire (old name for Barbados). In a year or two I shall look out for a parish with better school facilities. At present the children will be all right while they are young. The people are all very kind and we have made some good friends. The winter travelling is a difficulty but I live from week to week and hope for the best. I am getting used to the Churchmanship and am sometimes surprised at the quiet unassuming way at which it regularly shows a tendency to mark a higher plane.*
>
> *My Church worker who poses as an extreme Evangelical sometimes makes some startling "High Church" remarks. I am afraid that my friends in Barbados who looked on me as "an advanced Anglo Catholic" would have been surprised to think that I have fought one battle to prevent candles being put on the Altar at one of my churches. Nova Scotia is not quite ready for them yet, but in a few years time, I believe that all the churches will have them. I presented one Candidate 10 years old at my Confirmation. I spoke to his parent about it, and he only smiled and said, 'I leave that to you as Parish Priest'.*

In the early spring of 1931, Archbishop Worrell told Braddy that for the sake of the children, they should move to another parish where better school facilities were provided. "At the present time," he said, "there are two parishes, either vacant or shortly to become vacant - Annapolis, where the rector had resigned because of age, and Hubbards, where the present rector, the Rev. George Ernst, had been appointed to Wolfville. Annapolis would be fine for you; but they have already intimated to me that they had a new rector in view. That leaves Hubbards, which I think would suit you and that you would suit them. Go as soon as you can; see the church wardens; look over the parish."

At the end of April Braddy drove to Hubbards, on the south shore, twenty miles from Halifax. In those days very few of the roads were paved; the best that one could expect was a gravelled one. The road to Hubbards from Halifax had been scraped but was not in very good condition. It had several mud holes, out of two of which Braddy had to be pulled by a tractor belonging to the Department of Highways. The tractor was standing by to help motorists in distress. However, Braddy eventually got to Hubbards and was interviewed by the church wardens, Neil Maclean and Rex Dorey.

After discussion with the church wardens, Braddy told them that he would take the parish and they promised to notify the Archbishop. They also asked him, if agreeable to the Archbishop, and if he could be released from his present parish, to endeavour to be with them by the beginning of June, as Hubbards, being a Summer Resort, they needed to have regular services for their summer visitors during the short season.

The evening of Braddy's return to the Musquodoboit Harbour rectory, the family was talking over their proposed move to Hubbards, when he received a telephone call which put them in a state of uncertainty. It was from Mr. Harris, the vestry clerk of the parish of Annapolis Royal. He asked Braddy whether he would be prepared to accept that parish as the Vestry were unanimous in their wish for him to do so. He told him that he had just gotten back from an interview with the church wardens of the parish of Hubbards. The clerk told Braddy that they had understood from the Archbishop that he was available and highly recommended him to them. He asked Braddy to think the matter over and let him know his decision as soon as possible.

Braddy wrote off at once to Archbishop Worrell and put the matter before him. He had a letter from him in reply saying that he was sorry for the mix up. He had not realized that Braddy was the one that Annapolis Royal had in view for the parish. He advised him to accept Annapolis and he would find another man for Hubbards. Annapolis, he said, was a better parish, being self-supporting, with a higher stipend and he thought that they would like it very much. When Braddy received this letter, they had staying with them for confirmation, Bishop John Hackenley, the Coadjutor Bishop of the diocese. Braddy asked him his opinion on the matter. Should he go to Hubbards or Annapolis? Braddy could recall his face as he closed one

Bishop Hackenley

145

eye and looked at him rather quizzically and said, "If I had given my promise to Hubbards to go there, I would keep it." He went on to add how necessary it was for them to have a resident priest during the summer months when there were so many visitors. That decided matters and Braddy wrote the Archbishop saying that he would go to Hubbards and he wrote to Mr. Harris, telling him the same, with regret that the offer of Annapolis had not come sooner, but that he felt that he was committed to Hubbards. After the Bradshaws had been in Hubbards two months, Braddy was once again offered the Parish of Annapolis. They thought that he might not be satisfied with Hubbards. Once more he declined, as it certainly would not have been fair to Hubbards for them to pick up and leave after such a short time. Braddy often wondered what different courses their lives would have taken if his choice of parishes had been different.

With mutual regret on both sides, the Bradshaws said their good-byes to the congregations in the parish of Musquodoboit Harbour at the beginning of June, 1931 and went to Hubbards.

10

HUBBARD'S PARISH
(1931 - 1934)

Life at Hubbards

Hubbards is a pretty little village, lying on both sides of a cove extending in from St. Margaret's Bay. Braddy was taken to the rectory which was quite an old house standing on a small hill overlooking the highway and the cove. It was probably more than a hundred years old; no one knew quite how old. It had, in the rear, an old kitchen with a huge open fireplace with a spit for roasting, side hooks for boiling the kettle and huge iron pots for stews and suchlike. This, of course, was no longer in use. The rectory also had two other open fireplaces, one in the dining room and the other in the living room. The rectory was about twice the size of the one in Smith's Settlement that they had been occupying, but with their growing family they could do with a larger house.

The Bradshaws soon settled into the rectory in Hubbards and were glad of the extra bedroom space. There were four large rooms and the bathroom, which before bathrooms had been considered a necessity had been a bedroom and was also pressed into service for Charles when they had visitors and extra space was needed. There was also a large room at the back which extended over the old kitchen. This room the children used as a playroom on rainy days.

The church, St. Luke's, was across the cove from the rectory and was a very fine building, - also quite old - with a very tall spire that could be seen out to sea. There were four churches in the parish. Beside St. Luke's, the parish church, there were St. James, Fox Point about two miles away on the shore, St. Mark's, Mill Cove, a fishing village three miles father on, and St. John's on St. Margaret's Bay at Queensland, about two miles from Hubbards, on the way to Halifax. Therefore the travelling would not be heavy.

St. Luke's Church

A parish priest, in the course of his ministry, is called upon frequently to make changes from parish to parish. He wondered if frequent changes of the spiritual head of the parish were good for the people and the church or long encumbrances better. There is much good that can be said for both. One thing should always be remembered and that is that the minister should avoid, at all costs, attracting those committed to his charge to himself. There is a great danger in being a "popular" priest. Retired clergy should avoid living in a parish after retirement, especially if their ministry has been a long incumbency in the parish. They shall often be, without intention on their part, a source of embarrassment to their successor.

There was quite a bit of land around the rectory, but was not much use for garden purposes as it was interspersed with many large rocks. There was a large old barn, which housed Braddy's car at first until the Vestry provided him with a garage nearer the road and thus eliminated the difficult climb up the hill when it was icy or slippery through rain.

In 1931 Braddy writes from his present parish at Hubbards Cove, Nova Scotia to the Codrington Magazine:

> *I moved because of the school - there is a good one here about one quarter of a mile from the Rectory. I like this place better than my late parish because it is much larger and more lively. By larger I mean that the population is greater and nearly all are church people.*
>
> *Hubbards is also a popular Summer Resort especially for U.S.A. visitors. I have met a host of chummy and interesting people this summer including Dr. Robert Norwood, Rector of St. Bartholomew's Church, N.Y. whose father was for years Rector here. Dr. Norwood has a summer cottage near the village where he spends three months every summer. They leave tomorrow. Perhaps you may have come across some of his books; I think that the latest was The Man who Dared to be God. He is of course a tremendous modernist. I raided his library before he left and brought away with me 24 books of various types to be my winter reading, a most miscellaneous collection, I can assure you. He has every up to date book in his library here and tells me that any book that I want, as it comes out, he will send me from New York and it can be added to his Hubbards' library as I finish with it.*

Other fine men that I met were Dr. John Dewey, the philosopher, Dr. Charles G.D. Roberts, the Canadian Author and poet - Moutague Norman of the Bank of England and Philip Grosset of the firm of Grosset & Dunlop, publishers.

The people are very kind to us, always sending in little presents. One good lady has been busy all the summer collecting to put a radio in the Rectory for the winter which will be a delightful gift. I have four churches as before, but not quite so far apart.

I like Canada but when I come to retire I hope that it will be to Barbados. I shall never find a place quite like it.

As a summer resort, Hubbards had many cottages and small tourist hotels for the accommodation of visitors during the months of July and August, In fact, during these two months the whole population might be said to be engaged in catering to the tourist trade. There were summer homes around the shores of the Cove; out at the beach on St. Margaret's Bay, about a mile distant, there were also a number of cottages on the lake at the back of the village. This meant that during the season they met many interesting people who came year by year from Canada and the United States. Among them, was Dr. Robert Norwood, whose father had been, some fifty years previously, Rector of Hubbards. Dr. Norwood was at the time of Braddy's encumbency of the parish, Rector of St. Bartholomew's Church in New York and was very well known as a forceful preacher, lecturer and poet. He had a very beautiful summer home, called Tedholm, not far from the Cove. It was named after his only son, who some years previously, had lost his life in a hunting accident near Hubbards and was buried in the cemetery there.

Dr. Norwood was an exceedingly interesting character but not very orthodox as a priest of the church. He was continually at odds with Bishop Manning, who was then the Bishop of New York, and was also rather a thorn in the side of Archbishop Worrell. He told Braddy that he expected at any time to he inhibited by either or both of them, but managed to avoid this, although skating over very thin ice at times. He died quite suddenly in 1933 at the age of 58. His death was a great shock to the whole community.

Dr. Norwood had spent his early years in Hubbards. He was born in New Ross, where his father had been Rector before moving to Hubbards. He attended King's College and was ordained. His first cure was that of the little fishing community of Neil's Harbour, at the northern tip of Cape Breton. From there he had various cures in Nova Scotia and Ontario and at last became Rector of the fashionable New York Church, St. Bartholomew's. He preached his first sermon in St. Luke's Church, Hubbards, and by a strange coincidence, also his last. It came about in this way. When he visited Hubbards in 1933, he had been ordered by his doctor to take a complete rest - not to preach or lecture - as was his custom during the summer months. He had had some heart attacks. During that summer, Braddy had had one or two fainting attacks; in fact, one Sunday he collapsed in the pulpit, much to the consternation of the congregation. His doctor said that he must get away for a rest; he had not had any holiday that year. The job was to get someone to take Sunday duty for him. He happened to meet Dr. Norwood on the street and asked him whether he could manage one Sunday service for him. Braddy knew that he would be leaving the following week to return to New York. He said that certainly he would, and added that he was feeling fine after his summer's rest and relaxation. Braddy went off to Prince Edward Island and got a terrible shock when he read in the paper that Dr. Norwood had arrived back in New York and had collapsed and died at the luncheon table on the day of his arrival. Thus it came about that he preached his first and his last sermons in the little church of St. Luke's in Hubbards. Braddy returned straight

away to Hubbards and the funeral took place there that week. His body was laid to rest next to that of his son in the little cemetery on the hill above the church. The church and the churchyard were crowded for the funeral service. He was much beloved and through his writings, especially his poems, had achieved wide fame. There were many who thought that his vocation was more that of a poet and actor, than as a priest of the church. He was exceedingly kind to

Dr. Robert Norwood inset and his Funeral   Braddy, who always enjoyed his visits with him during his summers in Hubbards. He could and would talk interestingly on many subjects. He had at his home in the village, a library of the latest books on many subjects and each fall, when he left, he would insist on Braddy taking away as many of them as he wished for his winter's reading. Then when he returned in the spring, they would discuss much that was written in them. Dr. Norwood had such a wide knowledge of the various subjects that it made them doubly interesting. He was a strange, often baffling character, but one whom Braddy felt had indeed had a place in the purpose of God.

Dr. Norwood was instrumental in bringing to Hubbards many well-known and interesting people, chiefly men of letters and science. One of these was Sir. Charles G. D. Roberts, the Canadian writer of nature and adventure stories. Another was Dr. John Dewey, a leading philosopher and economist in the United States. It was a great privilege to come into close contact with men such as these, with their clear well-stocked minds.

Another frequent visitor to Hubbards that Braddy came to know quite well was Philip Grosset, a member of the publishing firm of Grosset and Dunlop. Several of the people in the community were anxious to get a good lending library in the village, and Braddy spoke to Mr. Grosset on this matter feeling that he might be able to help them, which he promptly did when he returned to New York, by sending several large cases of novels published by his firm. He promised further help when Braddy saw him the following summer, but soon after their conversation, later that same evening, he met a tragic death by drowning. He had gone on the lake in a canoe, with a lady companion. She was saved, but he must have received a blow on the head, because he went down and was beyond help when they got his body. His untimely death cast a gloom over the village, as he was a favourite with all.

The Bradshaw's four children managed to get established in the school, which was a two-room one about a quarter of a mile from the rectory, across the Cove. Of course, they only had a few weeks there before the school recessed for the long summer vacation.

One of the leading families in the village was the Shatford family. During the time the Bradshaws lived in Hubbards, there were two brothers - Frank Shatford, who was the manager of the general store, Shatford's Ltd., and A.W. Shatford, who was the owner and manager of the Gainsborough Hotel, the only fairly large one in the community. It was well run and was very popular with the summer visitors. Mr. A.W. Shatford was very well read and took a great interest in all community affairs. He was also the postmaster and, unfortunately, an agnostic. He and Braddy used to have some great discussions, neither of them, of course, convincing the other in the slightest. They were, nevertheless quite good friends. Being a great reader, especially of the classics, made him a very interesting conversationalist. His brother Frank at the store, was of a different type - business man all the time. He was very kind and fond of children. He and Braddy's eldest daughter, who was then in her 12th year, had a little competition, which with her father's connivance, Beryl won. It happened in this way; at a tea or something, in the Shatford house, their host broke a nut that had two kernels in it. Braddy thought he called it a Phillipino, but he did not know why. Anyway, he gave one of the kernels to Beryl and ate the other himself, and told her that if either of them accepted anything from the other they must give that other a dollar. Well, for a week or two, both of them tried to get the other to accept something from them. Finally, perhaps rather unfairly, Braddy took a hand in the matter. He wrote on a piece of paper, "Please give Beryl a dollar!", enclosed it in an envelope and told Beryl to take it up to Mr. Shatford and to say that it was from Dad. All unsuspectingly Mr. Shatford took the note, read it and said, "You've got me young lady!" and then handed over the dollar, which Beryl gleefully brought home. What skullduggery!!

Mrs. Frank Shatford had a small gift shop in a room attached to the hotel. She had quite a business during the summer season, and the profits from the sales were put into a fund to supply something for the rectory. While the Bradshaws were there she had enough to put a radio in the rectory. This was in the days when radios were not as cheap or as easily obtainable as now, so you will guess how much they enjoyed this kind of gift. Mrs. Shatford's work in her gift shop not only benefited the rectory but also added appreciable additions to the income of many in the district, especially women who made hooked and braided rugs and various articles of needlework which Mrs. Shatford sold for them on commission. Another well-known member of the Shatford family was the much loved Canon Alan Shatford, for many years Rector of St. James the Apostle church in Montreal. He was a cousin of the two brothers and was born at Indian Harbour on the other side of St. Margaret's Bay. He generally spent his summers in Nova Scotia at his cottage on the LaHave River and frequently visited Hubbards during that time. Quite as powerful a preacher as Dr. Norwood, he was of an entirely different character. He had no interest outside of the church and her work.

The church, St. Luke's, which stood across the Cove from the rectory was a small building but beautifully proportioned with an exceedingly graceful spire, which was a landmark for seamen out on St. Margaret's Bay and on the Atlantic beyond. Braddy stated, "To many of us of former generations, the modern church architecture has little appeal. Many of these buildings to be found in new suburbs of our large cities were, almost monstrosities that might be mistaken for picture theatres or in some cases Service Stations. One does miss the graceful lines of the Houses of God which our forefathers built, with, in most cases, lofty steeples holding aloft the Sign of our Salvation, as a constant reminder to all men of the love of the One Who Suffered upon it." Personally, Braddy was grateful for the witness of the village churches in our land, and he hoped that they would never be replaced by ugly "modern" church buildings.

One of the most common names in Hubbards then, was Dauphinee. There were numerous families by this name. A very happy one lived in a rambling old house, called the "Villa", on the other side of the Cove. Mrs. Dauphinee, quite elderly, was a widow and she had been living with her two daughters. One was Mrs. Copp, also a widow, who had her two daughters, Audrey and Marion, living with her. Mrs. Copp was a bookkeeper in the Shatford store. Mrs. Dauphinee's other daughter at home was Minnie, who looked after the house. During the summer months they took in boarders, and it was indeed a happy home for any who were fortunate enough to spend a holiday there. Miss Minnie was the type that was loved by all. Those who became guests in this house became, at once, members of the family. Although the caring for quite a number of guests must, at times, have been quite a job, Miss Minnie was never ruffled. Only once did Braddy see her a trifle peeved, and even then, in telling Braddy about it, she felt that the joke was on her and she could laugh about it. It came about in this way. The Executive Commissioner from the Boy Scouts headquarters in Halifax, Mr. Limbrey, was paying a visit to the Scout Troop in Hubbards and was being accommodated at the Villa. He came by train. The Dauphinees had a boat that they used to cross the Cove, saving the longer trip around by road. Minnie used this boat to meet Mr. Limbrey. When they got in she asked him if he would row; he declined inferring that he did not know one end of an oar from the other. What was her disgust, the next morning looking out of the kitchen window while she was getting breakfast, was to see him rowing up and down the Cove in a most professional manner. In telling Braddy about it, she said, "Was I ever mad! The great lump just sat there and was probably snickering at my amateurish rowing. You Englishmen have the most warped sense of humour."

Limbrey was one of the finest men Braddy had ever met. He had a great fondness for boys, and was heart and soul in the Scout Movement. He had a great sense of humour, perhaps sometimes rather warped as Miss Dauphinee said. He had a great joke on Braddy, when he made on one occasion a faux pas, which he never let Braddy forget. While Braddy was at Musquodoboit Harbour, he came there to endeavour to start a Scout Troop in the village. At the meeting of the parents, of which Braddy was Chairman, he said that women often made good Cubmasters. Without thinking Braddy said, "Well, we have some loose women around; it should not be difficult to find one for the job." Unfortunately soon after his visit to Hubbards, funds for Scouting were at a low ebb and the Scout Headquarters in Halifax could not afford to keep him on. Hoping that he might get back again when funds were more plentiful, he took a job as a Children's Aid agent in Truro. He gave to this work the same wholehearted service that he had given to scouting, the result was that he wore himself out, caught pneumonia and died in his mid-thirties. Braddy always thought that fitting words on his grave should have been those of John Oxenham's from his book "All's Well!"

> And when He saw his work below was done,
> He gently called to him, - "My son! My son!
> I need thee for a greater work than this.
> Thy faith, thy zeal, thy fine activities
> Are worthy of My larger liberties." —
> Then drew him with the hand of welcoming grace,
> And, side by side, they climbed the heavenly ways.

Not far from the "Villa" was another Dauphinee family, a young couple with two small daughters. They figured in a tragicomedy. One hot day in August - the husband, Park, being away at work in the village, and her children being at the beach with some friends - Mrs. Dauphinee decided to take a dip in the Cove. So she swam about for some time and finally went ashore further up the Cove and walked back home behind the houses to her back door. In the meantime, some neighbours who had seen her in the water suddenly missed her and thought that she had drowned. They spread the alarm and boats under the direction of the R.C.M.P. began to search for her body. Even dragging operations were begun. Her husband was sent for and he was nearly frantic with grief. In the meantime she had dressed and was sitting on the front steps of their house, taking a good interest in the proceedings, little thinking that they were dragging for her body. She asked some strangers standing by what all the commotion was about and was told that a woman had been drowned. She then happened to see her husband down by the water's edge and called out to him, asking him if he knew who it was that had been drowned. You can guess his feelings - great and overwhelming relief and then inclined to be a little mad! She declared that his first words were, "Where the h—l did you come from?" It is a pity that tragedies cannot more frequently have such a happy ending.

Still another Dauphinee family is worthy of note, the Basil Dauphinees. His wife was a widow, when Basil married her, with several sons by her previous husband, a Publicover. One of these sons distinguished himself in the war in the R.C.A.F. and rose to high rank. Basil Dauphinee was a very pleasant character, not overly fond of work, but making a fair living with his small yacht in the summer by taking tourists for sailing trips on St. Margaret's Bay to the various small islands for picnics. He also catered to fishing parties. He was very popular with the summer visitors.

There was one Dauphinee, however, who was the cause, all unconscious, of it, (you will see later that the word "unconscious" is very apt.) of giving Braddy one of the wildest experiences of his ministry. He was an old fisherman, Cyrus Dauphinee, who, lived alone in a little cottage on the shore obliquely across the Cove from the rectory. Every night they used to see old Cyrus with a lantern going down to his fish hut on the water's edge to see that all was shipshape for the night. He was very old, in his high eighties, and getting feeble. One winter it was decided by his family that it was not safe for him to be alone during the winter so he was taken to live with a married daughter at Bayswater, a small village along the coast. The following May he became ill and died. His son, who was a church warden, came to Braddy to make arrangements for the funeral. He was to be buried in the family lot in St. Luke's churchyard. Soon after Braddy went to Hubbards, he got the Vestry to pass a resolution doing away with a bad old custom at funerals of having the casket open in church and at the conclusion of the service, the friends and relatives passing around it for "a last look at the deceased body". The son asked Braddy whether they could make an exception and allow his father's casket to be opened as his being away all winter, there were many of his old friends who would like to see him again. Braddy rather reluctantly gave permission. Because of what transpired afterwards Braddy wished that he had not. At the conclusion of the service the casket was open, but to his surprise was not closed when all had passed around it. Braddy called a woman to him and told her to tell them to close the casket. She looked worried and said, "Reverend, he's sweatin'!" Braddy began to take an active interest in things then and went down the chancel steps to the casket and sure enough there were beads of perspiration on old Cyrus' forehead. Braddy wiped them off and they came back again. Braddy then sent to the vestry for a mirror which he held over his lips. There was no clouding. However, Braddy said that he would not go on with the interment until a doctor had seen him. Then came the news that the one doctor in the village was away in Halifax and would not be back until late that night. So Braddy said that the interment would have to wait until the doctor had seen him and that the completion of the service would be the next day. The doctor did see him that night and declared him to be dead. So they buried him. Braddy believed that there were still some who thought that they buried old Cyrus alive!

Since then doctors had told Braddy that the sweat glands go on working after death, and probably the sun beating down on the glass-sided hearse on the journey from Bayswater had caused renewed activity in the glands. Just to add another macabre aspect to the affair, that night they looked out from the rectory and there was old Cyrus' lantern bobbing down to the shore. To tell you the truth Braddy wondered for a moment whether the old fellow had left his casket in the church and gone on his usual jaunt to the shore. Braddy heard afterwards that it was his son looking after things at his father's fish hut.

Some years later when in the Parish of Maitland Braddy had another funeral experience, not quite so bizarre as the Hubbard's one, but still with an odd note to it. The husband of one of their devout church women died in the United States. He had been Baptist as all his family were, and he was to be buried in their family lot in the Baptist cemetery. Braddy was asked to take the funeral. He got permission from the Baptist minister to do the burial in their cemetery. He granted permission and said that he was rather surprised at it being asked. He said that everyone buried in their cemetery, and Braddy was the first that had asked permission to conduct a burial there. He never allowed the undertaker to put the lid of the rough box on before the words of committal were said and the service was finished. Being in the Baptist cemetery Braddy thought that he would allow them to do as was customary there, so as they lowered the casket they placed the lid on the rough box over it. When Braddy looked into the grave there staring him in the face was the following, in big red letters, "Rush! Fast Freight".

Braddy recalled that he had, for the most part, found that undertakers were always anxious to carry out the officiating minister's wishes with regard to the conduct of funerals. Braddy had one exception; this undertaker wanted to break up flowers and cast them on the coffin at the words of committal. Braddy told him that he required earth as our rubric directs. He did not like it at all and at one funeral asked, in what he thought was a whisper, "Do I throw the mud on her, or do you?"

The second story happened during Braddy's time in the Diocese. There was in one parish in the Annapolis Valley an old priest, who had been Rector for many years and was much beloved. He had occasion during one winter to conduct the burial service for an old man, who had been a well known reprobate. The following summer the Rector, because of age, and rather forgetful, met the son of the old man, and asked him, "How is your father standing the heat?"

As Braddy had already mentioned, the parish had three other churches beside the parish church of St. Luke's in Hubbards itself. Along the shore, about five miles from Hubbards was the village of Mill Cove, with its little church of St. Mark's. The people who lived here made almost their entire living from the sea, and very many of them were in rather reduced circumstances. They were also a primitive people, with little knowledge of the world outside of their own small portion of it. The years with their changing seasons passed bringing little change to the village of Mill Cove. Because of their poverty there was a considerable amount of hunting out of season. The authorities winked at a lot of this, but when it was reported that one family had shot a moose the game wardens had to investigate the matter. Moose were then beginning to show signs that their number was diminishing and shortly after this an entirely closed season on the shooting of moose was put into effect. When they went to the house and began to make enquiries about the breach of the law, the woman, who was the only one at home, flatly denied any knowledge of any moose, dead or alive, having been near them. In fact she inferred that she did not know what a moose looked like. However, the wardens, not satisfied, searched the house and yard around and very soon discovered - buried - some large leg bones, which had obviously been part of one of the lords of the forest, a moose. Holding them up they asked the woman, who was taking a great interest in the search, "What are these?"

Without any hesitation, she replied, "Oh them? Them's rabbit bones!"

Because of the obvious poverty of the family, only a strict warning was given against any infraction of the law and no other action was taken.

There was one old woman in the village, Mrs. William Jollymore, whom Braddy always liked to visit, as she was full of anecdotes of the present and past. One Braddy never forgot. It seemed that some years back when the railway from Yarmouth to Halifax was being built, it passed not far behind the village and a number of the men of the village were employed to work on the making of the track. One such man was her husband, William. He was a very meek soul, and as Braddy observed, he had to be to get on with his wife. Quite a bit of insurance against accidents was carried by those who were working on the line. Mrs. Jollymore, who was always one for the main chance, insured "Villium", as she called him. However, she told Braddy sorrowfully, some men were hurt; some were even killed but "nothing even happened to that damn vule Villium!"

Braddy had one battle with Mrs. Jollymore. He never really knew who had won. She had a tremendous admiration for Archbishop Worrell and had a picture of him, which she had cut out of the daily paper, and she framed it. One Sunday morning when Braddy went to take the service, he found this picture in the middle of the altar leaning up against the cross. He removed it and put it down at one side and went into the vestry to prepare the vessels for the Communion Service. When he came out, there was the picture again leaning on the cross. Once more he removed it. Finally when he came from the vestry to begin the service it was back once more in the center of the altar. This time, in the presence of a rather amused congregation, he moved it for the last time.

Towards the end of Braddy's ministry at Mill Cove, old Mrs. Jollymore was getting very feeble and he used to go once a month to give her Communion at her home. One morning, during the service, he sensed that she was excited about something. Hardly waiting until Braddy had taken off his robes at the conclusion of the service, she gave him her news. Her son, who had a good position with the railway, had sent her a gramophone and some records. "You must hear it." she said. "What would you like to hear, 'The Cat Sat Down on the Sticky Flypaper' or 'Jesu, Lover of my Soul'?" Braddy pleaded press of business and fled.

Charles' godfather, Canon Whippell, from Barbados, visited the Bradshaws for about a week before they left Hubbards. Charles re-membered him taking the children down to the General Store to buy them "ices". They were rather amused at his word for ice cream, which was totally English, and the Bradshaws were very much Canadian at this time. Canon Whippell was probably principal of Codrington College, Barbados, at this time.

158

One major event that happened in the life of the Bradshaws while at Hubbards was the birth (November 22, 1931) of their sixth and last child - a son, whom they named Malcolm Henry, after his two grandfathers.

NOTE: Braddy discontinued taping his memoirs after Hubbards as he always said the family could fill in from there. However, the reminiscences he had can never be duplicated by others but we have tried, through interviews and recollections to record some of the events to complete the life's journey of Alleyne George Bradshaw.

Memorial in Bishop's Park, Hubbards
The Park was dedicated in 1998 in memory of the
Right Rev. George F. Arnold, 11th Bishop of Nova Scotia
on the occasion of the 150th Anniversary of the laying of the Foundation
Stone of Saint Luke's Parish Church, Hubbards
A tree has been planted in this park in memory of
Canon Alleyne George Bradshaw by the Bradshaw Family.

11

MAITLAND PARISH
(1934 - 1942)

Upper Kennetcook Remembrances

Having moved to the Parish of Maitland, in Hants County, Nova Scotia, (in 1934) Braddy wrote to the Codrington Magazine, from the Rectory at Upper Kennetcook in 1940:

> *"Have joined the noble Company of 'rather Revs'. The clergy of the Deanery honoured me at our meeting in September by nominating me to the Archbishop as Rural Dean, and I was duly installed in that office at the beginning of November. I think that the plan of the nomination coming from the Clergy is rather a good one, don't you? We have just started a new plan in this Diocese, i.e. a Clergy Training School. The plan works like this; it has been established at a fairly large town parish, with a priest in charge and five Deacons. They will spend their Diaconate and the first year of their priesthood there, and then followed by others. It is hoped that this way will give our Deacons and Young Priests a much needed training."*

And two years later (1942) Braddy writes about his new duties in the war effort:

Rev. Hon.F/Lt.A.G. Bradshaw, BA, RD, RCAF

> *"I have an extra duty now, viz. Chaplain to a Flying School about 17 miles away. I go there on Sunday nights, and have a Service at 6.45 on Monday morning and spend the rest of the day there. I enjoy the work very much and meet boys from all over Canada, and the British Empire. I have a Commission as Flight Lieut. I was offered a full time Chaplaincy in the R.C.A.F., and would have liked to have accepted, but the Archbishop asked me not to, as we are so shorthanded in the Diocese, owing to 14 of our men having taken chaplaincies already."*

And the Editor of the Codrington College Magazine adds:

> *Mr. Bradshaw (Braddy) has very kindly sent us an excellent photograph of himself in his new uniform.*

Malcolm's Recollections of Upper Kennetcook

My memories about my life at Hubbards, Halifax County, Nova Scotia, where I was born on November 22, 1931 are nil. This is not surprising as I was only two when my family moved to the Parish of Maitland in Hants County. This was the only time when our family of eight was altogether. Shortly thereafter my brother Charles went off to Barbados to live with our mother's brother, Uncle Clyde. We did not see him again until after World War 11.

The rectory at Upper Kennetcook was relatively new; it was built after the former rectory at Maitland had burned down. We were the second rectory family to occupy it. It was situate very near the Kennetcook River which turned out to be our playground. In the spring we fished in it for the most plentiful sand suckers and in the winter we skated on its very winding way to Kennetcook. We also enjoyed the rather dangerous sport of ice-cake hopping. Many a chilly dip in the river was the result!

The railway line which ran from Windsor to Shubenacadie was nearby and although I cannot remember having a trip on it, I do remember my older sisters, Beryl, Joan and Dorothy, were forever using it to go to Windsor where Joan and Dot attended Edgehill, the Anglican Residential School and Beryl attended Windsor Academy.

I also remember that when there was no need for the train to stop at the station, the mailbag was hooked on a pole so that the trainman could grab it while the train was still moving. The trains in Nova Scotia were not known as fast means of transportation and this particular one was called the "Blueberry Special" as it was said that one could get off at one end, pick berries and get on the other end without difficulty. This reminds me of an occasion in the 1950's when I taught school at South Ohio, Yarmouth County, and took the train home on weekends. I was some distance from the train station when I heard the train blow and I asked Emerson Cook, the postmaster, if I ran could I catch it. He replied, "If you run you can beat it!"

One of my earliest remembrances of my father was trying to keep up with him when he went to the post office for the mail. My short skinny legs were put to the test. Dad learned early in life in Nova Scotia that

161

walking was the economic way to travel. I never knew him to take his car for short distances and I always thought his very good health was the better for it. I know from what I have heard that he was a keen sportsman, participating in bird shooting and tennis, but that was history for me as he was fifty when I was only ten.

The two-room schoolhouse at Upper Kennetcook was a short distance from the rectory and therefore I remember that my brother and I went home for dinner which at our house was always at noon. I don't remember any of my teachers but do remember that we sat at two-seat desks with ink-holes and places for pencils at the top. Single desks were becoming popular and I would compare having one of these to having a single room at King's College when I attended there in the mid fifties. A bee of activities took place in the basement of the school during recess and at noon hour. Most of the activity was not considered moral by teachers and parents and my parents must have been happy that we came home at noon.

The outhouses were behind the school, near the river bank and every Halloween they traditionally ended up in the river. As late as the fifties outhouses were commonplace in Nova Scotia. Many stories were told about them. I remember my father, who loved his 12 gauge shotgun, saying that the sure way of getting a long dweller out of the outhouse, was to throw some gravel against the door and at the same time fire a shotgun in the air. Many Nova Scotia rectories were among the last in the community to get the prized indoor facilities. Not so in Blue Rocks, Lunenburg County, where a dispute among the parishioners took place when the rectory was provided with a spanking new inside toilet, the only one in the community. However, shortly thereafter, when the rector left and the rectory became vacant, the new toilet became very popular as the parishioners attended there often.

Although the rectory at Upper Kennetcook had indoor facilities, it was the custom when the bishop arrived to provide him with hot water in the morning so he could wash up in his room. My father loved to tell this story. "Malcolm," he said, "the bishop will be arriving here shortly for his visitation to the parish. You, being the youngest child, it will be your duty to take hot water to him in the morning. You are to knock at his bedroom door and say, 'My Lord, the boy is here with the water'. You are to practice saying this so you will be ready and not be nervous when you arrive at his door." When the morning arrived I managed quite nicely carrying the large jug up the stairs and no doubt much to the bishop's surprise, said, "My boy, the Lord is here with the water"!

In the thirties community halls were generally a beehive of activity

162

and many socials took place there. Even then it was the custom to have a drawing and tickets were purchased and a prize given to the winner. I still have the image of a small plump boy being held shoulder high by my father when the draw took place. He won. The prize was a beautiful doll. My eyes widened. Now it would be mine. Not so. I will never know if my father thought little boys shouldn't have dolls or for some other reason I was not to have it. The doll was given by him to one of the small girls of a poor family of the parish. It is interesting to note that during his ministry he was never opposed to lotteries as a source of raising funds for church or charitable purposes provided they were kept within certain modest bounds.

Among my childhood classmates was Fred Currie and it was our habit to coast on the hill behind the rectory. In the summer we coasted on large pieces of cardboard. I remember on one occasion we disturbed a hornet's nest and the hornets pursued us, along with others, to the rectory. My mother who was in the yard working saw what had happened. She shouted to us to cover our throats and to get into the house as quickly as possible. She stood by the door swiping the hornets with her broom! To this day when confronted by any bee or hornet I think of the wisdom of my mother in telling us to cover up.

I remember Fred's sister, Lillian, with her long curly blonde hair and my attraction for her. However, she was not my first girl friend. That was left to the postmistress' daughter, Vivian Hennigar. We were both six years of age and spent considerable time playing together. She lived by the bridge leading to the railway station and the swimming pool under the bridge was our common playground. I remember on one occasion a man driving a hay wagon, saw a child in difficulty in the pool and he jumped into the pool from the wagon to save the child from drowning. In Nova Scotia with so many lakes throughout the province it was very common for parents to warn their children about the dangers of swimming. It has been said that a mother once told her children, "If you go down there and get drowned, don't you dare come home!" Soon after we left Upper Kennetcook, Vivian and her family moved to Annapolis County where her father, Barney, farmed. Her mother, Haley, named after the comet, lived to be nearly one hundred years old.

Over the years Sunday dinner has always been a special occasion. I remember one such occasion at Upper Kennetcook when after grace had been said by my father, an electrical storm began. To our astonishment, a barn across the river, which could be easily seen from our dining room, was hit by lighting. Everyone except Joan went out-of-doors to the fire. When we returned Joan had finished off the pie!

One of my most interesting play places was the barn. At one time the previous rector must have kept a cow or horse because there was a stall for such an animal and also a hay loft. We did keep hens which my mother attended faithfully. She sprinkled the eggs with water and always left one in the nest to encourage the hen to lay more. Among the poultry was my brother's pet rooster who terrified me, and my brother and sisters didn't add to the situation by telling me when my hair stood up that I had a rooster on my head. This rooster would sit on David's shoulder and pick his teeth. On the last Sunday before leaving Upper Kennetcook we had a grand meal of chicken and there was always some question of whether or not we had eaten David's pet rooster.

At least one time during our residence at Upper Kennetcook, the rectory barn was made habitable. The occasion was when my father had to move into it. I developed scarlet fever and the rectory was quarantined with a most prominent notice on the doors. From the barn my father carried on his priestly duties for a period of six weeks. My mother claimed that I caught scarlet fever from one of the children that my father was always picking up on the highway. I remember two stories that support her claim. On one occasion he picked up four girls and as they drove along he said that he was sorry that he didn't have room for their three brothers. "That's alright," said one of the girls, "they're on the rack on the back of the car!" On another occasion he picked up several children and later noticed that one small child was missing. He inquired where the child was and was told that he had fallen out a few miles back. Dad rushed to the child's home where he saw the child over the knees of the mother who was picking gravel out of his bottom.

All around the rectory were groves of alders where rabbits ran wild. In the thirties rabbits were a main source of meat in many small communities and it was not uncommon in the winter to see a great number of pairs of rabbits being transported out of the woods. My brother set snares and occasionally I would tend them. I remember seeing a rabbit caught by the hind leg and still very much alive. I beat it with a stick as it put up a lively fight and it was not a very pleasant experience for a small boy. To this day rabbit is still one of my favourite meats and over the years I have regularly "built" rabbit stews for my own satisfaction. My wife, Shirley, having been country bred, has had her full of them.

The alders around the rectory served another purpose and that was for furnace fuel. I remember one of my chores was to cut them, haul them on my sleigh and store them in the basement with the other furnace wood. I often think of this when I see the many alder groves along our Nova Scotia highways and wonder if they could be put to some useful purpose.

One of my other favourite foods is apples. I acquired the taste at a very early age. As I have previously mentioned the former rectory was at Maitland, at the extreme eastern end of the parish. On this rectory land was an apple orchard. Several times each fall my father would take us in his Chevrolet car to pick up the apples and pears which would be stored in the rectory basement for use during the winter months. On the back of Dad's Chevy there was a rack for holding luggage and other packages. On this rack we placed a very large bag of apples and off to Upper Kennetcook we went not realizing that there was a hole in the bag. As you can imagine, over rough gravelled roads, the apples, one by one, dropped out and by the time we reached home only a handful was left. My father was not pleased!

One of my father's great joys while he was rector of Maitland Parish was his appointment as chaplain of Stanley Air Force Station. It was located between Kennetcook and Windsor, a short drive from the rectory. The British Commonwealth pilots were trained there and my father, with his British background, felt very much at home. Padres were designated officers and he looked particularly splendid in his uniform. I remember during the early WW2 years the sky over the rectory being filled with the two-winged training planes. Very seldom did one crash even though some might fly under the telephone wires or hop over the stone-walled fences. It was even said that one had flown under the Kennetcook Covered Bridge. No doubt among the young enthusiastic flyers some betting took place on that one. Because of poor eyesight Dad was not accepted in the services. His consolation prize was that he hoped he might continue as chaplain at the Yarmouth Air Force Base when he was appointed Rector of Holy Trinity Parish in 1942.

My father loved dogs. He had several during his lifetime. He even had one at college. I can't imagine anyone having any kind of a pet in residence when I was at King's College. However, my brother, David and I, have had some strange pets. I have already mentioned David's pet rooster. In Yarmouth we had white mice in the attic and white rabbits in the backyard.

The dog I remember at Upper Kennetcook was a Samoyede named Mona. She loved to chase cars and at the speed cars travelled then she

Mona, the dog, held by David, Mac on right.

could keep up for several miles. My father could not break her of this habit and the only solution was to lock her in the house when we went driving. This did not always work. I remember on one occasion when we were at a summer cottage on the Northumberland Strait, she went right through the screen when she heard the car start. It is sometimes strange what one remembers but I remember the Sunday morning that Mona died. David and I had been fighting and Mum said that bad things happen when we misbehave. I have often wondered if there is any truth in this.

I close my remembrances about our life at Upper Kennetcook by saying that it was not always easy being the son of a minister as a pre-teenager. I was eleven when we left Upper Kennetcook and at that age was often called a sissy. Wearing knickers did not help matters. Neither did being the youngest of six help. I was often teased by my brother and sisters but my mother would always take my part. In those days I considered my father a strict disciplinarian but I could always depend on my mother drying my tears.

In June, 1942, we moved to Yarmouth.

Interview with Pearl Neil

The Bradshaws arrived in Upper Kennetcook during the winter or spring of 1934, following the departure of Rev. Fowlow and his family. Mrs. Pearl Neil, who was only eleven years old when the Bradshaws arrived. Pearl was the first person that the Bradshaws hired there to help with the children. Beryl, Joan, Dorothy, Charles, David and Mac were all there then. Charles left that summer to go to Barbados to live with his Uncle Clyde.

Maggie and the family used to talk about out west. It was difficult for Pearl to understand Maggie who at that time had quite a pronounced Barbarian accent. Beryl explained to Pearl some of the background of Maggie's life in Barbados with lots of servants, but in Canada she had to

166

do so much work which she was not used to at all.

The parish was a large one and Braddy did a lot of travelling to visit his parishioners, especially the sick. Pearl remembered that it was a very hot summer and the first day that she was there, she, David, Malcolm and Braddy drove out to Northfield to see Albro Miller who had pneumonia, which in those days was a very serious illness. Braddy left all in the car (Chevrolet) and went into the house for his visit after which they drove back home. The drive was a special treat for Pearl who had probably only had a few drives before in her life.

The rectory in Maitland burned in 1931 and the rectory in Upper Kennetcook was built in 1932. At that time the local people thought it was a huge building with four bedrooms and a bathroom upstairs, kitchen, dining room, living room, very large hallway and a library downstairs. The library had a beautiful fireplace as well as lots of books all of which needed dusting. Outside was a garage. There was no electricity until 1938. A holding tank for water was in the basement and water had to be hand pumped to the bathroom. This was one of the first houses in the area with a bathroom.

Rectory, Upper Kennetcook

The school was a one-room school with a wood potbellied stove and was often very well populated, sometimes with over eighty students. The teacher and others went home to lunch but about sixty of the children were left alone at the school and on the playground for the whole hour of noontime. In 1936, a new section was built on the school.

The year that Mac had scarlet fever Braddy stayed out in the garage in the loft where he made himself an office to do his work, - reading and preparing sermons. His meals were served to him there.

Braddy and Beryl often went to the river to sit and talk. Pearl recalls hearing Beryl talk to her father about the possibility of her getting scarlet fever. The whole family was quarantined and Maggie used to get someone to help out with washing and other work. The nearest doctor at that time was Dr. Grant from Noel.

The nearest dentist was Dr. Annie (Hennigar) Sandford from Noel who pulled teeth but did not do any other kinds of dentistry. She really was a general practitioner. She used to go around with a horse and sleigh or wagon to deliver babies.

Braddy used to tell the story that when he took David to her to have a tooth pulled she gave him a bit of chloroform on a mask over the face and Dr. Annie said after some dripping, "He's gone!" David asked, "Where?"

Pearl worked during the day that first summer but in later years she stayed at the house and helped out and would sleep there and go to school from there.

The sleeping arrangement was that Braddy had one room, Maggie and David and Malcolm shared another room. Beryl had another bedroom by herself. Joan was at Edgehill at this time. Dorothy and Pearl were great friends and shared a bedroom when Dot was there. Dot went to Edgehill too. Beryl used to go by train to Windsor and got her grade 12 at Windsor Academy. On stormy days Braddy would drive her to the train but on fine days she would walk.

Pearl remembered the seating arrangement at the kitchen table. Maggie had the loaf of bread and a cutting board on the table and cut the bread as people wanted it so it was always fresh. Braddy and Maggie sat at opposite ends of the table. Braddy would serve the meat and Maggie the vegetables.

Braddy had a very large confirmation class that first year - about forty - and held the classes in the church. Braddy also started Anglican Youth Group, Guides, Scouts, badminton and a ball team which became provincial champions one year. During Lent, activities such as dancing were stopped. Church services were held every Wednesday night. He had an annual picnic in Upper Kennetcook.

Pearl and her family all had to attend church regularly and because Pearl could not understand what the minister was saying; her mind and eyes would wander, and finally focused on the two tablets at the front of the church on which were written the Ten Commandments. She would memorize them and eventually was able to remember them all.

Pearl recalled that when she first went to work for Maggie, Maggie took her upstairs to teach her how to make a bed properly. Pearl could recall still seeing Maggie shaking out the sheets and saying to Pearl, "If you can say The Ten Commandments, I will buy you an ice cream cone." Pearl recited them right off.

Maggie would go up to the village store to buy groceries and often with the dollar Braddy gave her, she would buy meat and other things and would also buy candy for Pearl, Malcolm and David.

Pearl remembered the time Maggie bought bananas and warned her and the children to leave them alone. However, they went and peaked in the window and Malcolm, David and Pearl all craved them. While Maggie was resting in the afternoon, the three of them sneaked in and got one which they divided into three parts and each ate their share. Maggie never even missed it !

People fished in the river, swam in the summer, skated in the winter and in the spring did ice-cake jumping - a very dangerous sport.

People would go to the church and rectory to get married and Pearl remembered Maggie saying "That's another dollar, or two dollars." They really had very little money. On Thanksgiving day the parishioners would take lots of fruits and vegetables to the church and this was then given to Braddy for the winter.

Maggie was always afraid of bee stings especially around the neck. One day the children hit a bee's nest and all went running to the rectory with their collars up around their necks. Maggie was standing there with a broom swatting the bees; then, she locked the children in a room upstairs for awhile.

Pearl remembered what kindness the Bradshaws showed her which

Left to right, Malcolm and David in hockey sweaters

gave her such confidence and a feeling of self-worth which she lacked prior to this.

Jenny Patterson, a spinster, was a staunch Presbyterian but she liked Braddy so well that she went to the Anglican church to hear Braddy's sermon but just before the collection plate was passed she would get up and walk out because any money she had would go to the Presbyterian church at Five Mile River. On her father's birthday on March 4, there was an annual birthday party. One year Braddy was invited. This was a major event and a great honour to have the minister attend. There was real cream for the event, probably used to make a Washington pie, a special gift for her father. Eventually they saw Braddy coming - walking - and it was a long walk especially in the winter. Braddy said grace and then they ate.

At this time there was a United Church in the area but no Baptists or Roman Catholics. There were some Presbyterians but they had no church there then.

People from Hubbards used to visit the Bradshaws and would bring food. Pearl recalls them bringing peanut butter and that was the first time she tasted peanut butter sandwiches.

Clara and Harold Clarke were quite close to the Bradshaws and visited regularly.

Braddy was well respected in the area. He treated all people the same. He liked people and was so dedicated to everyone regardless of whether they were rich or poor. He defended everyone and never said an unkind word about anyone.

At Christmas time, parishioners would take gifts to the church and Braddy would put them in a barrel and send them out west. This was a sort of mission as there were many poor people in Upper Kennetcook too.

Pearl's father was in the army in Yarmouth during the war and he used to go to the rectory where the Bradshaws welcomed and entertained servicemen. He was very impressed with the open house policy of the Bradshaws toward all the service people and wished he would have gotten to know Braddy better when he was in Upper Kennetcook.

Braddy took books from Maitland to Upper Kennetcook since they had no books there. This library was very popular with many of the people who had no books of their own.

The impression of the people was that Braddy seemed to do and present his sermons so easily.

Pearl recalled keeping house for the Bradshaws when they went to see the movie, "Gone with the Wind". The next day Pearl told Maggie that she heard someone say that Scarlet looked very much like Joan. Maggie flew and said, "Why the very idea! She can't hold a candle to Joan! Joan is much prettier!" Pearl remembered how pretty Joan was and how happy she was - always laughing. Pearl and Dot were in the same platoon in Guides. They travelled together. At one time they had to draw a picture of Upper Kennetcook and they would go "viewing" - mostly walking and talking - in preparation for this project.

The train station was a favourite gathering place in the community. On Saturday there was a special one. The train would go to Truro in the morning and back at night. People would gather at six o'clock at night to see who had been to Truro and had gotten drunk during the day. There was a hook to catch the mailbag when the train didn't have to stop.

Sheehy, a blacksmith, was another well-known family; they also had the post office at one time.

On one occasion a man stopped at the rectory and told Braddy he was going in to Halifax and asked if he could get anything for him. Braddy said, "Yes. I want you to get me a haircut."

The Bradshaws, along with many other people from the area went to Halifax to see the King and Queen in 1939.

Interview with Elsie Clarke

Elsie, the daughter of Glen and Gladys Clarke, lived next to the church in Upper Kennetcook. There were four girls and one boy in the family - Myrna, Marjorie, Elsie, Audrey and Douglas. After each evening service Braddy always went to the Clarke home and although the kids went to bed the adults would talk and laugh. One thing they often talked about was politics.

Beryl and Elsie went to Windsor Academy together for their grade twelve. They travelled by train which they caught early each morning and returned at night. If anyone had a late lab or anyone had to stay late at school the train would wait for them. At that time, no one had much money. Elsie recalls that when she started at Windsor Academy her father gave her one dollar in case she missed the train sometime. At the end of the year she still had that one dollar. Joan and Dot went to Edgehill School for Girls in Windsor but when they came home they always got together. Joan, especially, visited the Clarkes often.

After the Wednesday night Lenten services, the young people always

St. Peter's Church, Upper Kennetcook

played badminton. Girls did not wear slacks to church in those days so the girls would put their slacks on and roll up the legs under their skirts so that they could go afterward and play badminton in the hall. One night as they were leaving the church, one leg of Joan's slacks fell down and all the other young folk gathered around Joan so her father would not see that she had worn slacks to church.

Braddy helped the young people very much. He always attended the AYPA meetings, and took them on picnics. Although Braddy didn't sing much the young people always managed to win the prize at the Avon Deanery picnics with their singing group.

There was a big group of young people at that time and Braddy kept the AYPA very active. This group included some from Northfield and some young people who were not Anglican.

There were two stores in Upper Kennetcook then. One was run by E. B. C. Solley and the other by Clarke Brothers. The Solley's were United so the Bradshaws dealt mostly with the Clarke Brothers. They had practically everything in their store that you would find today in a Zellers store. They had feed for cattle, fertilizer, hundred pound bags of sugar and even some clothes for children and adults. There were all kinds of groceries and hardware. In those days people did not travel easily as cars were not too plentiful so most people went to the Clarke Brothers for their needs. Each Christmas Clarke Brothers always supplied the rector and his family with a turkey. They had them in the store for sale and they made sure that the rector had one.

Harold Clarke was the church treasurer for many years. Glen Clarke and William Ettinger, an ardent church worker, were wardens for years.

Elsie recalls when Charles left Upper Kennetcook to go to Barbados. The children from the community went to the train station to see little Charles, who was then about eight, put on the train to go to Barbados. There were many tears shed as they watched him leave to go so far away. Braddy took him as far as Boston and then he went by ship to Barbados. He wore a tag to identify him.

Stanley, about eighteen miles from Upper Kennetcook, was the site of an airport which was built during the war to teach pilots elementary flying. Braddy was the Chaplain at Stanley and took services there.

The young girls in the community had a great time with all those airmen. The men would go to functions in the community - the church, dances, tennis or for the Queen's Canadian Fund (for the war effort). Whether they were good or bad dancers they were very attentive at the dances and the functions and they enjoyed the good home cooked food of the village families. Everyone in the community was very kind to all those serving the "war effort". There was also a Base in Selma and later at Debert.

The aircraft, called Moths, would often fly over the community when they were training and would "buzz" the people on the ground when they recognized them.

Often in the winter the roads were not plowed so the children could safely coast in the roads without fear of cars. Dr. Morehouse from Noel had a "snowmobile" to use when he had to visit his patients. Most of the local visits by the doctor would be maternity cases as all the babies were born at home, not in hospitals.

Bertie and Deanie Lantz - another prominent family in the parish - "helped" Braddy get to Northfield. The road wasn't fit for a car so he went up to get Bertie Lantz to take him in his horse and wagon. Bertie was milking at the time and he told Braddy he would harness the horse and he could take himself to Northfield. Braddy started out and when he got to the first hill the horse went about half way up the hill and turned around and went back home. No matter how Braddy tried he could not get the horse to go to Northfield. Soon the horse arrived back at his own barn. Bertie looked out and wondered why he had made such a quick trip. Bertie had to give up his milking and drive Braddy to Northfield.

Another day when Braddy visited the Lantz house, he sat down in the rocking chair, started rocking and the chair went over backwards and he ended up on the floor.

Braddy wit was known to everyone in the church and the community. He always liked to joke and was always ready for a good laugh. He was also very sympathetic and understanding and was a very well-liked rector.

Mr. O'Toole worked at the Clarkes on the farm. The large family lived up the road and were quite poor. The last baby was premature and several ladies from the community went to help with the delivery. The baby was wrapped in a blanket and put in the wood-stove oven, with the door open. This served as an incubator and kept the child alive. On one occasion Braddy won a doll at a raffle and gave it to the O'Toole children.

Another family in Upper Kennetcook that was very active in church and community was Addison and Mary Hennigar's family. They had twelve children but most of them had gone away to work - some to the United States. Helen, Bertha, Morris and Lloyd were still there and the whole family was very dedicated to the church.

The Hennigars lived on a big farm. Addison was often a warden of the church and helped in any way he could. Even as an elderly man he was still very active in the church. His brother, Havelock Hennigar, who also had a big family, was another active member of the church. His children were Elsie's age. He was the one who decided that the church should have a horse barn so that when people went to church with their horses and wagons they would have a place to put their horse. Most people who went to church did not have a horse so were not in favour of this but Havelock got the barn built.

Bertha and Cline Solley had a great deal to do with keeping the softball team going - practicing, and visiting other places to play softball.

Another dedicated family was Fred and Aileen Miller's family. Aileen was Elsie's aunt and all the kids in the community called her Antie (Auntie). Uncle Fred and "Antie" had three children. They built a sun porch on their house so the young people could go there Saturday nights to dance. They had an old Victrola phonograph that had to be wound up by hand and they would play records and dance to that music. One of the boys, Lou Garby, played the violin very well. He married Fred and Aileen's daughter, Claire, and they had three children. One year he became the senior fiddle champion. The Miller's son, Don, was a playmate of David Bradshaw. Aileen (Mrs. Miller) was the organist of the church for fifty-two years. Don and his wife, Madge had three children.

Basil Sheehy (the blacksmith) and wife Ivy came from the Noel area but originated in Northfield. They were Anglican. They had four boys and a girl in their family. Basil made skis for the children of the community and most of them learned to ski on the blacksmith-made skis. They did not have very much of a curve at the end but they worked. They also kept the post office for awhile, so everyone knew them. He later went to work in Windsor so the family moved there.

Barney and Helen (Hally) Hennigar took over the post office from the Sheehys and Barney was also the train station master for a long time. Barney's father, Ef, was a life-long resident of Upper Kennetcook. Hally was a school teacher who was courted by the bachelor, Barney, when she arrived in the community. They had two girls, Leone and Winnie. They later moved to a farm in Belle Isle, Annapolis county. When they took their oldest daughter to the church to be baptized she cried and cried so they finally took her outside. It wasn't long before Barney came in dragging a blanket and a diaper in his hand and whispered that they could not go on with the baptism so later Braddy went and baptized the baby at the house.

Wilbert and Susan Miller, with their big family, lived on what was called the Back Road. Mrs. Miller was a faithful church goer. Their oldest daughter, Beatrice, was about Elsie's age and always went to church with her mother or her grandmother. All the family took part in badminton and other sports and other fun things such as coasting and skating.

Another big family who lived on the Back Road was Millie and Bert Hennigars. Millie and her neighbour used to walk to the Clarke store for groceries in the winter and would carry them home in a washtub, which they had taken with them.

Fred Miller's brother was Whitney Miller and he was a neighbour of the Clarkes. Whit and Nellie were faithful church goers. The church was the center of activity so most people attended the services regularly and took part in the church-sponsored activities. Whit and Nellie had a son and daughter, Kay, who started school with Elsie. Later on they had a third child who was much younger that the first two. When Elsie's mother heard she was pregnant Elsie remembers her mother saying, "My Heavens, Nellie! How did that happen?"

"Well," Nellie said, "it must be the Holy Ghost."

One family that always went to the Anglican church because they did not have a church of their own as they were United was the Weirs. They did not have any children but all the children of the community used to go there because they had the first bathroom in the area. Elsie recalls having a bath in Mary Weir's big tub.

Addison Hennigar's sister, Lucy Joe, (She was called Lucy Joe because her husband's name was Joe Miller) was left a widow with a big family at a young age. She was a person who loved to introduce anything new. Elsie recalls a waffle party she had at one time and invited everyone to come. No one in the area had ever had waffles before. She, and Lois Lantz, were the midwives of the area and learned by experience without any formal training; they brought many babies safely into the world. Lucy Joe always had a "growly" stomach, which delighted the children in church, but she lived to a very old age.

After Aileen could no longer play the organ in church another aunt of Elsie's, Amy Darby, took over and she played for a long time. Her husband, Laurie worked in the community.

All the children in the community had a lot of fun back in the forties. They coasted and skated outdoors in the winter. The men would dam up the river so there would be lots of ice for the ice boxes, as there were no refrigerators in those days in that community. The backed-up water made an excellent place to skate.

Interview with Mildred (Clarke) MacIntyre

Mildred was the daughter of Harold and Clara Clarke. Harold was one of the Clarke Brothers who ran the store. He had been in the first World War and had met Clara, an Assistant Dietitian at the Sanitorium in Kentville where he was hospitalized for tuberculosis. After he was cured he went to Upper Kennetcook, started the store; lived in part of it and, took his brother in as a partner. Their kitchen was on the ground floor of the store, and their living room and bedrooms were upstairs over the store. All three children - Mildred, Gwen and Joan were born at the store but they moved around 1930, to a house up the road.

During the Second World War when two of the Bradshaw children (Dot and Joan) were at Edgehill they were students with children from the Anglican Church School in England because many of the children were evacuated. Because they did not have any friends or relatives in this country Braddy arranged homes for them to spend their holidays so they wouldn't have to stay at the school by themselves. One of the little girls, Enid Van Dyke, went to the Bradshaws but because the Bradshaws had such a large family it was arranged that the girl would stay with the Clarkes. It was quite interesting having a girl from another country and she was very interested in the way of life here as she was brought up as a daughter of a solicitor. She thought the people lived in rather an archaic style. Clara

176

used one of those old-fashioned washing machines with a wringer attached. One day Enid was writing a letter to her mother while sitting at the table and she kept looking at Clara at work so Clara asked her what she was doing and she told her that she was trying to draw a picture of that machine as she had never seen one like it before. Her parents used to write to the Clarkes, and on one occasion, when they visited England, they were invited to stay with them but they stayed in a hotel and were entertained by the Van Dykes.

Dot Bradshaw was Mildred's very best friend for many years, and they spent much time together either at the Bradshaws or at the Clarkes. They used to try to get away from Gwen when they were playing. Often when they were playing games one of them would say first, the other second and the last third. Usually Dot or Mildred would always have first or second place but one day when Gwen has a chance to say "First" she was so used to saying "Third" that she shouted "Third", although no one had said first or second.

Mildred remembered her parents playing a lot of Bridge with the Bradshaws. One night when they were playing, Braddy was facing the wall where the furnace pipe went through the ceiling. They burned wood in the winter and would take the big black pipe down for the summer and this left a hole in the ceiling. While playing Bridge, all at once Braddy got a funny look on his face and Mrs. Clarke said, "What are you looking at?"

One of the children was sitting up stairs beside the hole and was dangling her feet through the hole trying to attract attention.

During Lent, Braddy, who loved his cigarettes, and Mr. Clarke, who loved his pipe, made a pact at the beginning of Lent that they would give up smoking as their Lenten denial. After the first week it was very difficult and both men were craving their nicotine so they decided that Sunday was not a day of Fasting so they would go without smoking for six days and then they would smoke all day Sunday.

Once when Mrs. Clarke went to Halifax to a movie with the Bradshaws, Braddy opened up his coat to show his clerical collar and said, "You people get behind me and I'll get us in for half price because Ministers get everywhere for half price." He also said that when they travelled on the train they could travel for a cent a mile.

Long after the Bradshaws left Upper Kennetcook, the Clarkes and Bradshaws had many good times together. The Bradshaws encouraged the Clarkes to go to Barbados on vacations when they spent winters there following their retirement. Altogether they went there for five or six months and the Bradshaws always found them a cottage to rent and introduced them to their friends and family down there. They played cards down there too and the two couples were very close. Mildred went to Barbados and visited her parents several years when they were there and the first people to welcome her were the Bradshaws.

Dot and Mildred rather lost contact for a number of years when they both married and Dot was living near Toronto and Mildred was living in Digby County, Nova Scotia. Whenever they visited each other it was as if they had never been apart since they had such a close friendship when they were growing up.

When Mac had scarlet fever at the rectory, Mildred was the Bradshaw errand "boy". She would take the groceries, milk and mail and would leave it outside the door.

Eric Ettinger, down in Kennetcook, had a really old van and driving over dirt roads was very dusty. He had benches in the back and he used to drive the softball team in the back of this van to Windsor, Truro, Halifax, and different places to play softball. The team would start out dressed in white shorts, tops and sneakers but by the time they reached their destinations they were a dusty-looking crowd.

Harold Clarke built a tennis court of gravel which was rolled. High wires were around the court. Clara, who had played tennis for years, taught others in the community, including Harold to play. There were so many children who wanted to play that Glen Clarke built another tennis court at his place. The children could shout back and forth between the two courts. They would send messages back and forth with flags too. They had been learning Morse Code with flags in Guides.

Mildred went to school in Upper Kennetcook until grade ten and unfortunately she became attracted to a man in the village who was quite a bit older than she was and her parents sent her to live with her Grandmother in Lunenburg to take her grade eleven. Then she returned home to take her grade twelve in Windsor. She joined the others travelling by train each day to Windsor and back home each night. They called the train "The Blueberry Special". One of the conductors, Mel Whitman, from Kentville, was called Uncle Mel after the Uncle Mel of the children's radio program. He was very kind to the children and would always bring all kinds of goodies in his lunchpail which he would give to the children on their return trip at night. When his daughter was married they really had a feed.

A poem was written in 1936 entitled:

O Muse
A Contribution to the History in the County of Hants

O Muse, who sits aloft and writes at poetry all day,
Come sit by my typewriter as I finger out this lay.
Permit me, Muse, to introduce the heroes I have took,
The Travelling Man for Truro and the Priest from Kennetcook.

First to the Priest from Kennetcook. As good a man, by heck,
As ever wore his collar turned the wrong way round his neck.
He went to ride, this Man of God, within his Chevrolet,
And so began adventures, Muse, related in my lay.

The skipper took his daughter for to bear him company.
The priest was not a piker so he took his children three.
There's Dorothy, and David too, (I wish his name were Dennis,)
And Joan who camps, and also plays a nifty game of tennis.

"I pray you, gentle Father," said Ruel Garvey to the Priest,
"Take care about that tire. It is rotten. At the least
Have blowout patch within it." "Ruel, you're quite mistook,
You sell me no new tire," said the priest from Kennetcook.

'Twas half past ten, O Muse, perhaps about the time when you
Are hiding with a pretty hand what Frenchmen call a moue,
And calling for your candle. Ah, better far had they,
These four, been safe in bed, and not within the Chevrolet.

Bang went the tire, and hearts were bowed with sorrow, grief and pain.
The Priest got out to have a look and wished him in again.
Beside the car a six foot drop yawned like the gate of hell,
Where horrid fiends and damned souls, unpleasant folk, do dwell.

O Muse, there's sadness in the world, and broken hearts no doubt,
But none so sad as motorist who finds himself without
A flashlight or a match when tire is flat upon the road,
Talk you, O Muse, of loads of grief? That is indeed a load.

Long did the Priest with jack and wrench attack that tire, blind,
All poised upon a six inch ledge, a six foot drop behind.
And many priests and levites passed upon the other side,
With thumb to nose, until the holy Father could have cried.

But who is this that comes along, O Muse, like Galahad?
Yes you have guessed it right the first time. It is the very lad
Who is our other hero. Through the darkness of the night
The Travelling Man for Truro comes on flashing wings of light.

As a good Samaritan he would have rated mighty slim.
All his oil was in his crankcase, all his wine was inside him,
But he turned his headlights on the tire, and took his wrench in hand.
The way the work went on from there, O Muse, was simply grand.

"Goodby, goodby, O Travelling man for Truro," cried the Priest.
I wish you well, and thank you much. In sooth the very least
That I can wish you is that I shall never need to pay
You back in the same coin that you have given me this day."

Within his car the Travelling Man the road did now unravel.
Talk about speed, O Muse, I'll say that lad could surely travel!
His children three all safe inside, the Priest from Kennetcook
Stepped wearily upon the gas, and that dread place forsook.

But scarce two curves had passed before the Father had to stand
His car upon its haunches, for there with outstretched hand
Upon the middle of the road stood that same Travelling Man.
His head was bent in sorrow, and down his cheeks tears ran.

"Upon the waters cast thy bread and it comes back to you.
So says the book, Sir Priest, and I have always thought it true.
It also mentions many days, but we'll forget that utterance.
Pass the slice please back to me, and don't forget the butter.

There were two curves upon the road, and as I rode I reckoned
That I could take the first with ease, but I forgot the second.
That's my car fifty yards away, that field of oats within.
The way I feel right now, I'd give it to you for a pin."

"Fear nothing," said the Father, "Close by lives a Farmer
Whom well I know, a splendid man, a Mister Wolaver.
His horses twain will pull you out as quick as wink your eye.
I'll go and have them back to you before you can say 'Hy!'"

So off to Mister Wolaver he went with might and main.
He tumbled down the cellar hatch, but got him out again
He banged upon the knocker until almost in despair,
But finally a windowed head above him said "Who's there?"

The Priest explained. A Travelling Man, a car, a curve, a field.
He squeezed out all the pathos that he thought the tale would yield.
He spoke of Mister Wolaver and of his horses twain
To hitch on to the fielded car and make it road again.

"O holy Father, well you know that I would succour thee,
But my husband, Mister Wolaver, is now asleep with me.
If I should rouse him at this hour an awful row he'd make.
He's bad enough when he's asleep, he's terrible awake.

On yonder hill-top stands a house, all set about with trees,
And in it dwells our hired man, his name is Mister Lees.
He'll get the horses from the field and snitch you out with ease,
If well you understand the way his itching palm to grease."

The little house upon the hill stood in an orchard fair.
Here was a shady apple tree, there was a pleasant pear.
The small-fruit garden on the right, here lawn, there flowerbed
That in the sunlight was a blaze of roses pink and red.

Yes, in the sunlight, Muse, but this was half past ten at night,
When wandering through an orchard means you have to have a light.
The priest had piety and prayer, he eke had churches flue.
He'd have swapped the lot, that moment, for a lantern flame alive.

He bumped the shady apple tree, he bumped the pleasant pear.
He fell into a raspberry bush, and wished he wasn't there.
He tumbled o'er a garden rake and picked himself a rose.
He even tripped o'er wire. How he did that, Heaven knows!

It takes a lot, O Muse, to faze the Priest from Kennetcook,
But that wire got him down at last. If you will closely look,
Upon his hands and knees you'll see atoiling up the hill
A clerk whose form most clearly shows he has been through the mill.

Hurrah! He's reached the house, and knocks. Hurrah! A window opes.
Hurrah! He has an answer clear to all his fears and hopes.
"Our Mister Lees will be with thee, and eke his horses twain.
You'll find him almost there before you reach the road again."

An hour passes slowly for the travellers-to-be.
They talk of Mister Einstein and Eschatology.
They talk of women's winter-wear and wish they were in bed,
While the Universe majestic swings in long curve overhead.

The second hour begins, and then arrives the hired man,
With horses twain who almost - but not quite - put a ban
Upon the whole performance, for it really took a sight
Of work to make them leave their field at half past ten of night.

It took him full an hour to persuade these foolish ones
That half past ten was early and the road a lot of fun.
They were far too dumb to see it, though he argued loud and long.
It is possible, perhaps, that they were right and he was wrong.

However, when they did come they worked hard upon the car.
They pulled and hauled and dragged and yanked, until 'twas "There you are!'
The car stood firmly on the road, as right as right could be.
The horses had done all the work, the man he took the fee.

The Travelling Man for Truro, on flashing wings of light,
Shot down the road for Truro, and vanished in the night.
The holy Father watched him go, watched him with straining eyes,
Then in the clerical manner did thus apostrophize:

"Farewell, O man for Truro, upon the way you've went!
You say you're off for Truro, your speed, says you're hell bent.
But I pray to good St. Christopher that he may go with thee,
And guide thee to that Truro where thou sayest thou wouldst be."

*This Communion Set and the Trust Fund were blessed by Bishop
George Arnold in a Memorial Service at St. Peter's Church, Upper
Kennetcook, Hants County, Nova Scotia on Sunday, September 25, 1983.*

In Memoriam

This Holy Communion Set
and the
Margaret P. Bradshaw Trust Fund
are presented
To the Glory of God
and
In Memory of
Margaret P. Bradshaw
1890 - 1981
Wife of Canon A.G. Bradshaw
Rector of this Parish
1934 - 1942

The agreement with the Parish of Maitland states:" The trustee shall keep invested the Margaret P. Bradshaw Trust Fund and shall pay annually the net income therefrom in perpetuity to the Parish of Maitland, Diocese of Nova Scotia, to be used for the purpose of repairing, decorating and maintaining the Parish Rectory situate at Upper Kennetcook, Hants County, Nova Scotia, or any rectory designated by the Parish and the receipt of the proper officers of the Parish for each such annual payment shall be an absolute discharge to the trustees.

Margaret Praetor Bradshaw

Margaret Praetor Bradshaw (known affectionately to her children, daughters and sons in law as Mum) was an excellent partner and helper to her husband, Braddy.

She was born in Barbados in 1890 and was educated at Queen's College where a number of books awarded there attest to her achievement.

In 1917 she went to New York to work for the Council of Churches, until her marriage in 1919 to Rev. Alleyne George Bradshaw.

The young girl from the tropical island of Barbados had her first experiences as the wife of a priest in Alberta. Although quite a contrast to her life at home she coped exceptionally well and in later life when asked what she remembered best about those early years, she replied, " I only remember being happy".

This ability to be happy and content wherever she lived was an outstanding quality which exemplified Mum's life. As a wife of a parish priest for over fifty years in Alberta, Barbados and Nova Scotia she set a shining example through her unselfish devotion to her church, the lifelong work of her husband, and her family.

Her useful life might best be summed up in the words of an elderly parishioner, "The little mother had her hands and heart full".

The following letter (dated September 27, Hantsport, NS) was received from Bishop Arnold following this service:

Dear Mac,

To you and to the other members of your family, Mary and I send our warm thanks for your hospitality. The luncheon was a happy occasion made the more so by the relaxed atmosphere which you help to create.

As I mentioned previously, it was an honour for me to share in the Memorial Service and I appreciate your thinking of me.

To acknowledge adequately and briefly your generosity poses a problem. Will a sincere thanks do the trick?

If I may add this - and I am going to anyway - your Mother and Dad have every reason to be proud of their family.

With every good wish,
George

12   YARMOUTH PARISH
(1942 - 1959)

And in June of 1942, Braddy writes to Codrington that he has accepted a position at Holy Trinity, Yarmouth, his fourth and last parish in the Diocese of Nova Scotia and there he may continue as a parttime Chaplain at R.C.A.F. Yarmouth.

Holy Trinity Church, Yarmouth

We are moving again on June 2nd. I have been appointed to the Parish of Holy Trinity, Yarmouth, Nova Scotia. It is quite a nice town, with a very beautiful Church, valued at $100,000.00, a very comfortable Rectory, and a nice Parish Hall, all situated on one lot in the centre of the town. It will be a change to have only one Church to look after, and not to have the travelling. I have resigned as Rural Dean of this Deanery, as Yarmouth is another one. I have also had to resign as R.C.A.F. Chaplain at Stanley. It means quite a reduction of my 'letters'. I was the Rev. Hon. F/Lt. A. G. Bradshaw, B.A., R.D., R.C.A.F. Now I have just the B.A. left. The C.O. at Stanley has recommended that I be put on the reserved list of R.C.A.F. Officers, so I may retain my affiliation there.

And Braddy's last letter, written some 27 years after graduating from Codrington College, is from Yarmouth:

I do not find very much time for leisure; none of the days or weeks are ever long enough to get into them all that one would like. Of course here especially the war has increased my work tremendously, with so many service personnel in the Parish and the need which they cause for extra spiritual and social activities. It is a strange thing but I have met boys from all over the world except Barbados. Most of the other West Indian Islands have been represented in our Church services and dances, etc. in the hall, but no one from Bimshire. The nearest was a Fleet Air Arm Lietenant from Malborough whose mother was a Claumonte from Barbados, and I have seen and spoken to a goodly number during the past two years. Over 10,000 men have attended the dances and socials in our Hall and many more than that have attended Church.

Bishop Cashmore Visits Yarmouth

Bishop Cashmore, a colleague of Braddy's while at Codrington College, Barbados, visited the Bradshaws in Yarmouth. As president of the International Rotary Club he visited the Yarmouth Club and stayed at the rectory. Braddy recalled that while Bishop Cashmore was visiting two Cadillacs drove up to the rectory to chauffeur the Cashmores and Bradshaws to a Rotary meeting.

Interview with Mrs. Elizabeth Wainwright,
wife of the late Rev. Hastings Wainwright

Elizabeth was the daughter of Jean and Albert Hood. She had one younger sister, Esther West (died 1994) , a nurse, who had been married in March, 1942, by Rev. Gordon T. Lewis. Her husband was in the airforce. Her ashes were buried in Yarmouth. Elizabeth had gone to Edgehill, then to Kings, then to work in New Brunswick so was away from Yarmouth for a few years before her marriage and subsequent return to her home. Elizabeth and Hastings had five children - John, Anne, Charles, Esther and Emily.

The Wainwrights were married in January of 1941 and went to Granville for a few months but in May he was called to Headquarters, Halifax to work as a Chaplain so they moved to Halifax. From there he was sent to Debert. He was joined up with the Number 7 General Hospital in November and was sent overseas so Mrs. Wainwright came back home to Yarmouth to live with her parents. May 25, 1942, their son, John, was born and shortly afterwards, while Elizabeth was still in the hospital, the Bradshaws arrived, (June 2, 1942) at the rectory in Yarmouth which was right across the back lane from the home of the Wainwrights. Therefore they were always aware of the comings and goings to the rectory. From the time Elizabeth was a child she was in and out of the rectory and when Rev. Haslam was there, their two children were of Elizabeth's generation so as friends they visited back and forth very often.

Elizabeth thought that their son, John, was the first child that Braddy baptized. She knew that he visited her soon after moving in and was always very kind to them as to all parishioners. The Hastings were always very attentive and active people in the church, its ministry and administration. Usually she was included in the parties and entertaining that was always going on in the rectory. Elizabeth remembered Beryl, Braddy's oldest daughter, who worked for the War Time Price and Trade Board in Yarmouth and Dot, the third daughter, who was working in the bank when they first came to Yarmouth; she could not remember Joan, second daughter, as she was away in the navy and then went on to King's College.

All during the war years while Rev. Wainwright was in the service, Elizabeth stayed in Yarmouth and became very involved in the life of the church. She recalled the open houses that were held each Sunday and Wednesday evenings for the servicemen who were stationed in Yarmouth. The Fleet Air Arms were really young boys straight out of school and they began going to church and the social evenings at once and were made to feel at home which made the church and the rectory more like home than their barracks.

Originally Holy Trinity Church was frowned upon because they let the servicemen use the church hall to sing, dance and even play cards. At that time there was an evangelist, Rev. Parlee, who had a radio service each Sunday evening. Some Anglicans used to rush home after their 7 o' clock Sunday evening service to listen to him as he condemned the socials at Holy Trinity hall, often referring to it as Bradshaw's Dance Hall. Rev. Lewis who began the entertainment of the servicemen was considered very broad-minded and kind and felt it was important to treat these men well. Games, books, and the like were placed in what is now the Lady's Parlour of the church hall, and it made a very pleasant and good place for the boys to hang out to play checkers, chess, read or just sit and talk. Always there were refreshments supplied by the parishioners. Elizabeth recalled once when she and her mother were to assist in supplying refreshments and because the Wainwrights were a large family they had a lot of ration cards (Food and some other items were rationed during the war.) so they were able to make a great big batch of ham sandwiches. There were three people that night who took ham sandwiches. The boys were always treated to sandwiches, sweets, tea and coffee.

Beryl became engaged to one of the servicemen, Ernie Garber, from Bridgewater but he was killed during the war. She later married another serviceman from Liverpool, Randy Day. Dot also met her husband while he was serving in Yarmouth - Earl Patte - whom she married after the war ended.

Some of Elizabeth's memories include very pleasant visits to the rectory. One such visit was to meet a friend of the family from out west, Gay Armstrong, who was proud of his western homeland, his heritage and the fact that his mother was a full-blooded Indian. As usual the Bradshaws had invited some of the young people of the parish to meet him.

After the war Hastings come to Yarmouth several times to take services while the Bradshaws went on holiday. One such time was in August of 1952, when they spent the month in the rectory. Elizabeth remembers the family spending time at the beach and the children returning with clams in the sand buckets. These often were put under the porch and later discovered because of the odour arising from under the porch steps. During that time her father, Albert, had a stroke and died within a few days. Her mother died in 1979.

Elizabeth was a dancing student of coeducational classes of Anna Perrin Spicer. They used a gramophone for music to which the family
188

pet, a parrot, tried to sing. Whether the students were at all interested in the classes was debatable but they liked to go to see the parrot. Mr. Penn Spicer was church organist for many years.

When the Bradshaws arrived at the rectory there was a supply of photographic equipment in the attic. Rev. Haslam, who preceded Braddy, was quite a photographer and Elizabeth recalled one special picture he took of her mother's garden, which he had enlarged, tinted and gave to her.

The Wainwrights were good friends of the Rev. Davies, the immediate predecessor of the Bradshaws, and their family. In fact, Hastings stayed there the night before they were married. Mrs. Davies had painted pictures of swans on the walls of one of the bedrooms at the rectory which remained there for more than fifty years. They were papered over by the Rev. Ellis family during renovations of the 80 's. The summer of 1995 they were uncovered and photographed but because of the conditions of the wall plaster they had to be destroyed in repairing the walls. It was said that these swans epitomized several prominent ladies of the parish.

Swans on bedroom wall in rectory

Interview with Rev. Harold Kay

Harold Kay was the son of the late Arthur and Grace (Selbage) Kay. He had a younger brother, Robert, and an older sister, Barbara (Reading). Their father was Anglican, their mother was Roman Catholic and he was baptized at the Roman Catholic Church, Eel Brook, Yarmouth County. His ancestors were Salvation Army, Roman Catholic and Baptist. Later his mother and father decided to attend the Anglican church. Arthur had six sisters; the only one living now is Hilda in Toronto. (however died 1996) His mother's parents had eighteen children, sixteen of whom survived and most of them lived in Yarmouth in the thirties and all of them had large families so it became rather difficult to keep track of all of them. His parents divorced. His mother died in 1984 while she was living in Coburg, Ontario; his father died in Yarmouth.

Ray Reading, Barbara's husband, was in the army which he made his career. Robert was an X-ray technician and spent part of his career in Toronto and then in Woodstock and then they began to move around quite often.

In 1942 when Braddy first arrived at Holy Trinity the Kays were regular attendees at church, always present at Sunday School and at least to one of the church services each Sunday. Harold was in the first Confirmation Class held by Braddy and was confirmed by Bishop Hackenley on October 14, 1942. He served as crucifer and was always pleased and enjoyed the task as Braddy was very cooperative. The verger, Tom James, in his long black robe and staff, would ring the church bell and then knock on the door to indicate that Braddy and entourage were ready to process into the church for the service to begin. Harold left Yarmouth at the age of seventeen, June 30, 1944. One day after he finished high school - he did not even wait for the graduation - he joined the army. He did basic training and was assigned to the orderly office as he had Commerce from High School. When he became eighteen the following January, he became a real soldier, a Private, signed up for the Pacific and was doing advance training for the Infantry. Again his past training caught up with him and he was placed in a Regimental Office of the Third Canadian Infantry in Debert. After the war in the Pacific ended, Harold wanted to get out which he did in November, 1945, so that he could attend university.

Harold always felt that Braddy had been the one to instill in him the desire to become an Anglican priest. So when he began his pursuit of his career he had to go back to High School and get the grade 12 academic year which he had forfeited by taking Commerce when he was going through school. From November until June he obtained his necessary subjects and then went to King's College in 1946 and got his BA in 1950. From 1950-1952 he studied theology and also during the time, on May 12, 1951, he married, Edith Jost, a young lady he met around 1947 while taking a service at Tusket. After the service he was invited to the Jost home for lunch and he and Edith took an instant liking of each other. In the chapel at King's College Braddy performed the ceremony at eight o'clock in the morning. Both families were not very much in favour of the marriage and so the wedding was very quiet with very few family members attending. Braddy gave a lot of moral support to the couple and graciously married them without any financial payment at all. He became the surrogate family providing the support to the couple the families refused to give.

After Edith graduated in 1950 she went to Netherwood School in New Brunswick to teach. In 1951 Harold was assigned to be an assistant to a chaplain in Winnipeg so they spent the summer together in Winnipeg. They bought an old 1929 Ford out there and after the summer's work they drove down to Nebraska and Kansas to see some of Edith's relatives and then drove home to Halifax.

Harold was ordained a deacon at Trinity Church in Halifax. His choice was to be ordained at Holy Trinity in Yarmouth but as there were three students to be ordained at one time, Bishop Waterman thought it would be more convenient to be ordained in Halifax. Braddy gave the sermon for this ordination with his text from the Book of James which was a favourite of Harold's. In fact Harold's first sermon was also based on text from James. He felt he did this because of the impressions left on him by Braddy, who was really very much a people person, always encouraging and motivating people to do for others and to share their wealth with those less fortunate. Braddy was very involved in secular organizations especially those relating to children - Boy Scouts, Children's Aid, Library and the like. He was very earthly in that sense and a practical man who seemed to follow the directions found in the Book of James.

Harold felt that Braddy was a man who, at first impressions, was not one who would appear quite distinctive or have an immediate effect on one. It might be later that the strong influence he had on people would manifest itself.

Harold was ordained a priest in Neil's Harbour where he only stayed a short time as the rectory did not have a well and he had a small baby at the time. He then served in Port Greville, where his area kept expanding because of vacancies in surrounding parishes and the scarcity of priests. When Parsboro asked for Rev. Kay to come to their parish - he had been filling in there along with parish duties in two other parishes - the Bishop would not allow it as he said Rev. Kay did not have enough experience yet. So in 1956 he answered an advertisement for a church in Wichita, Texas and was hired. From here he came back to Canada to Clementsport, Nova Scotia. After a couple years he had an offer of studies in Philadelphia and a small parish with a minimum stipend so he decided to accept as he had always had in his mind that he would also like to teach. The church was in Woodbury Heights, New Jersey, and he attended classes each day in Philadelphia. After four years doing religious studies and Hebrew studies he was hired as a teacher of Hebrew at Huron College, Ontario. This came about while Harold was visiting his brother, Bob, in Woodstock, in August. In discussion with friends a local rector told Harold about Huron which he had never heard of before. Harold visited the campus and while he was looking around a short fat man, a clergyman, came out and they began talking. He was John Morden, the principal. As they discussed their respective occupations at the time, the principal informed him that they were losing their Hebrew teacher in the spring so Harold gave him his telephone number and in January he received a telephone call to ask if he would be interested in the job. Harold at first refused but was asked to think it over and a month later decided to accept. In 1966 he began his career at Huron and continued until his retirement in 1986. He enjoyed his work there very much and would often do fill-in services or other honorary assistant's work somewhere.

A Hole in the Surplice - Other Interesting Vestment

A little boy came to Yarmouth with his parents in 1942 and attended Sunday School at Holy Trinity. When visiting in 1999 with Christ Church Cathedral Choir from Ottawa, he discussed with Malcolm Bradshaw some of the things he remembered when he lived in Yarmouth. One of these remembrances was that as a little boy as he stood near Canon Bradshaw (Braddy) his eyes were level with a hole in Braddy's surplice. We assume this was the hole made by the spark which flew from the censer back in Barbados in 1921. Clergy were very poor in worldly possessions in those days and a surplice would never be discarded simply because of a hole - and such an historical one as that.

One other interesting vestment worn by Braddy for many years was a chasuble he received from the S.P.G. It had been worn by Bishop Henry Montgomery, father of the famed General Montgomery, who was secretary of the society when Braddy left England in 1913. It is now displayed in a cabinet at Holy Trinity.

The pelican on the chasuble in the picture is a feminine symbol of Christ. Here she is shown in all her piety with the Christ nimbus (halo)
192

around her head with a cross through it. The little pelicans at her feet are drinking the blood she has pecked from her own breast giving them life. The nest is a crown of thorns.

According to an ancient legend the mother pelican, if food is scarce, will feed her young with her own blood before she will see them perish.

Red Chasuble with Golden Pelicans
owned and worn by Canon Bradshaw
It is preserved at Holy Trinity Church Archives, Yarmouth

It is easy to see how the pelican could become a symbol of Christ and that image has been present in the Church for a long, long time. Lockeport Church in Lockeport, Nova Scotia (Holy Cross) has the same image under that of Christ in the window over the Altar.

NOTE: A history of the Society for the Propagation of the Gospel has been done by the late Rev. Sigmund Miller, of Ontario, but he served several parishes in Nova Scotia.

Not So Reverend

Archdeacon Hastings Wainwright in his memoirs entitled "Not So

Reverend" relates these stories about Rev. Gordon T. Lewis who after retirement assisted Braddy with church services at Holy Trinity, Yarmouth.

Deanery meetings used to last two days and the clergy would be billeted in private houses or in parish halls. Mr. Lewis was a great scholar and used to say his Daily Office in Hebrew, Greek and Latin. At Deanery meetings he would arise at 0600 to say his Office and, in cold weather, the others would be awakened by the sound of his puffing on his numbed fingers in order to turn over the pages.

He used a magnifying glass a great deal, even during the services in Church. When my sister-in-law's husband looked up during the marriage ceremony he saw the beard and nose of the Reverend Gordon T. through the magnifying glass. The sight was almost too much for him.

Mr. Lewis had been asked to take part in a quiz on the local radio station. He not only answered the questions which were asked him, but one could also hear his voice as he answered the questions which had been put to the other contestants.

Canon A. G. Bradshaw (Braddy) went to see the Reverend Gordon T. in hospital. The old man was near death, but he had the strength to tell the Canon what hymns and what tunes he wanted at his funeral. "I don't want any old tune played. I want these ones." Half an hour later, he was dead.

Rev. Gordon T. Lewis

Rector's Request

Note: Braddy rarely made any requests for any repairs or renovations and the following may explain why!

The Garage

The Vestry sat back with work nobly done
Repairs to the Church had been lots of fun.
The Rector rose to his feet and did say
What about a garage for my Chevrolet."

The Vestry sat back with faces of gloom,
For a garage in the estimates there hadn't been room
Then one bright lad said, "I clearly can see,
This is a matter for the Fab. Committee."

The F.C. didn't take the task with great joy,
As one of them said, after deep thought, "O Boy,
We can find the money in this day and age,
But where the heck do we put that darned garage?"

So they talked and they walked and looked the scene o'er,
And thought the best site right by the back door.
But one of them thought that the Rector might know
Where for his best use the garage should go.

Then full of resolve up spake H.C.,
"This job has been left to the Fab. Committee,
Like the Medes and the Persians our decisions we make,
Who doesn't like them can go jump in the lake."

So while the Rector a brief respite did take,
With his family to the city by Ontario Lake,
Although many thought the site very poor,
The garage was erected right by the back door.

His holiday over and right full of beans,
The Rector came back, though empty his jeans.
His mind was at peace with all of mankind,
No happier man would you be able to find.

He drove into the yard with his goods and chattels
The car had done well with very few rattles.
But he stopped so suddenly, that it threw up its rear end
And his wife tried with her head, the windscreen to bend.

The Rector, he said to his upended spouse
"Can you tell me what that is up by the house?"
"Do you mean that building, so broad and so large?
That my dear, she said, is your requested garage."

"Can you tell me", he said, "how we'll get the coal in,
They have planted the thing right in front of the bin.
Moreover," he said, and he began madly to shout,
"How the heck will I get the car in and out?"

And now day by day when you are passing that way,
You will see the poor man, gone considerably grey,
As he backs from garage to the lane in reverse,
Muttering about the F.C., it sounds like a curse.

The moral in all this you will easily see,
And not have to worry about what is to be.
And do not consider the use of a place,
As long as it fits a convenient space.

*Bradshaw Family Picnic, circa 1943. Back row, left to right: Beryl, Joan,
Maggie, Dorothy, Braddy; Front row left to right Malcolm, David.*

My father was appointed Rector of Holy Trinity, Yarmouth in June of 1942. He succeeded Rev. Jack Davies who joined the Armed Forces as a Chaplain. My father always said that during his sixty-year ministry, his early years at Holy Trinity were the only time he had a one-church parish. Later when Father Lewis died he served St. Stephens, Tusket, as well.

War is horrible! However, for an eleven year old boy living in war-prepared Yarmouth with 10,000 servicemen, it was also exciting. The rectory was situate at the corner of Forest and William Streets, in direct route from

Mac in College Days

the Royal Canadian Air Force and Fleet Air Arm Stations to Main Street. During the war the three main streets to downtown Yarmouth were Forest, Cliff and Parade. Next door, along William Street, were the church and parish hall.

Prior to my family's arrival in Yarmouth, my father had preached at Holy Trinity and had been accepted as the new Rector by the Church Vestry (now called Parish Council). However, he had in his possession, authority from his Diocesan Bishop to be inducted as Rector of the parish. The reason was that the parish had been vacant for six months and after that period of time the bishop had authority to appoint. My father's thoughts on the matter were that as he had been accepted by the Vestry he didn't think there was any point in disclosing the bishop's authority. The appointment remained unopened in his possession. He later found out that his cautionary action was appropriate as the Yarmouth Parish had a history of disagreements with diocesan authority. One of the most notable disagreements was in the 1870's when Rev. J. Roy Campbell (author of *Campbell's History of Yarmouth County*), the architect and curate of the new church, wanted to become rector but was turned down. On other occasions the fact that the parish was so far from central diocesan authority was unfortunate as parishioners did not always understand the church canons that govern the Anglican Church.

On our arrival in Yarmouth we were met by several parishioners who were to billet us for our first night. There were five of us - Dad, Mum, Beryl, David and me. My brother, Charles, of course, was still in Barbados and we would not see him until after the war. Two of my sisters, Joan and Dorothy were studying at Edgehill, the Anglican residential school at Windsor. I was to go to the Israel Porter residence, a short distance east on Forest Street from the rectory. This was the beginning of a friendly association with Mr. Porter who was a faithful Anglican churchman and a prominent Yarmouth business man. He owned a women's clothing store on Main Street in what was called the Porter Block. He employed a number

Holy Trinity Rectory, Yarmouth, circa 1942

of ladies, among whom was Gerry (Teed) Brittain, another prominent Anglican. In later years both David and I worked there as janitors. The Dominion Store, a groceteria, was next door and I clearly remember the large rats living in the basement. That Upper Kennetcook kicking hind-legged snared rabbit was nothing in comparison to one of those rats. How I could have used Benjie, our later rat terrier, on many an occasion! On the death of Israel Porter's widow, his Forest Street property was purchased by the Roman Catholic Corporation and is now the Tabitha Centre run by the nuns.

The adjacent property, on South Park Street, formerly owned by another prominent Anglican Yarmouth family, the Seymour Bakers, is now the Bishop's Palace. As is the case with many small towns in Nova Scotia, Yarmouth had its share of prominent families. It was once said that the Farishes talked to the Killams, the Killams talked to the Bakers and the Bakers talked to God!

After a relatively small rectory at Upper Kennetcook, my parents must have been delighted with the large spacious house at 65 William where we were to spend seventeen years. Downstairs there were a total of five large rooms, all entering from a large hallway. Stairs led upstairs at both the front and the back of the house. The dining room contained a butler's pantry between it and the kitchen, which had its own pantry. As was the custom with many Yarmouth homes, there were three fireplaces - two back to back - in rooms that were to become Dad's study and large sitting-room. The third was in the small sitting room. No doubt to my father's delight, there were built-in bookcases in two of the doorways between the study and large sitting-room, although these may have been established later. Upstairs there were five bedrooms and two bathrooms. Four of the bedrooms were in the front part of the house which gave Dad and Mum separate rooms and my three sisters, at one time or another, separate rooms as they were not at home together at any given time. To David's and my delight, the so-called back section was ours. It consisted of a bedroom, bathroom and long spacious hallway with stairs leading to the downstairs kitchen.

A door led to the attic where we played on a swing attached to the ceiling. One of the former rectors was an amateur photographer and he had left some interesting equipment for us to explore.

There was something new to us in the cellar - two bins for hard and soft coal. At first we thought coal an improvement over furnace wood and for adequate heat it probably was. However, it was much dirtier and accumulated dust everywhere. Fortunately there were hot-water radiators instead of hot-air registers which kept the dust down. The coal was delivered in bags by a low-bed wagon and was shot down shoots into the cellar. The soft coal was used mainly in the fireplaces and the hard coal in the furnace. There were no thermostats in those days and the furnace would be "banked" in late evening for overnight and early morning heat.

On another subject, that of heating churches, it is interesting to note that during the 1940's Holy Trinity's sexton, Tom James, would sleep over Saturday night in order to keep the church furnace fed so that the church would be warm for the eight o'clock Sunday Morning Holy

Communion. How appreciative I was of this as my father always insisted that I attend this early morning service!

This spacious rectory would be well used during the war years. My mother, having been accustomed to servants in her native Barbados, would be unable to cope with all the preparation of meals and the vast amount of cleaning. Help in the way of maids was essential. Due to the scarcity of laborers during the war, both domestic and other, jobs were at a premium. You could say that it was a worker's paradise. Consequently Mum's help came and went on a short term basis. One of her maids, Amy (Sanders) Whitehouse, who stayed for a relatively long period of time, has spoken to me about her work at the rectory near the end of the war. No doubt she remembered some of David's and my antics which she kept to herself. Not all of Mum's helpers were adults. Dad loved to tell this story about one of the young helpers who came to the rectory. She was a member of the Conrad family, one of the larger and poorer families of the congregation. When asked to stay overnight she said she had better call her mother. When told by her mother that she should come home and get some things including a tooth brush, she replied, "Mum, no need for that;

Left to right: Gay Armstrong, Dorothy and Joan Bradshaw, Andy Gow

200

there are lots of toothbrushes in the bathroom here"!

For my parents, together with the normal problems of raising two teenage boys, the war brought a host of servicemen into the rectory where they expected to be fed and entertained. No doubt three unmarried and eligible daughters kept them coming. The town was filled with ten thousand military service personnel, mostly men.

Included were basic training for Army recruits, other training and duties for Air Force and Fleet Air Arm personnel. A large number of these Fleet Air Arm men were from England and other parts of the British Commonwealth and were Church of England by faith. Sunday after Sunday, Holy Trinity was filled to capacity and my father was - most of the time - the only priest. Occasionally a military chaplain would assist him. At the time Eucharistic ministers to assist with Holy Communion were unheard of. Some services, especially at Christmas and Easter, would run to two hours or more. However, there were few complaints as the power of prayer during the war years was on everyone's mind.

Servicemen were entertained at Sunday and Wednesday evening dances held in the Parish Hall. The Sunday evening dances were not considered in good taste by the local Evangel Assembly minister, Rev. Parlee. He had a radio broadcast Sunday evening over CJLS and some of the parishioners would rush home after our evening service to hear what Rev. Parlee had to say about, "Bradshaw's Dance Hall"! My father generally never entered into any denominational conflicts and I often wondered if he felt he would have had to justify these Sunday evening dances. No doubt he would have said, "War times are not normal times," and left it at that. David and I were, on occasion, recipients of the generosity of the servicemen. One of the Fleet Air Arm men, who quite often spent week-ends at the rectory, took us to the Community Theatre for the popular Saturday matinee. From him we learned some "Lyme" language - boot for trunk, lorry for car and for theatre tickets, "one pint and two half-pints".

During my youth the two theatres, the Community on Cliff Street and the Capitol on Main Street, were considered institutions. The evening shows at seven and nine were out for us youngsters as the nine o'clock curfew was strictly enforced, if not by the police then by our parents. However, the ever popular Saturday matinees were crowded. Very few adults attended these and no wonder as the noise was deafening. There were shouts of joy when the cartoons were shown. These were followed by the war news which always quieted us down a bit. Then came the main feature, generally a comedy; my favourite was Laurel and Harding. I remember the children's ticket price to be eleven or twelve cents. The advent of the so-called "Blackout Nickel" which was made of a cheap alloy replacing the much more expensive metal, nickel, was a blessing for me. It came about for this reason. My mother couldn't distinguish between the pennies and the blackout nickels, which were the same color. This quite often resulted in me getting one dime and two blackout nickels.

My father often spoke of his tennis playing days in Barbados and I might add that he was considered a better than average player. Although I never knew him to play in Yarmouth he must have enjoyed talks of our exploits at the local tennis club situate on "Lover's Lane" (now called Park Lane), a short distance from the rectory. At various times there was employment at the courts for both David and me. David rolled the clay courts and I ran the canteen. I remember that soda pop was sold for 7 cents a bottle with a profit of 2 cents. Both my sisters, Joan and Dorothy, played and no doubt enjoyed the company of other local players including George Amirault, Matt Epstein, Ron d'Eon, Olga Davis, Cliff and Moira Seeley and Lorraine d'Eon. When brother Charlie was home from his seafaring on Imperial Oil Tankers, he too enjoyed playing tennis. Tennis tournaments were very special events and I remember that we had a home and home series with Windsor. Charlie told me that in one tournament he was paired with John MacDonald who was an excellent player. He asked John where he was to play and John replied, "Get up by the net and stay there"!

One of the games played in the tennis club house was chess. A visitor at the club might be very surprised to hear one of the young players say to the other, "Your move, Judge." That comment would have come from Ivan Hemeon, the friend of Tommy Judge with whom he was playing. Tommy's uncle, Peter Judge, was a prominent local lawyer and at one time, if political considerations had been slightly different, he may have become Judge Judge. Peter was a dedicated Anglican Churchman and Vestry Clerk for many years. He was a great supporter of my father in all church matters. My father always said that when he was made an All Saints Cathedral Canon in 1953, by the Diocesan Bishop it was Peter who had supported his appointment. Peter and his wife, Barbara, lived near the rectory and my mother visited them with some difficulty. The difficulty was a wire-haired fox terrier, named Toby. He was generally tied in the front yard and was very excitable. On more than one occasion she was in fear of losing one of her costly nylons. I know something about that as many years later, in the seventies, Shirley and I owned a similar dog named Benji. If he saw a cat outside the sitting-room window he would get very excited and try to pull the drapes down. My brother, David, told me that you could train a dog by throwing a bucket of water over him each time he misbehaved. However, that was not a good remedy in the sitting-room!

My father was a great reader of detective stories. His passion was shared with other members of the community. While visiting Jane Annable, a dedicated Altar Guild worker, living in an upstairs apartment, he met Mrs. Alan MacKinlay. She was also a reader of detective stories and for many years they exchanged books. Recently at Alan MacKinlay's funeral I met his daughter, Frances, who told me that my father was her hero. The reason was that as a small girl she played outside the apartment house and he always stopped and talked to her. This did not surprise me as I have always known of his great love for children. He once told me that in answer to the biblical question, "Who is my neighbour?" his answer was that it is those with whom you come in contact. That small girl was one of those with whom he came in contact and one half a century later she remembered him with affection. How often, during my lifetime, have people spoken to me about my father's concern for them or their loved ones!

His interest in detective stories held him in good stead on one occasion. It came about this way. My mother had a favourite ring which she wore. The stones in it spelled "dearest", that is diamond, emerald, amethyst, ruby, emerald, sapphire and topas. While visiting her next door neighbour, Gretchen Baker, she lost it, but did not discover her loss until the next day. Extensive searching ensued but it was no where to be found. What had became of it? My father put his detective powers to work. He called Mrs. Baker and asked if her maid had vacuumed recently and if so had she emptied the vacuum cleaner. She replied that the maid had vacuumed but had not emptied it. The cleaner was emptied and there was the missing ring - fine piece of detective work.

While on the subject of neighbours, my parents always had some good ones. The Wilsons lived across Forest Street from the rectory. Ted and Maude had one daughter, Susan, who was about my age and a son, George, who was a bit younger. Ted was the local Royal Bank manager and also a faithful member of our Anglican Choir. Maude was one of those caring persons who are always mindful of the needs of others. Both were always looking out for the financial welfare of the church. It is very interesting to note that both were good friends of the Killam sisters who in later years were the great benefactors of Holy Trinity. No doubt this relationship was a major factor in the most generous gift by Constance Killam and Elizabeth Killam Rogers to Holy Trinity.

I remember on one occasion, while my father was away on one of his infrequent trips, my mother had found some bullets in the rectory. Probably David or I had found them somewhere and carried them home, not an unusual occurrence during the war years. Mother was very apprehensive about them so she called Mr. Wilson and instructed him to bury them in the garden. I often wondered if anyone had uncovered them in future digging and planting.

In later years the Wilsons moved down Forest Street to be near Mrs. Wilson's parents, Dr. and Mrs. G.W.T. Farish. Their former Forest Street house was then occupied by the Courtland Baker family. Court was an excellent singer and had a prominent place in the church choir. He learned to sing the service responses ordinarily taken by the minister and this was a great relief for my father as he had no singing ability. Court had a great sense of humour and my father enjoyed his antics and their playful exchange of tricks on one another. I remember that my father had an old mangy stuffed goose in our attic, likely bought at a house auction. In order to get rid of it he put it on Court's back porch. To my knowledge Court never did find out who put it there.

Social Time with Parish Family in Hall. Clockwise from front around table:
Mrs. Charles Dyke, Robert Horton, Braddy, Jean Horton, Gertrude King,
hidden face unknown, Douglas King. Standing at right Kathryn MacKenzie.
In background are left to right: Barbara Judge, Ann Corning, Peter Judge,
unknown back to camera and Charles Dyke.

There was another occasion which was not humorous. It came about as the result of a conflict between my father and Kathyrn MacKenzie, the church organist. Court, as both a choir member and warden, was in the middle of it. The conflict was over what hymns could be used for Sunday services. It is the practice of the Anglican Church that the hymns be in keeping with the particular service on any given Sunday. There are appropriate hymns for each season of the year. However, the organist, who as well was the choir director, had different thoughts and chose those that were not in keeping with the season. My father would not give way. He was often quite lenient in church practice but not when it was laid down in very strict terms in the church canons and Book of Common Prayer. The matter went before the Church Vestry and was resolved in my father's favour. Miss MacKenzie was furious and called the members of the Vestry "communists", which was the very worst name you could call a person at that time. My father was an expert at keeping his cool and no doubt he did so on that occasion.

I remember on another occasion, after being on the telephone for a long conversation with a parishioner, my mother asked him who had called and what it was all about, he calmly answered, "Someone else who thinks I am God!"

The Don Chipmans lived next to the Court Bakers and both he and his wife, Marg, were Anglicans. Don had served overseas and returned to Yarmouth with his bride after the war. He was one of many veterans who went to college after the war. In Don's case it was to law school to continue his family's tradition in law and to practice in the century-old law firm of Chipman & Sanderson. Many years later, in the early sixties it was at that firm that I did my law articling and was admitted to the Bar of Nova Scotia.

Marg loved to tell stories about her daughter, Donna. On one occasion my father was visiting and Donna saw him coming up the walkway and rushed to tell her mother and said, "Here comes God"! On another occasion Donna told a friend that she must come to church as my father had a mysterious voice. Many Yarmouth youngsters who attended Central Town School will remember Mr. Baker and his ice cream cart. Donna remembered but was confused as to exactly who Mr. Baker was. Prescott Baker, who lived next to the church, on William Street, was known by Donna. Prescott had just died when Donna went to his house and knocked on the door. She asked Mrs. Baker who answered the door,

"Is Mr. Baker at home?"

"No Donna," Mrs. Baker replied, "he died and went to heaven."

Donna responded, "Did he take his ice cream cart with him?"

Dad's biography would be incomplete without reference to some interesting parishioners he encountered while at Holy Trinity. One of these was Harry Daley who lived on Kirk Street and attended Holy Trinity. He was one of the early supporters of the Fish and Game Association and this interest was carried on by his son, Edgar, and grandson, John, who became Superintendent of Schools for Yarmouth District. The incident that amused my father was associated with the fact that Harry was considered frugal. After a rather quiet wedding on the occasion of Harry's marriage to Fannie Phillips (Harry's third wife) he turned to my father, reached in his pocket, pulled out a handful of change and said, "I must go give something to the organist". Knowing that the organist would be very upset and outright insulted by a gift of some change, my father quickly said, "Harry there is no need to do that," and fortunately Harry readily agreed.

The Martell family arrived in Yarmouth in 1944 when the father, John, was transferred here by his insurance company. The mother, Mary, daughters, Iris and Laura, along with John all immediately became active members of Holy Trinity; Iris and Laura in the choir, John on the Vestry and Mary in the Women's Auxiliary. Iris always involved herself in church affairs. She was born in Cape Breton and her many relatives there were among prominent Anglicans on the island. No doubt from them she learned an extensive knowledge about Anglican traditions, especially about its liturgy. She had strong opinions and did not hesitate to express them. After several conflicts at church annual meetings my father came to an understanding with Iris. He had the English custom of keeping his handkerchief in his right sleeve. It was agreed that when Iris had said enough and was still going on he would take his handkerchief and wave it. This was a signal for Iris to sit down. It worked!

My father was a great promoter of "good works". Although he didn't live to see it he would have been very pleased that Iris was in 1980 recognized by the University of King's College with an honorary doctor of civil law degree for her "good works" over so many years to the causes of education, the church and community.

During my father's ministry in Yarmouth some of the most prominent businesses on Main Street were owned or operated by members of his congregation. These included Dyke's Jewellery, Central Pharmacy, Porter's Ladies Wear, Woolworth's 5 & 10 and Hood & Brown's

Auctioneers. Dad could always depend on Clarence Strickland, who was the manager of the 5 & 10 to provide prizes for the Sunday School Christmas Concert and Annual Sunday School Picnic. I am told that my father helped Clarence overcome his problem with alcohol and as a result Clarence was inspired to start the first Alcoholics Anonymous in Yarmouth. To this day the AA's have always found a welcome meeting place at Holy Trinity.

As Holy Trinity was far distant from other Anglican parishes, the closest being at Weymouth and Barrington Passage, my father had very little association with his fellow Anglican clergy. The Anglican Communion has always been considered ''middleway'' between Roman Catholicism and Protestantism. He had no formal contact with the Roman Catholic Church but did belong to the Ministerial Institute comprising Protestant clergy. At one time he was president of the institute when it decided that Sunday funerals would not be permitted as the clergy were too busy with Sunday Church Services. This caught the attention of the American magazine, *Time*, and printed it in their news of unusual happenings. On another occasion, at a dinner meeting, Rev. Blanchard, the Central United Church minister, turned to my father and said, "Look at that". He looked and saw in front of each of several Baptist ministers a glass of milk. Blanchard commented, "the Milky Way!"

Among the Anglican clergy who visited Holy Trinity, two were of particular interest to my father. The first was Father John Wilson whom he formerly knew at Upper Kennetcook when the Wilsons, including their sons, Bill and John, had a summer residence at Maitland, Hants County.

Mrs. Wilson came from a very rich American family and they had built, in the thirties, a fantastic entertainment facility at Maitland called "The Purple Dog". I remember that it had a theater and it was the first time I had seen movies; those, of course, were of the silent type. As well, I remember the clockwork trains. Father John, after naval military service during the war, became Rector of Trinity Church, Liverpool. There he was responsible for the establishment of a clergy training school which Canon Russell Elliott described in his recent book, *The Briefcase Boys*. The Wilsons owned a large cadillac

Canon C. Russell Elliott

which in those days was a gasoline "guzzler" and it was even necessary for it to be gassed-up between Liverpool and Halifax. On one occasion, having imbibed too much, Father John was known to have driven into his bishop's parked car. This was probably the only time a bishop had his car damaged by one of his clergy.

A recent letter from Joan de Catanzaro reminded me of the second Anglican clergyman whom my father found most interesting. Joan writes, "It is interesting that you are publishing a book about your father... because Carmino was converted to the Anglican Church partially by what he learned from him".

Carmino de Catanzaro spent a part of his youth in Yarmouth when his mother, an Italian Countess, owned one of the large houses on Parade Street which she donated to the federal government during the WW2. It became either the Officer's or Sergeant's mess, I don't remember which. His cousin, Peter Campbell, son of a Yarmouth physician, Dr. Rae Campbell, was one of my playmates. He was very scientifically inclined and I remember he once made a device from a pipe to shoot at seagulls. I also remember that the seagulls didn't have to worry. Father Carmino once came to visit Dad at the rectory and I remember him standing in the doorway of Holy Trinity and he completely filled it. He was a large man and in his vestments looked very large indeed. His strong objections to discussions concerning union with the United Church of Canada and the ordination of Anglican women caused him to leave the Anglican Church. He joined the Anglican Catholic Church and before his death he became one of its bishops.

During his sixty year ministry my father saw much of what in the Anglican Church is known as "high" and "low" churchmanship. Perhaps it can be said that Carmino represented the "high" and Father John the "low". The distinction may seem important to many people but my father handled it with a great deal of tact. I think that Canon C. Russell Elliott, in a recent letter to me, puts it very well. He writes, "I have great memories of your father. He was older, wiser, gentler and more committed to his ministry than some other priests, I had for a model. Though the term 'Father' was not as widely used in those days as now, yet to me he was a genuine 'father-figure'."

My father was well known for his sense of humour. He was never mistaken for anyone other than a religious minister or priest because he was never without his black suit and prominent white clerical collar. This often made for some interesting situations. He told that on one occasion he was caught in a police traffic trap on the lakeside road and a constable on seeing his white collar asked if he needed an escort. My father politely declined as he was going to a cocktail party at the Lakeside Inn. On another occasion while we were travelling by car through Quebec, on our way to visit in Ontario, his old Chevy's radiator boiled over. He saw a water bucket hanging on a gatepost next to the road and took it to the nearby farmhouse. He found out that nobody there could speak English and as a result he returned to our car with the bucket filled with vegetables. When my sister Joan became seriously ill in London, England, my father went overseas to be with her. One night while walking back from the hospital to his accommodations he was doing some window shopping. Peeping into a window he heard a voice behind him say, "Hello Dearie, what are you doing tonight"? He turned around to see the very surprised face of a prostitute looking straight at his white clerical collar. On more than one occasion when he visited the local liquor commission he would be met by Mrs. Ellsworth Ritchie, a strong temperance advocate. He would hold up his packaged bottle and say, "Communion wine, Mrs. Ritchie!".

On occasion his sense of humour was not appreciated. Leo Mooney, Sr., an ardent Roman Catholic, was one of my father's friends, and was curious about Anglican liturgy and theology. He asked why incense was used at funerals. Dad, with tongue in cheek said that it was because of the smell, which in earlier times had some truth to it. Leo reported this to his priest, Father Penny, who called Dad to ask why he had told Leo this. Fortunately, all went well as Father Penny had a sense of humour too.

My father always enjoyed a sense of humour in other people. He once took his dog, Flicka, to the vet, Dr. Goudey, who when asked if Flicka had any fleas on him, replied, "Flicka doesn't have a single flea on him; they are all married and have children!"

My father loved baseball. During all of his ministry at Holy Trinity, Yarmouth was a very active baseball town. First, during the war there were the military and town teams playing at the William Street Baseball Park. Who could forget

Braddy and Flicka, circa 1950

209

Murray Veinot hitting home runs, rounding the bases and doing headstands on home plate? Then, after the war, there was the Halifax and District league. He was forever discussing these games with Major MacLauchlan, Judge Elliott Hudson and Leo Mooney Sr. Later, when he became deaf in retirement and used earplugs, he would watch one game on television and listen to another on radio. He said he was wired for sound!

I always admired my father's attitude concerning material things. I remember that he once held a drinking glass in his hand and said that it was a wonderful thing that the glass had a dual purpose. It was one that originally contained strawberry jam and then could be used as a drinking glass. That glass manufacturer was well ahead of his time and my father clearly saw the benefit of it. He never seemed the least bit concerned that he never owned a home property. I know that on one occasion he was offered a house by one of his parishioners but it was not in his nature to accept such a gift. His Canadian cars were always of the very modest type. While in Yarmouth he traded his 1937 Chevrolet for an English Austin and was proud of the fact that the trade-in value was more than he paid for the car!

It is very obvious from his memoirs which constitute the major part of this biography, that what he cherished more than anything else was his relationships with people. He had a very long memory in this regard. Many years after he had retired and returned to Yarmouth he told me he

Joan Cecilia

was giving a ciborium to Holy Trinity in memory of Jane Annable. When he first came to Holy Trinity in 1942 Jane was a dedicated Altar Guild worker and continued to be one until her death in 1952. He was a regular visitor at her apartment on Church Hill. She was buried nearby in the Old Anglican Church Hill Cemetery. My father had a great liking for that cemetery and his last wish was that he be buried there. His wish was granted. Later, in 1980, my mother and in 1987 my sister, Joan, were also buried there.

At the time of Dad's retirement from the ministry in 1959, my husband, Earl, our daughter, Margaret Anne and I were living on Wexford Boulevard in Scarborough, Ontario. Dad and Mom came to live with us from November of 1959 until the summer of 1971, spending approximately six months with us and the winter months in Barbados with the family there thus avoiding the cold winter months in Ontario.

Dorothy Praetor

Dad enjoyed assisting our rector, the Rev. Canon Robert McLaren, with services at St. Jude's, our family church, and was often called upon to assist at other churches in the area if a priest were ill or on vacation. There was one strange occurrence while Dad was preaching at St. Jude's. Dad mentioned that when he was a chaplain in the Air Force in Nova Scotia during the war years, we had an elderly lady, a Mrs. Smerdon, in our congregation, whose son Allan, who had been a pilot in the R.C.A.F. taking his training in Nova Scotia and before going overseas, expressed a desire to be confirmed so was prepared for confirmation by Dad. Mrs. Smerdon had carried a clipping in her wallet concerning this and had always wanted to meet the Padre who had prepared him for confirmation. So, here he was preaching in her church. She spoke to Dad afterwards about it. Strangely enough, Allan's son Kent, was later in the Air Force with our son-in-law Jim Reith. In fact they were buddies and Kent was best man at our daughter and son-in-law's wedding and are good friends to this day. Kent and his wife Liz are godparents to our granddaughter Marin. A small world!

Once when Dad and Mom had tea with our neighbours, the Matthews, an elderly English couple, Mr. Matthews asked Dad, (I guess Dad forgot to wear his hearing aid.) if he would like to say grace before eating and Dad said, "No". Afterwards Mom told Dad he was very rude when Mr. Matthews asked him to say grace and he said, "No thank you". Dad told Mom that he thought he had said, "Would you like a drink?"

We often went to Toronto to shop and Dad's favourite eating place was the Georgian Room at Eatons in downtown Toronto. We also went for lunch at the Guild Inn at Scarborough Bluffs quite often. It is now apartments.

David Bernard

While with us, Dad had a couple of visits to Scarborough General Hospital for heart problems. At that time, Scarborough General was run by the Sisters of Misericord, a Roman Catholic order of nuns. During one stay there, my brother David, his wife Shirley and daughter Catherine were visiting us and went to visit Dad in hospital. There was a crucifix over his bed which Catherine had noticed. When we returned home, Catherine wanted to know why Grandpa was lying in bed, in Church!

One of the trips we made was to Niagara Falls which Mom and Dad had never seen. We spent a holiday at Wasaga Beach in a cottage there. Dad enjoyed walking on the beach and Mom met and visited with women in other cottages.

Earl worked at Rio Tinto Mining Company when Mom and Dad were with us so we visited Blind River (Elliot Lake) when Earl had to make a business trip there. We stayed in a trailer and Dad visited the mine with Earl.

I have many wonderful memories of those days and I was so happy that during their visits to us they were able to meet so many of Earl's relatives and all of our friends in Ontario.

13   BRADDY REPORTS AS RECTOR
OF HOLY TRINITY CHURCH, YARMOUTH

Braddy arrived at Holy Trinity in June, 1942 and at the end of that year his Annual Report to the parish contains the following:

Seven pleasant months have passed since we took up residence in your midst, and I assumed spiritual leadership in this Parish. This time of course, has been all too short for me to assess adequately the strengths and weaknesses of the Parish. I have tried to carry on the work, so faithfully done by my predecessors, with as few changes as possible.

In my experience I have found changes, unless absolutely necessary, disturbing to many and upsetting to normal Church Life. At present we are not living in normal times, and are faced with many problems not met with in times of peace. One of the greatest and most pressing of these comes from the influx of many men and their families, who have been brought here in the course of their service in the various Armed Forces. I have felt very deeply, almost with a feeling of shame, the fact that I have not yet been able to visit all members of the congregation in their homes; this has been mainly due to the presence in our midst of these men, members of our Church across the Dominion and from overseas. You will agree with me the need of keeping these in touch with the Church of their fathers. We are proud of the fact that our Church is catholic (universal) and its catholicity is most beautifully realized by those far from their own homes, who find a welcome in the same dear old Church of their childhood, and receive the same familiar administrations. Will you therefore do all in your power to make them feel at home, all those who from many congregations of the Church Catholic throughout the world, now find themselves in our midst?

If I were asked what I considered the most encouraging feature of our Church life I would, without hesitation, reply 'The entertainment of the Service men in the Hall on Wednesday and Sunday evenings'. I believe that of this effort we may be justly proud. Many of the men thus entertained have made a point of coming to me and uttering their thanks for this effort on their behalf. I had a letter from a clergyman in Halifax expressing the gratitude of his brother for the great privileges that has been his while at the Training Centre, viz. the inspiring Services of the Church and the kindly welcome and entertainment in the Hall afterwards. Some members of our congregation have been rather unhappy about the Sunday evening entertainments, they have feared that there was a danger of dishonouring the Lord's Day. We must remember, however, that He whom we worship in Church, was the honoured guest at the wedding feast of Cana of Galilee, and His presence is assured wherever His children gather in innocent amusement.

And on the matter of finance he has this interesting point to make:

We scorn indeed those who claim that Canada could have been defended from enemy attack by keeping all our Forces at home, and thus defending our own shores. Are we much better in our spiritual warfare, if we say that our concern is only with our own parish and its needs? We must take our part in the warfare against the powers of evil, which is world wide, and we can best do this by contributing our share to the work of God beyond our parochial boundaries. If every member of the congregation would contribute Sunday by Sunday their fair share towards the parochial and extra-parochial expenses of our Church, then there would be no difficulty in meeting all our obligations and much time spent in considering ways and means could be better applied to real progressive work.

Braddy, during his sixty-year ministry, was ever mindful of the spiritual training and welfare of the Parish children and at the end of 1943 reports his concerns to the Annual Parish Meeting as follows:

As we look back over the past year in our Parish life, we see abundant evidence of the Presence of God in our midst; there have been for priest and people, much of encouragement and enlightenment, but we cannot at the same time be unconscious of weaknesses in our spiritual life in this portion of God's Vineyard. May I mention one such weakness which has become increasingly apparent to me, causing me many hours of worried thought, with earnest prayer that God may give us strength here, in place of weakness. I speak of a general sad lack of interest in the spiritual training and welfare of the children and young people of our Church. That this is not only a weakness in our own parish, but is causing increasing concern throughout the Church, does not lessen its seriousness for us, but should intensify our desire to face the problem, and each and every one of us to assume responsibility with regard to it. I have frequently been told since assuming spiritual oversight of this parish, that 'we have no young people.' This is not true, but will come dangerously close to being true, if the neglect of the younger members of our congregation continues at the same pace as at present. The children in our Sunday School are a credit to any church; they are regular in attendance and attentive to instruction, but they often suffer sadly through the paucity of teachers.... It can indeed be said that 'The harvest truly is plenteous but the laborers are few.'

This lack of interest in the Sunday School as evinced by unwillingness to sacrifice a short time each week for the religious training of the little ones is tragic but equally as tragic is the way in which the young people who have been confirmed and left Sunday School are allowed to disappear from our Church membership. Perhaps someone will say that it is clearly my business to keep them in touch with the church; so it is and so I try to do, but I am only one and what I am convinced is needed is a greater interest on the part of the older members of the congregation in the welfare of these young people. I was deeply distressed at the smallness of the congregation on the occasion of the last Confirmation in August. A great day in the lives of twenty-one young people and yet how few were there with them to give them the support and encouragement of their presence and on the morning of their first Communion fewer still knelt with them in the fellowship of the Altar. No wonder so many drift away from such coldness, some to other religions, others into carelessness and indifference. Common sense, if nothing else, tells us that the future depends on the right direction received by these young folk in their early days and yet we feel that it is anyone's business except ours to assume responsibility for that direction. Is there not sternness in the Face of the Master when He says 'Inasmuch as ye did it not to one of the least of these my brethren, ye did not to Me'?

215

Braddy was always aware of the power of prayer and reported his thoughts to his congregation in 1944:

I have heard from many of our young men who are serving on the various battle fronts, and nearly all of them make some mention in their letters, of the gratitude which they feel for the weekly remembrance of them in our Services of Intercession. Frankly are we backing them up in this manner which they evidently value, as well as we might? I will not believe that more cannot spare the time each week to intercede with Almighty God for those who are enduring so much for us, and moreover to pray that the world may be worthy of their sacrifices. Is it fantastic to think that the slowing up of the allied advance on the Western Front corresponded with the slowing up of prayers on the Home Front? Read again the story of Israel's battle with Amalek, given to us in the 17th chapter of Exodus; read especially the 11th verse, 'And it came to pass when Moses held up his hand that Israel prevailed, and when he let down his hand, Amalek prevailed." Has the letting down of his hands - our feebleness in prayer - been the reason for the stemming of the tide of victory, which at one time seemed to be running so strongly? Let us take the opportunity of this coming Lent, to deepen our spiritual life by more earnest prayer, and at the same time make more real in the world spiritual values.

And in 1945 he continues:

...there are still many troubled spots in the world, where it seems that men are not yet tired of warfare, but our gratitude to Almighty God should be intense for the complete defeat of the chief disturbers of the world's peace and equally decisive victory for our military forces. We, all of us know, however, that the task of bringing the world back to sanity, is not yet finished, and much has to be done before we can once again replace weapons of warfare with the tools of peace. This is a job for each one of us, let us give ourselves to it with the same determination that marked our efforts to win the war.

And in his same yearly report he praises his fellow priest:

During the year there have been removed from active service in our midst several faithful members of our congregation. I mention one, who held a unique position, as he looked upon himself as a member of this parish, and at the same time was a Parish Priest of a parish outside the boundaries of this one; I speak of course, of the Rev. Gordon Tallman Lewis, who entered into the Higher Life on October 11th, after over fifty years of faithful service as a priest in the Church of God. He was known and loved so well that words are inadequate to express the sense of loss which his passing caused, but I for one cannot think of him without a feeling of great happiness, when one considers the joy which must now be his. Never was his studious inquiring mind satisfied while on earth, now many of those perplexities, to which here he could find no answer, are made clear; and in converse with those he knew so intimately through his study of God's Word, he must indeed be content.

Always interested in the welfare of the church beyond the parish, Braddy concludes his 1945 Report as follows:

I must say a word about the great 'Recall to God Movement', which has been launched by our Church in Canada - The Anglican Advance Appeal - and it will run concurrently with similar appeals from the other non-Roman religious bodies in our land. ...What are the aims of this Appeal? Briefly, they are to make of men and women, boys and girls, Christians indeed, and not only in name, in order that there may go into the world, those who through the practice of Christ's teachings in their own lives, may show that they are not only beautiful admonitions to good living, set forth in the Book of Books, but wherever practiced will give to the world stability and peace, which otherwise it will seek in vain.

On the occasion of the 75th Anniversary of Holy Trinity in 1947, Braddy writes in a letter to his congregation:

During the five years that have passed since I came among you as your Rector, I have spent many odd moments looking through the old records of this Parish, and intensively have I studied them during the past few weeks in preparing this special

217

edition of our Monthly Bulletin in commemoration of the 75th Anniversary of the Consecration of the present Church. We must not lose sight of the fact that this 75 years is only half of the period of time that our Church has administrated to the people of her faith in this extreme South Western tip of this Province by the sea. This House of God, not only one of the most beautiful buildings in this town, but also one of the most beautiful Churches in Nova Scotia, only came into being through the love and loyalty of those pioneers of our faith, to the ancient Church of their fathers, who 150 years ago, not only gave thought to laying the foundation of material prosperity in a new land, but were constantly mindful of the need of those spiritual things which they felt could best be realized by building a House in which they could worship God. First an 'unpretentious frame building', then an 'upper room' in a store on a wharf, and finally when they acquired land and built a Church they for a time worshipped there, with the building uncompleted, with plank benches for seats. What a tale of patient endeavour and achievement our Church records relate. As present Rector I am humbly conscious of the spiritual leadership and ability of the long line of my predecessors from Ranna Cossit to John Davies, each in his generation according to the Grace given unto him through the Laying on of Hands, 'studied to show himself approved unto God, a workman - that needeth not be ashamed rightly dividing the word of truth' (ed. from II Timothy, 2;15)

*Brighter still and brighter glows the Western Sun
Lighting with it's gladness all our work that's done.*

(Note - from a verse of the hymn, *Saviour, Blessed Saviour* which was inspired by the words of Psalm 47:6, "Sing praises unto our King". The words were written by Godfrey Thring in 1862. The verse goes like this:

Brighter still and brighter glows the western sun,
Shedding all its gladness o'er our work that's done;
Time will soon be over, toil and sorrow past,
May we, blessed Savior, find a rest at last.)

218

We lift up our hearts with glad thanksgiving on this occasion of our joyful anniversary, but there must be more than this if we are to be worthy of those who have built on such a firm foundation in the past, let us each and everyone go forth from our Services of Thanksgiving determined to give ourselves unstintingly to the service of God. Let us make this glorious House of His into the building of which so much love and adoration was poured, a Power House, from which men and woman, boys and girls may go forth into the world to make practical their love of God, by their service for their fellows.

In 1948 Braddy comments on the care of the Old Churchyard Cemetery on Church Hill where exactly thirty years later, at his request, he was buried and where his oldest daughter, Beryl, says in his Memorial Service pamphlet, "Where the seagulls drift down the wind and the sunsets glow at eventide."

This year in our Parish has been marked by the undertaking and completion of a long-needed work, I refer to the fencing and renovation of the old Churchyard on Church Hill, and the erection of a Memorial Cairn to those whose bodies rest there. ... and it will now be the duty of the Parish to see that for all time to come, this now beautiful little spot is maintained in a condition befitting its sacredness.

Braddy's 1949 Rector's Report on finance reveals his concerns about the use of current receipts as opposed to bequests:

You will see by the Financial Statement that our position financially is about the same as at the end of 1948. This can only be improved by an increase in the weekly contributions. There has been some improvement in this direction, and it is hoped that the year ahead will see a much more marked one. I have heard often the suggestion that the interest from the bequest ... could be used for liquidating our current deficit, but this would not be sound finance. Surely it is the obligation on present members of the congregation to provide the means of meeting the current needs of the Church, and reserve for the upkeep of the fabric and what is known as capital expenditure, the interest from bequests in the wills of former members. We have, unfortunately, had to use the interest from some endowments to meet current expenses, but your Vestry has put the bequest ... in a separate fund and has designated the interest from that fund to be used only for necessary capital expenditure. I know that you will concur in this action.

And as always, there was praise where praise was deserved:

I am indeed pleased and gratified, as I know that you are, that we have this year overpaid our Missionary apportionment. I think that only once before in the past eight years have we met it in full.

At the beginning of a new decade (1950) Braddy records the death of a beloved Archbishop:

... I feel that I must open on a note of sadness, yet a sadness with a halo of glory, reflected from that of the cross; I refer to the sudden taking from us of our beloved Archbishop on November

20th. His death was a loss to the whole Church on earth. It has been said that God buries His workman and still His work goes on. The great power of lives such as that of Archbishop George Frederick Kingston lies in the fact that they inspire others with fresh vigour to carry on the unceasing battle against evil. St. Paul exhorted Timothy 'to show himself approved unto God, a workman that needeth not be ashamed'. Our late Archbishop exemplified this exhortation to a great degree in his life and we can best show our gratitude for that life by endeavoring ourselves to be such workmen in God's service.

Archbishop George Frederick Kingston

And at the end of his report, Braddy once again reminds his congregation of the power of prayer:

In thanking all the faithful workers of the Parish may I add the reminder of the need to remember that it is God's work, and to be done efficiently it must have a foundation of prayer. The success of physical and mental activity for God depends entirely upon our spiritual preparation for it.

Braddy in his 1951 Annual Report again emphasizes the importance of work of the Church outside parochial boundaries as follows:

In the executive of our General Synod at the present time, there is considerable anxiety over the paucity of the fund supplied for the continuance of existing missionary work, to say nothing of the heartache for inability, for this same cause, to take advantage of opportunities for extending the work. That bug-bear, rising cost of living, has hit the work of the Church as it has private and business budgets. The result has been that missionary and other clergy and full time Church workers are faced with ever increasing difficulties in meeting their ordinary living expenses. We in our endeavour to balance our own parochial budget must not be unmindful of our obligations to share in the support of the Church's work outside of our parochial boundaries. This parish has during the past few years greatly increased its missionary giving and has for the past year overpaid its apportionment for this purpose. Many have discovered the truth, that that which is given for the work of God in never missed, and it has been proved equally true, time and time again, that the parish that gives generously beyond its borders to the needs of the Church, of which it is a unit, finds its own parochial needs fully met.

In closing his Annual Report of 1953 he reminds his congregation that the work of the Church must have a deep spiritual foundation:

Looking back over the past year we are conscious of much that might have been done and was not, some things which would have been better left undone, but nevertheless with humble thankfulness that God has been able to use us as individuals and as a parish for His purposes. Let us never forget that all we do must have one aim in view, viz the enhancement of His glory and in greater or less degree the restoration of His world to be His Kingdom. In again thanking all the Church officers and the organizations and their leaders for their work and co-operation during the year, may I remind you that this work, to be lasting, must have a deep spiritual foundation, and that foundation can best be assured by our regular attendance together in the family worship in God's House. All work needs prayer to make it really worthwhile and this is particularly so with regard to the special work of God.

In his 1954 Annual Report Braddy asks his congregation for their support for the work he was about to begin as both a Rural Dean and Canon.

All Saint's Cathedral, with interior view of alter

At the Diocesan Synod in June, the Bishop honoured me and through me, the parish, by conferring on me a Canonry in All Saints' Cathedral in Halifax. This he said was in recognition of my thirty-five years service in the priesthood and also of the parish's many more years of outstanding work and service for God in the Diocese. Just previous to this the clergy of the Deanery had honoured me by nominating me to the Bishop for appointment as Rural Dean. I ask your prayers that I may have ability and strength to acquit myself faithfully in both these offices.

Braddy was always mindful of his responsibilities as a Diocesan Official, (Rural Dean and Canon) to report matters of a Diocesan interest and in his 1955 Annual Report he does so concerning an interesting Thanksgiving proposal:

> As most of you have been informed the Synod of the Diocese will be observing next year during October the centenary of its existence as the legislating council of the Church in this diocese. The committee in charge of this celebration has suggested three means of preparation. A Thankoffering to be devoted to Church Extension work. In several parts of the Diocese new communities have sprung up, necessitating the providing of spiritual privileges, by the building of new Churches. Other Christian bodies have not been slow in taking up this work, and we must not fail our own people who move into new communities. For the purpose of this fund for Church Extension, coin cards, to the number of 2500, have been ordered and will be distributed to our Church homes throughout the Diocese after Easter. They will provide for the giving of 10¢ a day for forty days. If all take their share of this effort it will mean the raising of $80,000 to $100,000 as the beginning of a fund from which money can be borrowed for the building of new churches.

Braddy's Annual Report of 1957 conveys his thoughts about the faithful departed in these words:

> Death has laid its hand very heavily during the year, and there are several well loved faces that are missing from our midst. We can best hallow their memory by continuing to make as beautiful as possible the Service which we offer to God in His House which they loved so much, while in their earthly tabernacle. May they find rest eternal in the Paradise of God.

He concludes this report by giving his congregation notice that it is time for a long holiday:

> ... I have received permission from the Lord Bishop and from the vestry to be absent from the Parish for three months in order, with my wife, to visit her old home in Barbados, which we left 28 years ago. We have there a daughter-in-law that we

have never met, and two small granddaughters. So you may be sure that we are looking forward to the trip. During my absence from the Parish, for most of the time, the work will be in the charge of the Rev. F. C. Pemberton, Vicar of St. Paul's Church, in Bridgetown, Barbados. I have not personally met Mr. Pemberton, but he comes highly recommended by his Bishop. It will be his first visit to Canada so I ask for him and his family a kindly welcome from you all. They will be living in the Rectory during their stay in Yarmouth. Once again will you accept my grateful thanks for the many kindnesses extended to my wife and self and especially may I thank you for the generous Christmas offering, which particularly at that season of the year is very welcome. That God may bless you all in your work and witness for Him is the sincere wish and prayer of your friend and Rector.

Braddy's Annual Report of 1958, now being in his 67th year, again deals with the subject of Christian Education and congratulates those responsible for improved Sunday School facilities:

Through the initiative and the energy of the Ladies Service a very valuable addition has been made to our church plant, viz. the providing of four rooms to the South side of the Parish Hall for the use of the primary classes in the Sunday School. There have been some who have objected to the expense that this involved, claiming that there is room in the body of the Hall for all the classes. This criticism comes mainly from those who have never taught in the Sunday School and have had no intention of so doing. It is only fair that those who are willing to give of their time and also of their means, to instruct our little ones in the rudiments of the Faith, should be provided with the best facilities for doing this. We all should be very grateful to the ladies of the Service Guild for providing these rooms, and know that it will not be very long before the outstanding debt is paid off.

In his final Annual Report before his retirement, due to ill health, in September 1959, Braddy again reminds his people of their responsibilities as members of the Anglican Branch of Christ's Church:

Your Treasurer's report will show that financially our state has not deteriorated and is in fact in a more healthy condition *than for some years, considering the heavy outlay of money that has been made during the past year. We have achieved a gratifying "first" in that we have overpaid our missionary apportionment of $210.00. Considering the many years that we have underpaid, we hope that the parish may now have a permanent place in the plus column. In financial matters let us each set as our objective a steady advance towards tithing our income for the purposes of God's work. Our giving is improving, but there is still room for a further advance in this direction. There are still some who claim to be members of the Anglican Branch of Christ's Church, and all the privileges of that membership, but forget that the privilege carries also the responsibilities of membership in giving to support the work and joining in the corporate worship.*

Visits and Life in Yarmouth after Retirement

Although the Bradshaws retired in 1959 and left Yarmouth to share their time living with a daughter, Dot and her husband, Earl, in Scarborough, Ontario, in the summer, and Barbados in the winter, they visited Nova Scotia regularly. On one such visit while with Mac and wife, Shirley, at their summer cottage in Markland, Braddy thought dinner was rather late one evening and went around saying, "Oh Dear"! Meals to Braddy were to be precisely at a set hour and any deviation was cause for alarm.

In 1964 while visiting Mac and Shirley at their apartment on Cliff Street, Yarmouth, Braddy had a "fainting" spell. Shirley was alone with him at the time as Maggie was resting. She called Maggie and then ran to get a neighbour to help. After awaking and vomiting, we called an ambulance and got Dad safely in hospital. This was only one of the many times Dad "fainted" or had strokes while visiting in Yarmouth and often Shirley was the one who had to assist with the crisis.

A letter from Braddy after the Cliff Street event became a keep sake for Shirley. Braddy always seemed rather remote and sedate, though always very polite and friendly, but this excerpt from his letter of July 21, 1964 letter displays the most human side of him:

Dear Shirley,

Shirley Isabel Ford Bradshaw

... now a few lines from me to let you know how constantly you are in our thoughts and prayers.
... I cannot begin to tell you how much we enjoyed our stay with Malcolm and yourself, and we can never forget your unremitting kindness to us. I wanted to thank you at the airport, but my heart was too full and I knew that I would begin to bawl if I tried to express all that was in my heart. I am only sorry that my old hernia, or whatever it is, had to act up, and spoil to a certain extent, what was

such a delightful stay in Yarmouth. One thing is certain - not one of my other daughters could have given me more care than you did. Thank you for everything.

... Give our love to Malcolm.... Do take care of yourself and I do pray that perhaps, in God's good time, you may give to us our second grandson, in fact we will be satisfied with another granddaughter. ...

With love from us all. God bless you!

Affectionately,

Dad

Braddy and Maggie moved back to Yarmouth in 1971 to live in an apartment prepared for them in the newly purchased home of Mac and Shirley on Porter Street in Yarmouth. Daughter, Joan, also moved to Yarmouth that same fall and decided to share the apartment with her Mom and Dad so the parents and two of their children were together again in the same house and remained so until their deaths. Shirley claims to this day that she still hears thumps from the upstairs apartment - which is no longer an apartment but now just part of the home - and always says, "Oh! Dad just had another stroke and fell!" He never seemed physically

Retirement in Barbados - circa 1960
From left to right Maggie, Braddy, son Charles
sister-in-law Frances Greenidge and brother, Ralph Greenidge

to hurt himself when he fell but we rushed to his side and someone stayed beside him until the ambulance arrived. The last one in September of 1978 seemed no different from many before but he died in hospital about a week after the stroke. We were always so thankful that he never suffered any pain nor was he ever adversely affected by paralysis, loss of speech or anything.

Anniversary Reception
in honour of the 50th wedding anniversary of Braddy and Maggie
and the 50th Anniversary of Braddy's ordination to the priesthood.
Five of their six children were present to celebrate with their parents.
Left to right, David, Joan, Beryl, Braddy, Maggie, Dorothy, Malcolm
The other son, Charles was at his home in Barbados at this time.

Dorothy with husband Earl
daughter Margaret, 1971

David with wife, Shirley, and
children, Brenda, Catherine

During his sixty-year ministry Braddy received many letters of appreciation from parishes which he served. The earliest of these was in 1916 from St. John's Parish in Barbados and reads as follows:

Dear Mr. Bradshaw,

> *On the eve of your departure to take up Ministerial duties in Canada, your friends in St. John's Parish, Barbados, feel that they must express to you their appreciation of your four years' faithful and unostentatious labour among us as a Lay Reader, and wish you God-speed and every blessing in your new sphere of work.*
> *As a small token of their regard they would ask you to accept the accompanying purse, with which they hope that you will purchase some slight memento of them, and they would beg to assure you that you will not be forgotten by them.*

We remain,
Your sincere Friends,
C. G. Clark-Hunt E. Clark-Hunt G. A. Sealy (and all at Buckden) L. Hart D. M. Simpson J. Haynes M. Haynes and 36 others

Braddy's reply:

My dear Rector and friends of the Congregation,

> *May I take this last opportunity on the eve of sailing for Canada to thank you for your great kindness to me.*
> *Your parting gift shall be spent as you desire on something to be kept in memory of the St. John's days. But it will not require that to remind me of the happy four years which I have spent among you.*
> *Thank you again for the kindness which has been extended to me for over four years.*

Remember me in your prayers.
Yours sincerely,
ALLEYNE G. BRADSHAW

In a letter dated October 1, 1934, Braddy received the thanks of the Hubbards Parish, after four years of service there, as follows:

> *It is with deep regret that we meet here tonight, to bid farewell to you and your family, but what will be our loss, must be someone else's gain.*
>
> *During your period of service here, with us at Hubbards, there have been added to the Church through your zealous endeavours, four beautiful memorials, not only to those whose names they bear but to you, through whose untiring efforts they were obtained.*
>
> *Your deeds of Charity, although perhaps unknown to some, have brought cheer and happiness to the homes of many in our Parish. Through your friendly visits and your congenial manner, you have won a lasting remembrance in the hearts of those who knew you best.*

On retirement from the Parish of Maitland, Braddy received the following letter, dated April 23, 1942:

To Rev. A. G. Bradshaw and Mrs. Bradshaw

Dear Friends:

> *During the past Eight years as our Rector you have been a familiar and kindly figure in our community, always ready and willing to cheer the down-hearted and comfort those in trouble and we feel that you will be greatly missed now that you have been called to another Parish. It is however our desire that you take with you our hearty wishes that you will in the discharge of your duties find contentment and happiness without which no one can really do good work.*

And from the Parish of Holy Trinity, Yarmouth on his retirement a letter dated November 8th., 1959:

Canon Bradshaw:

> *The congregation of Holy Trinity wishes to express its sincere thanks to you for your spiritual and secular efforts during your stay with us.*

We wish Mrs. Bradshaw and you health, happiness and contentment during your forthcoming retirement.

We hope that your sojourn in Barbados will be pleasant and we look forward to seeing you in the future on your return to Canada.

*Holy Trinity Church, Yarmouth, circa 1942
showing the rectory on the left*

And from the church of St. Stephen in Tusket:

With deep regret we are met this afternoon to say farewell to our dear rector and valued friend. For seventeen years you have worked for our parish of St. Stephen in Tusket, coming in fair weather and in foul, truly a faithful servant of God.

Now, we present to you, Canon Bradshaw, this expression of our gratitude as we say: May God be with you always, in health and happiness to keep you safe and well.

BISHOP GEORGE ARNOLD READS AND REVIEWS

Bishop George Arnold (1914 - 1998)

George Feversham Arnold, son of Archdeacon Arnold Feversham Arnold and grandson of Rev. William John Arnold, followed the profession of his family and did so with a sincerity and dedication to his faith. Born in Mulgrave, Nova Scotia, he was educated at Sydney Academy, Sydney, N.S. and Kings College and Dalhousie University, Halifax, N.S. After graduating with a Masters in Classics in 1938, he was ordained as an Anglican priest in 1939. After serving in several Nova Scotia parishes he was made suffragan Bishop of Nova Scotia in 1967 and then Bishop in 1975. C. Russell Elliot described Bishop Arnold (in the 1998 Prayer Book Society of Canada Newsletter) as "...constant...with a calm and unperturbed attitude " and outwardly as "composed ... in the midst of disorder or dissension" and that he had " the ability to speak objectively ". He went on to say that "he never lost his grip on the real issue. Behind all superficialities, his mind and heart remained fixed on what was true, what was right, what was good".

Serving his church always came first to Bishop Arnold. It is no wonder that he was a true role model for Braddy who respected and loved him dearly.

Bishop George Arnold was the last Diocesan Bishop that Braddy knew well. He agreed to read and review the first drafts of the biographic material and copious correspondence resulted.

Quite some time ago I completed reading your manuscript which you so kindly sent me. It was of such interest to me that when something took me away from it, I could hardly wait to return to it.

And later in March he adds:

Equally with the other materials you sent, I enjoyed 'Alberta Bound' and the Barbados section. Your Dad had a gift for narrative; possibly because I share his vocation, his experiences are of special interest but I am confident that his work can stand on its own merit and will be read with pleasure by many people. As you progress with your task, don't forget to keep me up to date. I am getting a great deal of pleasure and enjoyment from the process.

On March -16, 1995 the Bishop writes:

As usual I have enjoyed your letter along with the contents of the manuscript. I have a couple memories of the Archbishop; one relates to a visit he made when I was serving in the Parish of Mahone Bay. We had some interesting theological discussions and shortly after that I was appointed examining chaplain in dogmatic theology. I have always suspected a connection'! The other was from a dinner party at Bishop's Lodge. After the meal we were exchanging limericks and this is one of his:

There was a young man with a hernia
Who said to his Doctor, Gal durna
When you cut down my middle
Just kindly don't fiddle
With gadgets that do not Concerna.

The bishop was known during his episcopate never to be at a loss to relate an amusing story. He tells this one:

This story is told of a Bishop in India early in this century who lived in great fear of a paralytic stroke and was constantly pinching one leg or the other to test their sensitivity. Once when dining out in formal episcopal dress he alarmed the company by struggling to rise from the table and saying tragically 'This is it! All feeling's gone.'

But it was not his own leg that he had been pinching - as was explained with some asperity by the lady on his right. Believe it or not - this is a true story.

Bishop Arnold never lost his sense of humour - again very like Braddy - and on one occasion relates the story of the Panda as follows:

A panda bear entered a restaurant and ordered a bowl of soup which he calmly ate. Then he gets up from the table, pulls out a gun and shoots the place up then runs from the restaurant. The owner of the restaurant telephoned the police who asked him if it was a panda who shot up the place. The owner was perplexed and asked," How did you know it was a panda?" The policeman told him to check the definition of panda in the dictionary.

So the restaurant owner did that and was most surprised when he read the definition of panda - "a large bear-like mammal with black and white markings, native of China and Tibet, eats, shoots and leaves".

Then the Bishop finishes his comments about the biography by saying:

You have trained me like Pavlov's dog. Everytime I see a good sized brown envelope, I run home for a paper knife

*This plaque, honouring the Reverend Canon Alleyne George Bradshaw as
Rector of Holy Trinity Church for seventeen years, was unveiled on October
14, 1979 by the Hon. John Shaffner, Lieutenant Governor of Nova Scotia and
was blessed by the Right Reverend George F. Arnold in a Memorial Service at
Holy Trinity Church, Yarmouth. Also assisting at this service were Rev.
MacAllister Scott Ellis, Rector of Yarmouth and Rev. Eric Irwin, Protestant
Chaplain at CFB Greenwood.*

Index